Smile for the Camera

Smile *for the* Camera

The Double Life *of* Cyril Smith

Simon Danczuk
and Matthew Baker

Biteback Publishing

First published in Great Britain in 2014
This edition published in 2015 by
Biteback Publishing Ltd
Westminster Tower
3 Albert Embankment
London SE1 7SP

ISBN 978-1-84954-875-5

10 9 8 7 6 5 4 3 2 1

A CIP catalogue record for this book is available from the British Library.

Set in Caslon

Printed and bound in Great Britain by
CPI Group (UK) Ltd, Croydon CR0 4YY

Contents

Acknowledgements

First and foremost, thank you to all those who gave their time to make this book possible. We particularly appreciate the time given by the victims of Cyril Smith who co-operated with us and we also remember all those victims who suffered at his hands.

We are also especially grateful for the time and efforts made by former police officers in helping us with this book.

Obviously, there are some people who assisted us who do not wish to be named – we pass on our thanks to them.

Whether by allowing us to interview them for the book or for helping bring this important story to light, we would like to say thank you to: Jason Addy; Jonathan Ali; David Bartlett; Dominic Carman; Maureen and Roy Cooper; Jonathan Corke; Father Paul Daly; Ashley Dearnley; Martin Digan; Michael English; Richard Farnell; Lord Fearn; Nick Fielding; Barry Fitton; Lorna Fitzsimons; Paul Foulston; Roy Foynes; Edmund Gartside; Jim Hancock; David Hencke; John Hessel; Simon Hoggart; Ed Howker; Lord Hoyle; Simon Hughes; Eileen Kershaw; Ibrar Khan; Liz McKean; Chris Marshall; Stephen Moore; Khandaker Abdul Musabbir; Ronald Neal; Liam O'Rourke;

Mohammad Pasha; Steve Panter; Lyndon Price; Steve Roberts; Sue Rothwell; Derek Smith; Mike Smith; Ann Stott; Jack Tasker; John Walker; Elwyn Watkins; Tom Watson MP; Paul Waugh; and Jennifer Williams.

When it comes to assembling, editing and constructing this book we must thank Rebecca Winfield at David Luxton Associates and Hollie Teague and Olivia Beattie at Biteback Publishing – their comments on the manuscript were invaluable. Suzanne Sangster at Biteback must also be commended for her advice and public relations expertise.

In researching the book, we thank Rochdale Central Library; Touchstones Arts and Heritage Centre; the North West Film Archive; the London School of Economics; and the Working Class Movement Library in Salford. We also credit the *Rochdale Observer* for some of the photographs reproduced in this book.

Simon Danczuk would like to express his gratitude to the following: John Walker, who was one of the founders of the *Rochdale Alternative Press*, helped me decide on the need to write this book, his conversations and thoughts stimulated me to start the project and I am very thankful to him. Obviously, I also pay tribute to my co-author, Matt Baker. I'm appreciative not just for him being the wordsmith on this project but also for his continued excellent advice and support on a whole range of matters, his dedication to Labour politics and, most of all, for his friendship.

Let me also thank Allen Brett, who is my political agent in Rochdale, my eyes and ears when I'm not around. I must also put on record my thanks to Professor Roger Penn for his ideas, thoughts and encouragement over many years. The same applies to Sir Bill Taylor who has been and remains a very good friend.

Staff in my constituency and parliamentary offices have been invaluable, so thank you to Neil Emmott, Iftikhar Ahmed, Shah Ali and Tom Railton.

One of the greatest privileges is to serve as a Member of Parliament and I say thank you to the people of Rochdale for giving me the opportunity to do this. Rochdale Labour Party have also been very generous in choosing me as their candidate and for supporting me so strongly. They have also provided me with ideas and thoughts which stimulated me to produce this book.

Finally, I say thank you to my lovely wife, Karen Danczuk, for being so understanding and supportive. Not only does she assist and advise me on a daily basis but she helps create space for me to take on a project like this. Our children, Milton and Maurice, are also thanked for allowing me time off dad duties during the course of writing this book.

Matthew Baker would like to express his gratitude to the following: I was inspired to get involved in this project by the moving stories from men who had been abused by Cyril Smith when they were boys. This book is a tribute to them and an attempt to set the record straight.

I'd like to thank David James Smith, Rebecca Winfield and Chris Dean for their advice and encouragement, and, above all, my wife Margaret and our children for their love and support.

That a paedophile was able to hide in Parliament is one of

the most shocking elements of this story, and a reminder of how it's been skilfully hidden for so long. There are far too many people to list whose efforts have allowed the real story to finally come to light but they include many local and national journalists whose tenacity deserves high praise.

I'd also like to thank the kind people of Rochdale for taking the time to share their extraordinary reminiscences about Cyril. In doing this, many also spoke proudly of the town's rich history. From Cobden and Bright to the Pioneers and Gracie Fields, Rochdale has a remarkable history and it's incredible that, in my lifetime, these names have been somewhat overshadowed by Cyril Smith, who became synonymous with Rochdale. Now that Cyril's fall from grace is complete, it's my hope that this book can help Rochdale reclaim its true history and heritage.

S. D., M. B., March 2014

Preface to the updated edition

Secrets, it's been said, are like plants. They can stay buried deep in the earth for a long time. But eventually they'll send up shoots, pop up everywhere and give themselves away.

Once one big secret is exposed to the light, others, it seems, will inexorably follow.

That certainly seems to have been the case where the unmasking of Cyril Smith as a predatory child abuser is concerned. When we started writing this book back in 2012, we could not have foreseen the consequences of its publication. This was, we believed, a parochial tale. An unflinching portrait of a charismatic, innovative, albeit minor politician of the twentieth century. A cautionary tale for our times, as we edge towards a new era of personality politics.

But since *Smile for the Camera* was published in April 2014, this story has taken on a life of its own and has become something else – a vital part of the unfolding investigation into the abuse of power by our politicians. Parliament has always had its share of corrupt Members, but child abusers? Paedophiles? Was there a network of powerful paedophiles in and around Westminster? Were MPs guilty of collusion and cover-up to protect child abusers in Parliament? When we first asked these questions, an overwhelming sense of incredulity stopped us in our tracks. It seemed far-fetched to even entertain the notion. But now it looks very much like this was the case.

Piece by piece, the continuing revelations around child abuse committed by senior political figures is starting to show a much bigger picture. An inevitable day of reckoning looms. Some already know what's in store and that's why former Cabinet ministers from the 1980s are talking about a need for a thorough purge of those who so spectacularly brought Parliament into disrepute. It's why the Home Secretary has said the cases exposed so far represent only 'the tip of the iceberg'.

If there's one lesson from child abuse that we all should remember, it's this: that for every child abuser there are usually many more accomplices covering up their crimes. This book is not just about a terrible abuse of power; it's about those who knew that abuse was taking place but looked the other way. This is how abusive networks are formed and how the corridors of Westminster became a safe haven for paedophiles like Cyril Smith.

This was certainly a difficult story to tell, but there are some books that simply have to be written. Once we began to listen to the voices of those trampled underfoot by Cyril, we realised their story had to be told. Little did we know that these voices were signposts to a much bigger secret.

We are still uncovering more details in this awful history. In the weeks and months that have followed since publication, many more people have contacted us with powerful stories that shed more light not just on Cyril's double life but on the troubling activities of other politicians.

Police officers have visited us to talk about other high-profile investigations of politicians who were serial child abusers. Select Committee hearings have taken place, criminal investigations are now underway and the Independent Police Complaints Commission has announced it is investigating claims that Scotland Yard covered up child sex offences because of the alleged involvement of MPs. The Prime Minister has indicated that it may be time to make not reporting child abuse a crime. And the Home Secretary has launched a major child sex abuse inquiry into establishment cover-ups.

Such action is welcome and the repercussions are already being felt. What once looked like a far-fetched conspiracy theory is growing in credibility week by week. The public know there have been too many child sex abuse scandals featuring prominent figures for it not to have been widely known at the time by people in power.

That such momentum has been helped by the publication of this book is a timely reminder that stories can still give voice to an unspeakable truth. Stories have the power to unsettle and force action. The voices contained in this book forced Greater Manchester police officers to come and interview us both and then launch a criminal investigation into the cover-up of child abuse at Knowl View School in Rochdale.

This, like other events of the last year, represents one of many breakthroughs. But the one we remember most didn't happen in Parliament and wasn't made through a police announcement. It happened as we listened to the wavering voice of a survivor of child abuse who had come to visit us to tell us about his experiences at Knowl View School. In his fifties now, his hands were visibly trembling and tears welled in his eyes as he spoke about Cyril Smith and the terrible abuse that he and his fellow pupils experienced.

The detail was distressing, but it was the slight gleam of hope in his eyes, offering a sense that something good may come out of unloading a terrible burden, which affected us most.

'I would not have been able to talk about this ten years ago,' he said. 'It would have been too embarrassing and no one would have believed me. But the environment's changed. It feels safe to talk about it now.'

This was the moment we realised that change was happening. As a country, we've reached tipping point and the public will no longer tolerate such abuses of power, nor the old ways of covering them up. The faintest whiff of cover-up nowadays creates an almighty stink. The barriers preventing stories being told like those accounted in this book are slowly melting away. Of course vulnerable people will always be silenced and powerful people will continue to abuse their position, but there's less certainty now that they'll always get away with it – and that can only be a good thing.

Introduction

In 2007 I was selected as Labour's prospective parliamentary candidate for Rochdale. We were in the tail-end years of the New Labour government and the omens weren't good. In his last budget as Chancellor, Gordon Brown scrapped the 10p tax rate, increasing the tax burden on the poorest. I knew that it was going to take a Herculean effort to win the seat.

As we filed out of the Labour Club on Oldham Road into a cold, grey drizzle, I resolved to live and breathe this town, to throw myself into political life and try to understand what made Rochdale tick.

It didn't take long before I ran into the legend of Cyril Smith.

If you thought Cyril was big in a physical way – he tipped the scales at twenty-nine stone – that was nothing compared to his legend. To say his reputation preceded him would be an understatement. Cyril was now in his late seventies and largely stayed confined to his modest, terraced home on Emma Street. But his mythology dominated the town. Mayor of Rochdale in 1966, he was soon elected the town's MP in 1972 and he never lost an election after that. He stood down twenty years later, undefeated and one of the most popular faces in politics. You'd hear stories about Cyril everywhere in Rochdale. In the pubs, on the streets, in community centres, at bus stops. Everyone had something to say about him.

It might have been fifteen years since Cyril stood down as MP for Rochdale but you'd never know it. The current Liberal Democrat MP was still struggling to emerge from Cyril's shadow, acting more like a historian than a politician, devoting his energies to keeping Cyril's flame alight and clinging on to a political past.

Cyril Smith had cast a spell over Rochdale all right. And, as I began to find out, far too many people were still marching to his tune.

Like most people of a certain age I had a fuzzy awareness of Cyril. Even if you had just a passing interest in politics Cyril would have been on your radar. In his day he was one of the most instantly recognisable politicians in the UK. He used his oversized appearance to good effect, combining humour and an in-your-face northern style to stand out as a colourful personality in a world of grey, indistinguishable politicians.

He was approachable, too, and spoke a language that anyone could relate to. Few did more to narrow the distance between Westminster and the factory floor. Cyril made politics accessible. He had a common touch that helped him break down barriers. But, while Cyril was one of a handful of Liberal politicians who had made an impression on me – I'd seen him on television joking with chat show hosts, recognised him on *Spitting Image* and heard his straight-talking schtick on party political broadcasts – I knew next to nothing about him.

After a few months of knocking on doors and introducing myself to people on the doorstep, I began to wonder who this person really was. I like pavement politics, but Rochdale people are tough to please. They don't suffer fools gladly and they were naturally suspicious of a newcomer with no local track record. Every day was hard work. And Cyril Smith's name came up time after time. Cyril had not only won their vote, but also their respect. He comfortably survived two decades and six general elections with no real party political machinery behind him. After all, the Liberals were less a political party back then than a cause. And all too often a hopeless one at that. So how did he do it?

Trying to discover the real Cyril was almost impossible. He'd spent years and years carefully honing the perfect political myth. He'd built an impressive political legend. In the three years I spent campaigning in Rochdale to become the town's MP it followed me everywhere I went until I was sick of it.

Sometimes I'd be woken at two in the morning by people calling to ask for urgent help on an immigration case. 'Do you know what time it is?' I'd ask.

'Cyril Smith would always help us whatever time it was,' came the reply.

When I was presented with difficult casework on the doorstep, resolute eyes would meet mine and people would mutter the same thing. 'Cyril would have been able to sort it.'

It got so absurd that at one point someone even claimed

Cyril had helped end the Indo-Pakistani war of 1965 and brokered the Tashkent Declaration.

Although he was officially 'retired' from politics, he could never really give it up. It was his life and even if he tried he couldn't keep his nose out of local affairs. Prospective Liberal Democrat candidates would compete for his attention, making trips to his home in Emma Street as though it were some kind of pilgrimage. Lucky ones would get an official Cyril Smith endorsement letter, which would be posted through thousands of letterboxes on the eve of local elections. Many councillors would never have been elected without his backing.

He'd frequently fire off letters to the local newspaper. Most weeks I'd read Cyril's ramblings on some issue or another. And when local elections came round, party activists would leaflet streets the night before announcing: 'Cyril Smith's armchair will be on your street corner between 5 and 6 p.m. tomorrow'. Sure enough, they would plonk an old armchair on the street and hoist Cyril into it. The old man of Rochdale would sit there smiling like some saintly monk while a queue of people waited to hear his familiar homespun homilies. It was like some bizarre medieval ritual. This was politics all right, but certainly not as I knew it.

Some say the highest honour a politician can get is to be made freeman of the borough, an award bestowed on people who have rendered eminent services to their community. There are usually plenty more deserving candidates for such an award than politicians, who tend to get it for lasting a long time more than anything else. This, however, was one award Cyril did deserve. He had an umbilical link with Rochdale that no one can deny. Cyril showed the difference between being involved and being committed. For all his serious faults he was a politician who never sat in the grandstand. Cyril understood street politics. He was no effete intellectual. And he knew the connection between a voter and politician had to be an emotional one to really mean anything.

It's true I came to respect Cyril. This will sound strange, abhorrent even, given the details that have subsequently emerged about his other life. To many Cyril has become a monster. But there was another side to him that the people of Rochdale knew well. We shouldn't forget that he was one of the most successful politicians of his era. He won election after election, demolished his opponents and his public adored him. He had an aura that most politicians would give their right arm for. And he was brave enough to stake everything on his character. I don't know of any politician past or present that would have stood on the strange slogan that Cyril used at elections. 'Vote Smith the man', it read. This was just one example of the supreme confidence he oozed. While many in the town recoil in horror at the very mention of his name now, there are others who still speak highly of him.

There was an element of his politics that was honest, simple, noble even. In an age where politicians go out of their way to avoid constituents and most could walk down their high street unrecognised, Cyril actively courted his constituents and had a real bond with them. He was an early pioneer of the grassroots activism that was to serve the Liberal Democrats so well in years to come. Far too many politicians come across nowadays as having an innate distrust of people. Cyril was the opposite. His was eye-to-eye politics, spit and sawdust, grit and passion. Where many of his contemporaries struggled to put their finger anywhere near anything resembling a pulse, Cyril was swimming in the bloodstream. His was in many ways the antithesis of ivory-tower politics; it was street-level politics.

But Cyril was from the Pennines, not ancient Greece. Towns like Rochdale have a history of brutal politics and no one knew how to play rough quite like Cyril. For all his efforts to bring politics to the people, he was also guilty of conning them on a huge scale and there was a dark, repugnant side to Cyril's politics that I came to see. In time, the scales fell from my eyes and I was confronted with absolute horror. It was well hidden from view all right. But once you tore down the veil of mythology and looked beyond the TV image and the jolly clown playing for the camera, there was a sickening dark heart. This wasn't a man of the people. This was *Bad Lieutenant*. I saw it in police files that had been hidden for years and I heard it in the desperate voices of grown men that Cyril had abused as boys. Politics is rarely pretty but this was both ruthless and chilling in its ugliness. So far removed was this from the popular image he enjoyed that once you caught sight of it you questioned whether your senses were being deceived. Where did child abuse, bullying, asbestos-championing, electoral fraud and ruthless power-lust sit with the larger-than-life friendly face laughing from the chat show host's sofa? I don't remember it making *This Is Your Life*.

Just as the beauty of seaweed viewed underwater becomes a slimy mess when lifted out, so too did Cyril's well-polished public image fall away once he was seen from outside a protective media bubble.

In the three years I fought to become Rochdale's MP it became less a battle to win at the ballot box and more a crusade to clear the air in Rochdale and smash stubborn myths that I became convinced were holding the place back. Forget the garlands, the accolades and constant tributes that Cyril received all his life. This is a book that goes in search of Cyril Smith's dark side. It has always been spoken about in Rochdale – and the whispers had echoed through British politics. But for years the truth had been concealed from the wider public. When he died, Nick Clegg said that everyone in Rochdale knew Cyril 'as a friend'. Another Liberal Democrat MP said Cyril 'gave politics a good name'. They couldn't be more wrong. I do, however, agree with Clegg on his final observation. 'I think we can safely say there will never be an MP quite like Cyril Smith again.'

That gives me some comfort. But Cyril's legacy still endures. Over the last seven years I've seen the ghost of Cyril Smith everywhere in Rochdale. The town I had come to love had settled in to a bad way of doing things. There didn't seem to be anywhere that Cyril's toxic influence hadn't reached.

Terrible political orthodoxies were in place demanding complete subservience to a style of politics that had no place in modern Britain.

Whenever I caught sight of a dodgy planning deal, a blatant cover-up to protect people from being held accountable for serious wrongdoing or some cynical electoral wheeze, all roads led back to Cyril. 'This is how we do things round here,' was the unspoken article of faith.

It's hard to imagine any politician nowadays having the same kind of influence on a local level as Cyril. The 'Westminster bubble' has put paid to that. Cyril was well aware of that long before the term was coined. 'Parliament is the longest running farce in the West End,' was how he put it. The House of Commons, he argued, was just a 'daft, end-of-the-pier charade'. Few politicians have the same visceral connection to their constituency. Even fewer know how to build the same kind of local power base like Cyril did. Leader of Newcastle City Council T. Dan Smith did on the Tyne, but he went to jail. Cyril built an equally rotten power base in Rochdale and was feted all the way to his grave.

His is a story that provides big lessons for us all. It's also one that offers a fascinating insight into a world of politics that probably no longer exists. Now and again we can still catch a trace of it, though, like a gossamer thread that's barely visible. It's a world where big political characters bestrode the world like colossuses. In an age of Austin Allegros, small-town banality and near permanent recession, the big beasts emerging from a fug of smoke and the glare of popping flash bulbs looked as though they could shape the destinies of communities through their own hands. They couldn't, of course. And no one illustrated their failure quite like Cyril. But for a while they gave the impression they could. It was both exciting and horrifying. And they certainly put on a great show.

Simon Danczuk
February 2014

Chapter 1

Hunger

They came from all corners of Lancashire. And they marched. The rhythmic thud of lace-up leather boots, the beating of drums, enduring songs of protest and the spirited defiance of the brass band was the soundtrack to what became known as the hunger marches. Throughout the 1920s and into the Depression era of the 1930s, thousands of men and women joined this social protest. They marched to Manchester. They marched to London. They marched everywhere to demand an end to the degrading unemployment means test.

By the early 1930s industries across the north were crumbling, unemployment soaring and entire communities suffering. A mood of grave civil unrest had taken hold of large parts of the country. The hated household means test carried out by the Public Assistance Committee would see investigators search through food cupboards and order families to sell valuables before they would award unemployment relief. Unemployed workers would be given food vouchers or, worse still, public assistance pay. A plate of bacon fat boiled in water poured over a few small potatoes was the kind of meal on offer for a day's labour. But while the north felt the worst effects of the Depression era, stories had begun to emerge across the country of mothers starving to death to feed their children. Annie Weaving was one. After the 37-year-old starved to death in London to feed her seven children, a 'Hungry England' Inquiry was commissioned. She 'sacrificed her life' for her children, observed the coroner. 'I should call it starvation to have to feed nine people on £2.8s a week and pay the rent,' he concluded. In Lancashire this battle for survival was made worse by the fact that the lowest unemployment payments in the country were awarded.

To proud workers it was an intolerable indignity. Degrading. A third of Lancashire's 800,000 unemployed had been struck off benefits completely. Only 7 per cent of children in elementary schools were receiving meals and the county medical officer warned that large numbers were suffering from malnutrition.

Public anger was palpable. In 1932 almost a thousand marched towards Lancashire County Council's offices to demand change from the Public Assistance Committee. Songs were sung. Women carried banners that read 'food for kiddies, not for cannons'. Unemployed weavers, spinners and dyers joined from towns en route as the protest converged on Preston.

As they arrived at the county town, police lines blocked their route and batons were drawn to stop the marchers reaching the hated Public Assistance Committee. Accounts say the violence was ferocious and indiscriminate. Batons were swung wildly and blood and teeth flowed along the cobbles. Bricks and stones hurtled through the air. Screams were heard above the din. But the police stood firm and ensured the seat of local government remained protected.

Scenes like these were common during the Depression era. Violent clashes between the police and the unemployed happened on a regular basis. A year earlier the army had been called to guard Rochdale Town Hall during a protest against hunger and unemployment.

Against this backdrop of poverty and struggle, Cyril Smith entered the world in 1928. Born in Birch Hill Hospital, Rochdale, he was, in his own words, 'illegitimate, deprived and poor'. Like many of his generation, Cyril was scarred by the extreme hardship that shaped his childhood and his early years were tough. He shared a room in a one-up one-down house on Falinge Road with his grandmother Sarah, his mother Eva, his younger brother Norman and older sister Eunice. Both his siblings would end up marrying and his brother followed Cyril into politics, becoming a Liberal councillor in the town. As children they were part of a tight-knit family living in extremely cramped conditions with only basic amenities. The communal outdoor toilet was 300 yards away down a back alley.

To keep warm, Cyril and Norman would scavenge bits of coal dropped on the pavement from the horse-drawn drays. Other days they'd collect pieces of wood from derelict mill sites. Plenty of other children were out on the same mission and the task often became a fierce battle to seize the best logs. On occasion, they burned bits of their own furniture in order to cook a meal. Food consisted of dripping on bread, a single egg shared between three people, potato hash and penny bags of stale cakes.

But if Cyril was aware of the poverty around him, he was far more conscious of the fact that he and his siblings had no father. It was customary in those days for the *Rochdale Observer* to print details of all the births at Birch Hill Hospital. But if you check the records for June 1928, Cyril's name is conspicuously absent. Illegitimate children were not recorded. Being poor, he acknowledged in his autobiography, 'was just simply how life was'. Being illegitimate was socially unacceptable.

In a town such as Rochdale – medium-sized, surrounded by the Pennine hills – one wasn't afforded any anonymity and everyone knew each other's business. There were shops in the town that would not serve Cyril and his brother and sister. His sense of being an outsider was very real and painful. One day, after his mother burst into tears out of frustration at having no money for food or coal, a young Cyril eavesdropped on a conversation downstairs. As a neighbour tried to comfort Cyril's upset mother, he remembers hearing him tell her that she should have taken his advice and put young Cyril in an orphanage. All of this never would have happened, he said wearily, if only she'd taken his advice.

The terrible stigma attached to children born of unmarried parents was something Cyril could never quite shake off. He saw it in the way people looked at him. It was an open secret. Many people believed illegitimate children were from such a morally weak bloodline that they could corrupt others just by being in their presence.

Cyril became acutely aware of the pressures on unmarried mothers to get rid of illegitimate children. 'I myself could have been aborted if my mother had taken some of the advice given to her at the time,' he told the BBC years later. In Parliament he was to become one of the fiercest opponents of abortion. When a Liberal bill to reduce the time limit for abortions to eighteen weeks failed, Cyril was forced to apologise to the Speaker for shouting 'murderers' at other MPs.

Yet while a growing sense of injustice cast a long shadow over Cyril's early years, his home wasn't a miserable place. Hunger often gnawed away at him, but laughter and song filled Falinge Road. Cyril had fond memories of the time, singing in a tin bath before the fire, playing with his brother and sister, and hungrily breathing in the tantalising aroma of the little food being cooked on the open fire in the grate. Although his diet didn't vary and meals were often the same, the smell of food cooking never failed to excite him.

Being his mother's first son he was always her favourite. Of all her children, Cyril was the one she had highest hopes for and from an early age would get preferential treatment. This came at a cost and, with all three children said to have different fathers, none of whom played any part in their upbringing, Cyril took on that mantle of male head of the household. He had to. His mum worked seven days a week as a live-in maid for a cotton family. The responsibility of bringing up three children fell on Cyril's grandmother, Sarah, and, as soon as he was able, on Cyril. From an early age he carried a sense of expectation and responsibility was thrust upon him. It was obvious straight away that he was bright and very able. If the family were going to fight their way out of poverty then Cyril would lead the charge.

Cyril grew up in the heart of a bustling mill town that was one of the first in the world to be industrialised. Situated on the edge of the stunning and dramatic natural landscapes of the Pennines, not many towns could boast Rochdale's proud history. By the eighteenth century Rochdale was full of wealthy merchants and it became the centre of textile manufacturing during the industrial revolution. It spawned luminaries such as Samuel Bamford, the celebrated weaver, radical and poet; John Bright, one of the first Quakers to sit in the House of Commons; and Reverend Joseph Cooke, the inspiration behind the Methodist Unitarian movement. It was also home to the Rochdale Pioneers, who established the co-operative movement in 1844.

Like many northern towns at the time it had fallen on hard times, but it wasn't all drudgery and grinding poverty. As one of the town's most famous daughters, Gracie Fields, ably demonstrated, Rochdale had a thirst for glamour, too. The Depression of the 1930s conjures up some of the most striking images of poverty in the twentieth century. But it was also a time of great social and technological change that was to usher in a new wave of prosperity. Squalor and misery were sharply contrasted by the emergence of cars, cinemas and the expansion of electricity to power homes. Only the wealthy had access to these new advances at first, but gradually modernity started to spread. Despite the grinding poverty all around him, the young Cyril did not have to look very far to see the first hint of glamour, excitement and the prospect of an altogether very different life.

A few months after Cyril's birth, Gracie Fields opened 'Rochdale's Super Cinema', a first for the town and a symbol of the new entertainment era that was dawning. During the 1930s, Gracie became one of the world's biggest stars and Britain's highest-paid actress. She was a rare combination of glamorous Hollywood star and down-to-earth Lancashire lass. Typically, in her 1934 film *Sing as We Go*, she played a champion of workers' rights fighting the closure of the mill where she worked. Gracie, too, had tasted her fair share of poverty as a youngster and though her star had long since ascended from squalor to the stratosphere, her roots remained strong. For Cyril she was an inspirational reminder that talent and determination could always overcome poverty. She gave Rochdalians a sense of pride and identity. She radiated hope.

Gracie was part of a cinematic golden age that offered a retreat from everyday life. *Gone with the Wind*, *The Wizard of Oz*, *City Lights*, *King Kong*, *Frankenstein* and *The 39 Steps* were among the big films of the time. But the film that Cyril remembered best was *Boys Town*. Starring Mickey Rooney and Spencer Tracy, *Boys Town* tells the story of an American priest who set up an orphanage for deprived boys and it was to have a major influence on Cyril's life. Indeed such institutions and the boys that were in their care became a strong feature in almost every decade of Cyril's adult life.

Looking at the grainy 1938 trailer now it's easy to see how a nine-year-old Cyril would have been captivated by this tale. Over footage of hundreds of boys pouring into an orphanage, a distinguished voice booms out, 'This is the story of one young renegade who came from the back streets...' As the camera zooms in to the scowling face of a young Mickey Rooney, no doubt Cyril would have recognised some of the outsider's defiance that burned in Rooney's eyes.

A school trip had been planned to see the film, but Cyril was unable to attend because his mother couldn't afford the twopence admission fee. His teacher, Mrs Halstead, however, didn't want the poorest children to miss out and secretly paid his admission. Thirty years later, Cyril returned to school to speak on the occasion of Mrs Halstead's retirement and the memory of this gesture overwhelmed him. Tears poured down his face as he recounted the story of her kindness.

Evidently, the film gave the young Cyril plenty of ideas. The thought of setting up a home for boys appealed to him greatly, as did the journey made by Mickey Rooney from wayward youth to mayor of Boys Town. Years later, Cyril confessed that he had come from that cinema determined to find out what a mayor was. Whenever he managed to find any spare time he would run down to Rochdale Town Hall in the hope that he'd catch a glimpse of a real mayor. Marvelling at the Victorian Gothic architecture and its magnificent balcony, where the King and Queen had stood a few years earlier as part of their coronation tour, Cyril would stand alone for hours on end, his eyes fixed on the hall steps waiting for the mayor to appear. When the mayor did finally appear, draped in robes and a chain of office, something clicked. For the first time in his life he dared to dream. If Mickey Rooney could do it, he thought, then why not me?

Despite his keen sense of alienation, Cyril was not short of confidence. He'd assumed extra responsibilities from an early age and carried his mother's hopes for him like a lucky charm. Although the looks of disapproval he received from 'respectable folk' hurt and the experience of being turned away from shops and shunned pained him, it sparked a fierce determination to be accepted, to succeed and, above all, to have the last laugh. But if poverty and illegitimacy already provided long odds of him succeeding, he was soon going to have to contend with another barrier that would only add to his status as an outsider.

Playtime at Spotland Primary School was never the most enjoyable part of school for Cyril. While other boys raced out of the doors to play football, he would bring up the rear knowing he could never properly compete. But he would try – with severe consequences.

One day, as a tan leather football skimmed across the yard and through the puddles chased by a huddle of boys, Cyril held his position and watched the action come towards him. A determined young face bore down on a goal of jumpers and schoolbags and skipped over desperate tackles. But he wasn't agile enough to evade the colossus defence provided by Cyril. A headfirst collision ensued and both boys scattered to the floor, grazing their knees on the tarmac.

Cyril was the first to get up. A trickle of blood rolled down his shin and he silently winced at the stinging pain. But he made sure no one could see his discomfort and lumbered back to resume the game. It was only a few days later that the consequences of his fall emerged. Collapsing at school, he was taken to hospital. A piece of gravel had entered the cut and made its way into his bloodstream to lodge in his kidney. He was diagnosed with nephritis, a condition so serious that it could be fatal. Indeed, many soldiers in the First World War had died in the trenches from the disease.

For eight months he lay in a sick bed, living off barley water for the first six weeks. After that he was fed rice pudding to help get his strength back. In those pre-NHS days, access to medical treatment for the poor was reliant on the goodwill of the family doctor and it is to the philanthropy of his family doctor that Cyril credits his survival.

After a further nine-month stint at an open-air school for convalescent children, Cyril returned to school determined to pass his eleven-plus in order to get into grammar school. Despite his setbacks, Cyril looked at the challenge in front of him as well within his grasp. He was so certain of passing his scholarship exams that he told his mother to start saving for a high school blazer. Sure enough, he passed.

But if this was to mark the start of Cyril's ascent to better things, it was tempered by another troublesome development. His weight started to balloon and his body began to assume the girth that made him so instantly recognisable years later as a politician. Cyril has always argued that his obesity owed to a medical complication caused by nephritis, which left him unable to burn off excess calories. This was a side effect of kidney damage. He did, however, acknowledge that his poor diet, born of economic necessity, was a contributory factor. Bread, boiled potatoes, chips and dripping were his staples. The irony that he was born at a time of starvation was not lost on those who viewed his growth with disbelief. He was also deemed medically unable to take part in sports at school and physical exercise quickly became an alien concept.

He arrived at high school weighing in at twelve stone. By the time he was fifteen he'd shot up to fourteen stone, which was the same weight as the then world heavyweight-boxing champion, Joe Louis. While the other boys enjoyed football, cricket and athletics, Cyril was sent off to play table tennis. At playtime he cut a lonely figure. Mocking voices, cruel taunts of 'fatty', 'jumbo' and 'fatso', and the sound of laughter followed him wherever he went. And it hurt.

Some evenings he would go home and sit alone in the bedroom, brooding. But he never cried. He wouldn't allow it. A tough identity was forming and long before he left his teens Cyril was battle-hardened and resolute.

'I didn't grow up as someone's son,' he said, 'I grew up as me. Cyril Smith, individual. It was one of the first lessons of life, perhaps one of the most painful...'

Hurtful as his overweight figure was in making him the target of playground cruelty and endless taunting, he soon realised he could turn his size to his advantage. He learned to accept that he was always going to be fat and stand out from the crowd. Obesity as a child may have made him an easy target but it strengthened his sense of being an individual. He wasn't like the others. And the mocking voices in his ears helped build a strong defence against ridicule in later life.

Like the obese hero of John Kennedy Toole's posthumous novel, *A Confederacy of Dunces*, Cyril began to combine the same mixture of clown-like antics and wonderful oratory that made Ignatius J. Reilly such a memorable character. Ignatius was described as 'a mad Oliver Hardy, a fat Don Quixote, a perverse Thomas Aquinas rolled into one'.

Cyril was more a strange blend of Les Dawson, Alan Sillitoe and John Bright, but his sense of individuality was equally striking.

Being bullied, poor, fatherless and carrying a strong social stigma was painful, but it set Cyril apart from others, and this wasn't always to his disadvantage.

The more his outsider status was reinforced the more self-assured he became. Cyril was never going to shuffle off into the shadows, doff his cap and know his place. He was going to show people how wrong they were to judge him. His self-belief started to translate into a fine northern eloquence and his large frame gave him an unmistakable identity. Years of poverty, struggle and ridicule had helped forge a determined outlook. He was soon picked to play table tennis for Rochdale. 'He was probably the best table tennis player in the world for his size,' Roy Cooper, an acquaintance at the time, remembers. 'He really was good.' As an early indication of Cyril's resourcefulness, it showed how he was able to make the best of his situation. Most boys denied the right to play football and forced instead to play the more gentle sport of table tennis would have nursed resentment rather than thrown themselves enthusiastically into mastering a new sport. Not Cyril.

He umpired in the Central Lancashire cricket league as well, and began to show a willingness to discover new experiences. The shy, withdrawn boy standing on his own outside Rochdale Town Hall peering up the steps to catch a glimpse of the mayor had grown up and was barely recognisable.

The extra-large figure prowling round the table tennis table, swatting the ping-pong ball back and forth, pulling faces in between points, dancing the occasional little jig and clowning about as though he were on the northern comedy circuit was a different beast entirely. An extrovert was born.

But behind the silly antics lay a keen mind. Books, religion, girls and politics signposted a dizzying journey of self-discovery. First he devoured history. The Dutch Golden Age, the French Grand Siècle, the General Crisis, the Enlightenment and French and American revolutions. Then the great British reforms of the Liberal governments of Campbell-Bannerman and Asquith: primary education for all children, the first sickness benefits for the poor, old-age pensions and controls on the House of Lords' powers.

Among the Liberal titans of this era were northern figures that Cyril developed a special kinship with. William Gladstone, the son of a Liverpool merchant, who served as Prime Minister four times. Herbert Asquith, the son of a Yorkshire wool merchant, who, until Thatcher, was the longest-serving Prime Minister in the twentieth century. And, of course, John Bright, the son of a Rochdale Quaker who helped repeal the Corn Laws to create a free market for goods.

Bright is a fascinating figure in British politics and his statue still stands proudly opposite Rochdale Town Hall today. Opinions remain divided on Bright, though. He undoubtedly helped achieve remarkable reforms, including the 1867 Reform Act, which gave most urban working-class men the vote. But he also stands accused of hypocrisy, campaigning against slavery while blocking efforts to improve the slave-like conditions of children working in his factories in Rochdale. He also provided terrible-quality housing for his workers in some of the worst slums.

Nevertheless, it is Bright's reputation as a determined reformer and ardent Nonconformist that ensured his legacy in Rochdale. A restless religious sensibility informed his radicalism, and Bright campaigned against and won the fight to oppose payment of a tax to the Anglican Parish Church.

One branch of Nonconformism is Unitarianism, which has strong roots in Rochdale with churches dating back to the early eighteenth century. For several generations Cyril's family had been committed Unitarians and he quickly fell in with what he called a 'left-wing religion', which deliberately encouraged rigorous independent thinking among its followers.

Unitarianism has no standard set of beliefs and is a very broad church, accepting Christians, Jews, Buddhists and atheists, for example. Central tenets include the belief in religious freedom and diversity, tolerance of other religious ideas, including humanism, and religious principles founded on conscience, thinking and life experiences.

Cyril credits the Unitarians for helping develop his fiercely independent and anti-establishment streak, and his involvement at Sunday school soon began to take on a greater commitment. A dedicated singer in the choir, he quickly became first a teacher and then assumed the more senior role of school superintendent. It was Sunday school that soon tested Cyril's outspoken and critical nature and as the first signs of Cyril's straight-talking style emerged, he made it clear that no one was free from his sharp tongue – including the Unitarian church itself.

First this manifested itself in a violent outburst. At the end of each weekly meeting tea would be poured for the congregation. As the steam rose from a cracked teapot and trays of old, chipped cups were brought out, Cyril would grumble at the state of the crockery. Surely we can do better than this, he'd moan. Weeks passed and still dusty, chipped crockery was used to serve the tea. And then Cyril exploded. His face turned a violent red, expletives poured out and he smashed every single cup in a fit of rage.

Then, after securing the new crockery he'd demanded, he followed his physical outburst with a moral one. Taking to the pulpit to preach the Sunday sermon at the Blackwater Street chapel, years of pent-up disgust at the hypocrisy of the establishment tumbled out. Pointing to the church elders, he accused them of double standards, of condemning drinking and gambling from the comfort of their chapel pews, only to go home and do the same themselves.

The chapel council immediately passed a motion. Cyril Smith was never to be allowed access to the chapel pulpit again.

This forceful response did little to dampen Cyril's confrontational style. His inhibitions were melting away, his struggle to find a voice was paying off and the lure of politics was starting to grow stronger.

While the likes of Asquith found their political voice debating at Balliol College, Oxford, among men he described as having 'the tranquil consciousness of an effortless superiority', Cyril's early debating days took place in a far less grand environment.

From the pulpit of his local church he made the journey to Rochdale's Town Hall Square on a Sunday evening. Here, speakers of different persuasions, along with evangelists, firebrand preachers and doomsayers, would mount soap-boxes and express their views.

This outpouring of passionate oratory fascinated the seventeen-year-old Cyril. He'd stand for hours listening to arguments about communism and fascism, following every last intonation of a rapid-style oratory delivered by all kinds of characters. He'd revel in their presence, their charismatic delivery and how they commanded attention. It was, he recalls, a place that was teeming with life. On some occasions, Cyril would join in the debate and heckle the speakers, including one old-style communist who he'd regularly argue with. Very soon he would climb on to a soapbox himself and be forced into a decision that would change the course of his life.

By now he'd left education due to economic necessity and was working hard to bring as much money as possible into the family home. The family had endured enough under his mother's meagre wages and it was time for him to start bringing home the bacon. Even though he had no choice, this was still a decision that rankled and Cyril long nursed a regret that he didn't go on to university. He later identified this as the barrier preventing him ever becoming leader of the Liberals. But his thirst for knowledge and wish to immerse himself in the great thinkers of his age had to be balanced with more humdrum requirements for now. The money he'd bring in to the home made all the difference. He was able to buy much-needed clothing for his sister; the word 'paid' was soon stamped on the bottom of the electricity card; there was food on the table and the family became free from debt. It was about keeping the family's dignity.

He threw himself into work. Whitewashing lavatories, selling rail tickets, delivering telegrams for the post office; Cyril showed plenty of entrepreneurial flair. There wasn't anything he wouldn't turn his hand to. Deciding to put his grammar school education to good use, he eventually landed the job of a clerk at the Rochdale Inland Revenue Tax Office. It was a solid start and his mother was proud of the respectability it afforded – at seventeen he was told he had a good pension to look forward to! But it was never a job to satisfy Cyril's ambitions. He still craved excitement and with the 1945 general election looming, he had other things on his mind.

With the Second World War having disrupted the routine of politics, this was the first general election to be held since 1935 and politics soon captured the nation's imagination. Voters were driven to the ballot box by a message of hope, a new social order promising better housing, free health treatment and employment for all. Much was at stake and Cyril was determined to play a part in rebuilding Britain after years of war.

A well-known local Liberal, Frank Lord, convinced Cyril to join the party and introduced him to other members at the Liberal headquarters on Drake Street. Here, Cyril made his first bond with the wealthy mill-owning class of Rochdale, as he shook hands with Charles Harvey, the Liberal candidate. The director of the Fothergill and Harvey's mill in Littleborough (which is still running today), Harvey was one of the richest men in Rochdale and a highly influential figure.

Cyril became a fully fledged activist and he could barely

contain his excitement when he was asked to speak at a rally in Rochdale alongside Sir Archibald Sinclair, the Liberal party leader, as part of the general election campaign.

As he made his way to Packer Spout Gardens by the town hall, little did he know what impact his speech would have. Joining Charles Harvey on the platform at the fountain, Cyril looked out at the faces before him, cleared his throat and began to speak. He was a little nervous at first, but he finished strongly and the passion in his voice was clear to everyone present. He stood down to polite applause, but across from the gardens in a nearby red-brick building, a man peering out of a window was not clapping.

Alf North, Cyril's boss at the tax office, had heard everything he needed to hear. He pulled his window shut, lit a cigarette and pondered what action to take.

The next day Cyril was summoned to North's office and told that he was in breach of civil service rules. Members, he explained, were not allowed to take part in political activities that would compromise their impartiality. He presented Cyril with a choice: a career in the civil service or politics.

Cyril stared back across the desk, dumbfounded. Only the sound of the wall clock ticking broke the silence. North said he'd give him a day to make up his mind. He was asked to bring his mother to the office tomorrow when he'd made a decision.

Cyril was torn. He'd only been in the job six months and he knew his mother would not be happy at the prospect of him becoming unemployed. But he knew in his heart of hearts that he had no choice other than to follow his political calling. As an aside, he now had wealthy mill-owning contacts to call on and he made the calculation that he wouldn't be unemployed for long.

The next day was a solemn affair. Cyril shifted uneasily in his chair in North's office while his mother's face betrayed a huge sense of disappointment. This has to be your decision, she stressed, knowing what he was about to say. North looked at him expectantly and asked for his decision. There was a brief silence. 'Politics, sir,' Cyril responded.

North nodded and Cyril's mum got up to leave. At the door North extended his hand and smiled. He told Cyril he'd made the right decision and would most likely do well in politics. Cyril shook his hand firmly and, after looking to see if his mother was watching, grinned back. His heart was pounding and it was all he could do to suppress a little squeal of delight. He was on his way.

After putting in an exhausting and committed campaign shift for the Liberal Party in the 1945 general election, Cyril's honeymoon thrill with politics woke up to a sobering reality. Charles Harvey had not even got close to winning the seat in Rochdale, losing to Labour by 11,836 votes. Nationally, the Liberal Party suffered a humiliating defeat, as Labour romped to a remarkable – and surprising – landslide victory. Clement Attlee was the new Prime Minister and Cyril licked his wounds and looked out at a new political landscape that had left his dreams in tatters. He'd now learned that wanting something badly and working hard to try and get it was not enough. He'd need to possess great stamina and persistence if he was going to see this mission through.

Despite his sorrow at seeing seventy-six Liberal candidates lose their deposits and the overall loss of nine seats, including that of their party leader, Archibald Sinclair, the 1945 general election presented one unseen benefit for Cyril. One of Cyril's great talents as a politician was his prodigious networking ability. Powerful contacts were carefully cultivated to help clear the way for him to progress. Charles Harvey was one of the first powerful people he met and, as Cyril had anticipated, he soon secured a job with him: he was offered a job at Harvey's textile mill in Littleborough as an office boy.

It was a new world for Cyril, who was still only seventeen. It wasn't just his first experience of a large, successful private enterprise; it was the first time he came into close contact with girls. Months of debating, campaigning and making public speeches had lifted his confidence no end, but he remained incredibly shy around the opposite sex and was extremely conscious of his weight, which by now was tipping the twenty-stone mark. By any teenage standards this was freakishly large.

Cyril's position became even more uncomfortable when he found himself the only male working in an office of eleven females at Fothergills. This was a new experience entirely. For a while the discomfort he felt was almost unbearable. He was so embarrassed he could barely speak. Puberty had hit Cyril like a train and it required monumental willpower just to stop himself from staring open-mouthed across the desk at the young women before him. Cyril's first approaches were, unsurprisingly, met with rejection. It was a massive blow to his pride and the humiliation stung. Things did not improve despite his best efforts to be noticed. For a man blessed with a forceful personality and strong character this came as a shock.

One woman soon captured his attention, however. She was indescribably beautiful, better dressed than the rest and a source of endless torment for Cyril. He would sit and stare at her when she wasn't looking, careful to quickly avert his gaze if she looked over in his direction. She became part of Cyril's fantasy life and he began to entertain all sorts of silly daydreams, which usually involved him walking arm in arm with her down the promenade in Blackpool.

Maintaining such a fantasy life required strict discipline. Cyril could never approach her for he knew she would reject him and his dreams would crash violently into the buffers. So he remained silent and never spoke to her.

But these dreams could only partially shield him from the cold reality of rejection that he felt everywhere in that office. The haughty laughter, the looks of cool disdain, the scornful flick of heads as the girls would toss their hair back and walk away from him. His sexual appetite had awakened with a jolt. And it wouldn't tolerate rejection forever.

In that textile mill office Cyril learned to deal with humiliation and found a way of earning respect. As teenage secretary of the works council people came to him for help. Complaints from the shop floor would have been communicated to management through Cyril. If staff had a problem with tea breaks being shortened or wanted more overtime, Cyril would make their case. Suddenly he served a purpose.

Teenage years are never easy for anyone. But for Cyril they were a titanic struggle, one where he was forever straining to find an identity and rid himself of the pariah status he'd felt as a child. He knew that acceptance, friendship, love and a safe passage would not come easily. He would have to defy all odds and fight. Cyril Smith the pariah was going to be killed off. A different Cyril Smith was going to replace him. One who people respected. And feared.

Cyril's tumultuous emotional life mirrored the colossal sense of struggle that was happening all around him. The post-war settlement promised to sweep away an old order, but the change that people cried out for would take a long time to arrive in Rochdale. The old-established way of thinking was crumbling and in Cyril's case he quite literally saw old foundations collapse in front of his eyes. One night there was a large bang and the cottage next door fell down in a heap of bricks. With the support of next door gone and a ton of rubble on their doorstep, Cyril's family had no choice but to leave their condemned home.

As they hurriedly gathered their belongings and left the one-up one-down terraced house for the last time, Cyril took one backward glance at his childhood home. Then he pulled his coat collar up, set his face against the sleeting wind and made his way to what would become his home for the rest of his life.

Chapter 2

My Kind of Town

A sense of optimism filled the post-war years even if wartime austerity dragged on for far too long. Rochdale had avoided the bombs that fell on many British towns and cities but war still cast a long shadow. The promise of a better life for the working class showed no sign of arriving in the town as rationing, bleak winters and potato and coal shortages meant the peacetime change that everyone cried out for was painfully slow to arrive.

'I have no easy words for the nation,' admitted the new Prime Minister, Clement Attlee. 'I cannot say when we will emerge into easier times.'

There were no comforting words guiding Cyril either. And he certainly wasn't relying on Attlee to help him find a better life. Hard work, determination and discipline were his watchwords. Fear of rejection still nagged away at him and cruel judgements continued to block his ambitions. Public service had long appealed to him and outside of politics he harboured ambitions to teach. His attempt to become a teacher, however, was knocked back after he failed a medical examination by the Education Authority. Fearful of his weight, Cyril had been assured by his family doctor that he was perfectly fit enough to teach, so it was a serious setback when doctors examined him and said otherwise. When he received notice that he was deemed unfit to become a teacher he was dismayed. It was yet another humiliating blow that was to scar Cyril. He blamed the fact that he was a Unitarian and illegitimate as the real reason why he'd been barred from entering the teaching profession.

Cyril and his family had by now moved into their new home. Situated in the heart of Falinge, just off Rochdale town centre, the word 'home' barely does this neat terraced house on Emma Street justice. It became more like a fortress for Cyril, a symbol of his roots and unbending commitment to the town and its people. Years later, when he became one of the most famous and instantly recognisable politicians in the land, Cyril would take great pride in the startled looks shown by distinguished visitors as they squeezed into his cramped living room, which was warmed by an electric bar fire. Cyril was never ostentatious in Rochdale. He knew it would offend too many people. When close friends asked him why he didn't move into a bigger house once he had the money, he'd respond that if he was going to be a man of the people he had to stay with the people.

Humility remains an important character trait in Rochdale. There is nothing flash about this town and people are not easily impressed. In the 1980s TV series *Brass*, Morris Hardacre once dryly commented to his dad, 'The nearest you came to high society was the Rochdale Mountaineering Club.' There certainly is many a true word spoken in jest.

The post-war years are often talked about as a whirl of social and cultural change yet this change was barely perceptible in Rochdale. The immigration boom started soon enough, and Cyril's Falinge neighbourhood was one of the first places to see an influx of Pakistani immigrants arriving to work in the textile industry, but the emerging consumer boom that was to signify an end to the age of austerity seemed about as far away as the moon.

Poverty was stubbornly clinging to many parts of post-war Britain and the Treasury was nearly bankrupt, dependent on loans from overseas. Ration books continued to be issued for nine years after the war ended. Frustration was evident all over the country and domestic violence and divorces dramatically increased. It was said that Britain believed it had won the war but behaved as though it had lost it. Across the north-west, where the Lancashire Fusiliers had raised seventeen battalions for service in the war, the mood was far from triumphant. The opulence of the royal wedding between Princess Elizabeth and Philip Mountbatten in 1947 was a million miles away from the reality of power cuts, food shortages and poverty in Rochdale.

But, slowly, prosperity returned in other parts of the country and the first signs of a new consumer lifestyle began to emerge. In 1946 the first bikini was shown in Paris. That same year the world's first credit card was introduced. And in 1949 television first arrived in Rochdale, as broadcasts were received on transmissions from the Sutton Coldfield transmitter.

Cyril began to hear about the first signs of a new age dawning, even if it hadn't reached him yet, and wanted to play a part in shaping Britain's future. Having licked his wounds following the Liberals' catastrophic 1945 general election defeat he set out again with renewed vigour to advance the Liberal cause. Politics was no longer just a calling; it had begun to consume him. It was the only place where he felt he had a chance of being noticed and the one place where he knew he could make a difference.

But it was also a place that had its own set of rules. And before Cyril was out of his teens – before he had even properly started shaving – a weary acceptance of the kind of pragmatic trade-off he would have to get used to had already set in. He was starting to recognise the basic tenets of power. In order to make change you either had to have your hands on the levers of power or be in a position to influence people who already had it. Power, he reasoned, was what politics was about – and without it, all his endeavours were meaningless.

'It is fashionable today to ignore this truism, to sweep it under the carpet as the Victorians did with sex,' he noted. If he was going to get anywhere, he figured, this axiom would have to guide him and he'd have to stay relentlessly focused. He already knew much more than many of his contemporaries and armed with this knowledge he would become a ruthless and formidable campaigner.

During the late 1940s, Cyril quickly learned the ropes of politics – and his ambition began to match his progress. As chairman of Rochdale League of Liberals he easily brushed aside the competition to win a north-west area debating competition. He already had a reputation in the area as a young talent to watch and national figures were starting to take note of his progress. His style of addressing audiences owed much to Nonconformist preaching and made him easily stand out. His treacle-thick Lancashire accent added to the effect and he was soon asked to make his first Liberal conference speech in Hastings. In Blackpool the following year, 1950, the BBC broadcasted one of his speeches. He began to get invites to the National Liberal Club in London and would frequently board the midnight train from Manchester and try to snatch a few winks of sleep in crowded, sweaty carriages of dilapidated trains that would slide into Euston at dawn. He'd walk the streets as the sun came up and cut through the gaps of tall buildings on streets waking up to the hum of metropolitan life. It was a heady time and his world was expanding fast. People who years previously he would have been running errands for were now inviting him into their mansions and speaking to him as an equal.

He met the elite sections of the Liberal Party, the Lords, the Knights of the Realm, the rich. He handled leather-bound books in the party treasurer's private library, brushed against expensive velvet curtains and was waited upon by house servants. And none of it left him particularly impressed. Looking on at the highly educated aristocrats of his party twirling their brandy glasses and lighting fine cigars, Cyril was left with the overriding impression that for some politics was merely a pastime. It was like a high-society debating club. They were dilettantes.

The wealth, social connections and expensive education of the *haute bourgeoisie* left him cold. These people seemed so remote from the people in Rochdale that politics was supposed to serve. They were in the wrong game, he thought, and they seemed to lack the appetite for the fight that was needed to get their hands on the levers of power. For all their expensive education, they hadn't yet cottoned on to the fact that politics was about power. And they no longer had any real power. Smashing a two-party hegemony would require a relentless, restless push for change. Were the Liberals really ready to break the system? Did they have the hunger or the drive, or were they content to remain a protest party? Cyril had his doubts. He'd seen the people running the party at close quarters. He knew they adopted different policies for different regions that often contradicted each other. It was a kind of selective truth. Ideals were sacrificed on the altar of political expediency. And it left in Cyril a sour taste.

But he had no time to dwell on these bitter truths. Since 1948, he'd been a paid Liberal agent in Stockport, busy laying the foundations of his political career. Yet despite being in a hurry to make his mark, the problems that dogged his party were to continually block his progress. Once again he had to face up to the harsh realities of defeat – and, this time, learn how to respond to it.

Back on the eastern rim of the Lancashire industrial area, where the moors and hills of the Pennines rose in the distance, Cyril took stock of what he'd discovered. Politics for him could never be simply a high-minded occupation based around the sport of a noble intellectual joust. It could never emerge from smoke-filled boardrooms and martini lunches. It would have to break away from the pseudo-aristocratic worldview that came to typify large parts of the Liberal Party and instead be shaped by the struggles of men and women in Rochdale. His experience of mixing with the great and the good of the Liberal Party had changed him. He was no longer cowed by his background, unsure of himself or hesitant in how to proceed. For the first time in his life he felt comfortable in his own skin and certain that he had what it takes to make it in politics.

In the dreams and hopes of men working the looms in weaving sheds, of women hanging the washing in backyards, of boys kicking a ball against gable ends or girls playing hopscotch, there was a crying need for real representation. Someone championing their cause, not simply patronising them. No one was doing this in the Liberal Party. It was time someone changed the rules of the game.

But, as the 1950 general election approached, a Sisyphean pattern was emerging both for him and the Liberal Party. As hard as they campaigned, the Liberals continued to get nowhere. While the country had seen enormous change, particularly in the creation of the NHS and the birth of the modern welfare state, the spectre of nationalisation loomed large over the campaign to determine who won the keys to Downing Street. Cyril was uncomfortable with Labour's programme of nationalisation – and the Tories were positively hostile towards it. As the votes came in, it soon emerged that many of the public also had doubts about increased state control over the economy.

In places like Rochdale, however, changes like the NHS were extremely valued. Providing a comprehensive service, funded by taxation, and free to all, its launch fifteen miles away at Park Hospital in Manchester had a huge impact. Far too many people were being denied medical help because they could not afford to pay for it. With spiralling tuberculosis death rates, and polio and rickets also prevalent, the service was needed more than ever.

Going in to the 1950 general election, the Tories pledged to keep the NHS, but that didn't prevent a deeply polarised campaign with Labour and the Tories locked in a class struggle, and the Liberals relegated as also-rans. Churchill accused Labour of presiding over an increased 'cost of living' and 'socialist mismanagement', while Labour campaigned on a record of establishing the NHS, nationalising the railways, electricity and gas. Its manifesto was titled, 'let us win through together'. Also standing that year for the first time, under the slogan 'vote right to keep what's left', was a young Margaret Thatcher. She lost by over 13,500 votes.

As the results came in it represented a new nadir for the Liberals. A record 314 candidates lost their deposits and only nine MPs were returned to power. In the end Clement Attlee just held on to power, with Labour scraping home with a five-seat majority. Within a year they were voted out of office and Winston Churchill returned as Prime Minister for a second time. It marked the end of the moderate centre, concluded Cyril. From that time on tribal divisions rather than individual conscience set the tone at Westminster.

Cyril's candidate in Stockport South clung on to his deposit but only after Cyril had demanded a recount. The day after the massacre, on 24 February, Cyril sat down in Stockport Reform Club and chewed mournfully on a sandwich, warming his hands round the cup of tea before him. He stared at the frost patterns on the window and blew out his cheeks. Politics was certainly a hard nut to crack. He was desperate for the chance to enter public life but the banner of Liberalism offered little hope of getting anywhere. The Liberals were entering a period of dramatic decline. A few years later they would reach a new low when Lloyd George's daughter won Carmarthen for Labour leaving the Liberals with just five MPs. Cyril could see the writing on the wall. The public had roundly rejected his party. What must he do to have a chance of getting on?

He didn't have to wait long before the answer came. Reg Hewitt, the defeated candidate, told him to pull himself together. After all, he was the one who'd just suffered a devastating defeat at the ballot box, not Cyril. He smiled and reminded Cyril that he had youth on his side. 'If I were you, son,' he said, 'I would join the Labour Party.'

Cyril finished his tea in silence and watched the frost melt on the window. He knew Reg was right. He would have to do whatever it took. A fustiness now clung to the Liberal Party and they were no longer in a fit shape to compete for the vote. Throughout the 1950s, the Liberal Party would come close to extinction.

In political terms it wasn't much of a leap for Cyril to change parties. Steeped in Rochdale's history of Nonconformism, Cyril was known for his contrary views and his pick'n'mix approach to politics. He saw no reason why a man shouldn't have the right to a wide spectrum of beliefs under one umbrella movement. Cyril was a big advocate of broad-church politics. He also wasn't the only Liberal defecting to Labour at the time. Well-known figures like Megan Lloyd George and Dingle Foot left the Liberals and went on to become Labour MPs.

Cyril flitted from left-wing to right-wing positions on

a regular basis, and was able to establish common ground in most camps. Where possible, he avoided ideology. He disliked dogma. His politics, he liked to think, reflected common sense thinking and the views of the working man and woman in Rochdale.

Joining the Labour Party in his early twenties, Cyril found, not unexpectedly, that he was viewed with a certain amount of suspicion by the rest of the Rochdale constituency party. He lost count of the number of times he heard 'turncoat' muttered behind his back. But, in true Cyril-style, he slowly began to win the respect of his fellow party members, and those that didn't respect him began to fear him. By now Cyril was quite an imposing figure. Standing at over six foot and possessing an immense bulk, he was not someone that was easily interrupted when in full flow. Few dared to openly challenge him. Nevertheless, it still took almost two years before Cyril was asked to stand as a candidate in local government elections – and even then he was given what was assumed to be an unwinnable seat.

In May 1952 Cyril's name appeared on a ballot paper for the first time. He was standing for the role of councillor in the ward where he'd grown up and lived. Falinge Ward, however, was not natural Labour territory. Cyril was up against a Conservative councillor who'd held the seat for eighteen years and played a major part in the running of the council, which was under no overall control at the time. Fred Greenwood was chairman of the finance committee and part of the town's furniture. He'd also been mayor in 1947. As far as Labour was concerned, he was unbeatable. Labour had never won the ward and there seemed little chance of anything changing. Yes, it had its fair share of poor districts, notably where Cyril lived, but once you moved beyond the slums Falinge soon opened up into more prosperous areas filled with Victorian and Edwardian houses where mill families lived. It was natural Conservative territory and it was going to take a remarkable effort to buck the voting trend.

Cyril had other ideas, though. He was not there to make up the numbers or earn 'valuable experience' as a paper candidate. As far as he was concerned he'd already earned his stripes. He was standing to win – and he quickly devised an ambitious strategy that would put him personally at the heart of the campaign. Cyril's big idea was a kind of 'pavement politics plus'. He was going to make himself known to every one of the ward's 5,000 voters. Not just shake their hands and hand them some party political literature. He was going to try to get into their homes and strike personal connections. He would win them over with his personal story and convince as many voters as possible that he was the best person to represent their interests in the town hall.

Over the next six months, he spent every free hour traipsing round his ward, covering every nook and cranny of Falinge, and forcing his presence on every voter he could find. He walked mile after mile, wearing out shoe leather and rapping doorknockers. And before long there wasn't a single person in Falinge who didn't know who Cyril Smith was.

It was during these mammoth sessions, when Cyril came face to face with thousands of voters, that he came into his own. Arguably, the remarkable alchemy that had transformed an awkward youth into a garrulous, confident man of the people had taken place years before. But this was the first time the real Cyril Smith was exposed to thousands of Rochdale people. He'd found a stage at last.

Perhaps it was because a somewhat patrician and aloof air clung to politics at the time or maybe it was because voters had never seen anything like Cyril before. Either way, an umbilical connection was made that was to help Cyril at the ballot box for the next forty years. On doorstep after doorstep Cyril quickly established a friendly rapport and was invited in for tea. Once over the threshold he'd tell voters about his life, his love of the area and his ambitions for the town. And they seemed to lap it up.

Michael English was a Labour member in Rochdale at the time also looking to become a councillor. He was later to become the MP for Nottingham West and spotted straight away why Cyril was set to take Rochdale by storm.

'He was just a natural extrovert,' he explained. 'A great communicator and he told it straight. He spoke their language. People can smell reality; they know authenticity when they see it.'

English watched Cyril on the doorstep and said his approach transcended politics. 'One of Cyril's greatest attributes was his memory,' he noted. 'He remembered everyone and he knew everyone. Once he got talking to people on the doorstep, he'd be talking about Johnny down the road or their uncle Billy. He connected with people's everyday lives. He didn't need to talk politics.'

For Cyril, the connection between a candidate and the voter needed to be much more than a party political one.

It had to be a visceral and emotional connection. It was about trust.

Even then, he noticed the growing distance between politics and the people. The mere mention of local government would normally make your average voter start to yawn, he argued. Politics for most people was an abstract, dull activity that wasn't on their radar. The challenge was to bring it to life, to make it matter. Cyril had learned his lesson from the last two general elections. People weren't interested in hearing about the Liberal Party's manifesto on the doorstep. And he wasn't going to bother trying out the Labour Party manifesto either. A strong personality was needed, someone with a real connection to people's lives.

Cyril employed a potent mix of persuasive charm, northern humour, blunt common sense and what he called 'straightforward effrontery'. To say he made an impression is an understatement. The sheer force of his personality drew voters to him like iron filings to a magnet.

But it wasn't enough just to get nods of agreement and promises that he had their vote. Cyril's sales technique had a further twist to guarantee their support.

In order to stand for election, every candidate must submit a completed set of nomination papers with the signatures of at least ten registered electors. Cyril decided to use this legal requirement as a tool to make people feel obliged to vote for him. He carried a huge wad of nomination papers with him and would urge supportive voters to add their name.

In recognition of your promised support, would you be so kind enough to sign my nomination papers? I would be honoured if you would, he'd say, flashing a smile and thrusting the paper forward. It was, he claimed, a good mix of cheek and common sense that made people feel part of a small, select group of nominees and, therefore, obligated to vote for him. He got 1,850 people to sign his nomination papers and each person who agreed to do it thought they were one of just ten signatories. He would carry these papers back home every night and count the signatures excitedly. His plan was coming together.

Then, in the week before polling day, he sat down and composed a letter that he hand-delivered to everyone who'd signed his nomination form. 'I know that having given your word in this way, you will turn out and vote for me on polling day,' it stated. 'In return, I will guarantee that, should I be elected, I will represent this ward and your interests to the very best of my ability.'

It was late when he finished delivering the final letter on the eve of the 1952 local elections and he trudged back towards Emma Street guided only by the street lamps. As he kissed his mother goodnight and collapsed exhausted into his bed, he was certain of one thing. He was no longer a pariah in his own town. He'd been invited into countless homes and made welcome. These were his people. And they saw him as one of their own. Whatever happened tomorrow, he could see a future stretching out in front of him in this town.

The next day Cyril headed to his former school for the local election count. It was an unusually warm evening and Cyril mopped a light sweat from his brow as he walked through the school gates. His eyes narrowed as he crossed the yard and for a second he could almost hear the distant echo of cruel taunts he'd endured for years.

He quickly settled into the hullabaloo of election night, with reporters, activists and candidates talking excitedly about the likely results as the first ballot boxes were carried into the hall. Aside from a few pleasantries, most paid scant attention to Cyril. He was considered to be making up the numbers and had absolutely no chance of winning. Cyril caught sight of his opponent Fred Greenwood smiling and laughing with supporters. The Conservatives were back in government and Greenwood looked relaxed and confident.

That all changed moments later when the shock result of the night was announced. The Labour candidate, Cyril Smith, had won the Falinge seat by a majority of 520 votes. Cyril raised his arms and nodded slowly and joyously at the result, as a few belated cheers from astonished Labour supporters broke the stunned silence.

It was an astonishing victory and he was overcome with emotion. Not yet twenty-four, Cyril was Rochdale's youngest ever councillor. Politics melted away for a moment. He had been given a mandate by local people. They'd placed their trust in *him*. The backing from voters all over his ward filled him like a surge of electricity. 'Winning that council seat in 1952 gave me the greatest sense of victory in my life,' he said many years later. Other local politicians had dismissed him and no one had given him a chance yet he'd proved them all wrong. It was the first hint of the seismic shift in politics he was about to bring to the town.

It was as though he had smashed through a barrier that night. Having only ever known painfully real limitations, he now saw a world of opportunities within reach. Cyril had shown everyone just how single-minded he could be and, while he received enthusiastic slaps on the back then, many in his party looked at each other blankly, unable to work out how he'd won the seat.

Cheered on to a local pub by his dazed supporters, he huddled round a table with Labour colleagues and let his victory soak in. As the beer flowed and the rest of those around the table began to get drunk, Cyril declined the offer of more drinks and abstemiously nursed his gill of mild. A calm sobriety descended upon him. Winning an election was all well and good, he reasoned, but now he had to put it to good use. Another tray of drinks appeared in front of him and there were toasts all round. 'You having another?' a councillor asked him, beckoning Cyril to the bar. 'No thanks, I've got to get back to my mother,' responded Cyril, and said his goodbyes, making his way slowly through happy supporters.

Celebrations would have to wait for another time. There was important work to be done.

Chapter 3

Power and Abuse

Throughout the 1950s Cyril cemented his position as a rising Labour star. He was comfortably re-elected and made good on his promise to work tirelessly for Falinge. Having worked so hard to get elected, he knew he had to fulfil expectations. He immersed himself in the world of local government and secured positions on as many committees as possible. It wasn't long before Cyril was known as the man to see if you wanted something doing. Problems getting your child into school? Difficulties getting planning permission? Need a new coal bunker? Go and see Cyril. He didn't disappoint, but he'd make sure people were under no illusion that they owed him a favour.

Becoming a councillor changed Cyril. It was his first taste of real political power and he was eager to broaden his political networks and look for opportunities to help him benefit personally. Cyril had already demonstrated his political opportunism in deserting the Liberals, and it was a trait that was to define his career. After all, being a councillor was an unpaid role back then. He helped everyone across town, but especially the rich and powerful, not least because he knew they were powerful allies.

When a by-election was called in Rochdale in 1958, Cyril's long-term ambition became clear. He wanted to become a Member of Parliament. On this occasion he watched his fellow party member Jack McCann take the seat from the Tories but he was already plotting at how to get a shot at Parliament himself.

The 1958 by-election was the first British election to be televised and Cyril could see that it represented a significant turning point. Granada's TV cameras changed the character of the British electoral process forever. This was no run-of-the-mill election; it was a glamour contest pitting the celebrity broadcaster Liberal candidate, Ludovic Kennedy, accompanied by his glamorous wife, the dancer and actress, Moira Shearer, against the dashing Labour candidate, Jack McCann. The huge interest in Kennedy and his charismatic media performances gave a strong hint at what was to come. It was the advent of personality politics. The glare of TV cameras made sure of that. A year later, at the general election of 1959, the viewers of televised party broadcasts outnumbered the radio audience for the first time.

Attitudes were changing, old orthodoxies were being swept away and the media had to adjust to change. Cyril joined McCann's victorious campaign group and can be seen cheering in the TV footage. It was an exciting time, but there was still some resistance towards television. Churchill, for example, never gave a television interview in the UK during his time in office. A few years earlier, Lord Reith had bemoaned the advent of commercial television, saying, 'It was sad that the altar cloth of one age had become the door-mat of the next.' As the three candidates discussed election issues in a live broadcast for the first time, Cyril observed the polished media skills of Ludovic Kennedy, and took note. In coming second to McCann, Kennedy achieved the highest Liberal vote since the 1920s.

Nevertheless, Cyril knew that if he wanted to become the MP for Rochdale McCann would be hard to shift. He was a popular figure and had respect across political parties. A year later Cyril tried unsuccessfully to become the Labour candidate for Heywood and Royton, the next-door constituency. It was going to take time to get into Parliament. But Cyril was happy to wait. Besides, it wasn't just in the world of politics where he was making an impression. He was busy getting his fingers into as many pies as possible in Rochdale. Despite making rapid political progress, he couldn't lose sight of the fact that he had a living to earn – and he began to advance in the business world.

Cyril's networking became legendary. If you were wealthy and influential in Rochdale the chances are you'd be one of Cyril's friends. Some of these newfound friends helped bankroll a host of business ventures by Cyril, including the purchase of St Mary's Gate newsagent and tobacconist in 1956. Cyril would have almost certainly known that the council were planning to issue a Compulsory Purchase Order on the land – and in 1959 he cashed in on the building and sold the newspaper rounds. But not before he'd annoyed some of the neighbouring small businesses that had campaigned against the demolition. 'Cyril joined our campaign group against the new development in the area,' one former businessman at the time told me. 'Then he turned up to a meeting one day and said he could no longer support our campaign because he was now in favour of the development. It didn't go down well.'

By now, Cyril was also starting to get a reputation as a handy fundraiser and his entrepreneurial eye didn't go unnoticed by others in the town. Rochdale football club chairman Fred Ratcliffe was an admirer and offered him a job fundraising. Cyril accepted and before very long was bringing his own brand of entertainment to the club. It was like nothing they'd ever seen before. Cyril was a massive wrestling fan and Rochdale's version of 'Big Daddy' began to host professional wrestling matches on summer evenings at the football club.

But as Cyril's fundraising efforts began to take off, he soon faced a reality check when he found himself in trouble with the law after selling a raffle ticket to the chief constable of Rochdale. Little did Cyril know he was in breach of public lottery laws, as raffles with prizes over a certain cash value must be sold only to members of a legitimate club or organisation. The police threw the book at him and Cyril ended up with a criminal record. He was bound over to keep the peace for twelve months.

Fortunately for Cyril, changes in the law, which allowed the development of commercial bingo, meant the police couldn't touch his next fundraising venture and in 1960, with the help of Ratcliffe, he set up Rochdale's first bingo hall. With Cyril as manager he and Ratcliffe took full advantage of the craze sweeping the nation.

As the doors swung open to welcome the start of a working-class gambling boom, Cyril stood proudly at the ready in his best tuxedo. Arms akimbo and with a grin as wide as the River Roch, he knew he'd found a winner.

He was right. By the mid-1960s a quarter of the population was playing bingo. The smoke-filled British bingo hall had more than a hint of glamour and decadence. There was some grumbling in the national media about it encouraging a moral decline, but Cyril took no notice of that. People queued round the block just to hear the 'eyes down' shout of the caller. Rochdale folk loved it. It was exciting. But most of all it was great fun.

And no one was having more fun than Cyril. It was the start of the 1960s, sexual revolution was in the air and the haunting, hypnotic voice of the Shirelles blasted out across the airwaves. Their song 'Will You Still Love Me Tomorrow?' perfectly captured the mood of sexual freedom that began to mark the end of an age of austerity and the decline of Victorian morality. The pill was approved for contraceptive use in Britain in 1961 and a new generation began to leave the repressed background of the 1950s behind. Suddenly it was no longer cool to hold the same values as your parents. Mini skirts were in vogue, promiscuity was becoming more commonplace and an emerging youth culture, fuelled by drugs and rock'n'roll, laid the foundations for much greater sexual freedom. The dawn of Beatlemania was approaching, the seminal working-class film *Saturday Night and Sunday Morning* started to address sex and abortion in a way British cinema never had done and bookshops all over the country sold out of D. H. Lawrence's sexually explicit novel *Lady Chatterley's Lover*.

One of the biggest political sex scandals ever loomed, with the Secretary of State for War, John Profumo, ultimately bringing down the government by lying about his affair with nineteen-year-old showgirl Christine Keeler. Stories of orgies and naked ministers were plastered all over the papers. One of the nation's favourite poets, Philip Larkin, later pithily observed that sex was invented in Britain in 1963.

Not since the roaring '20s had the pursuit of sexual pleasure been so open. But in the shadows of an increasingly permissive society, Cyril had embarked on an altogether different pursuit that would have to stay hidden.

He was abusing boys.

The origins of paedophilia are widely debated and there is no clear view on its causes. Arguments abound on whether it is a behavioural disorder or a type of sexual orientation. For those who view the desire to have sex with a child as a behavioural disorder, its roots lie in dysfunctional, psychological issues to do with power, anger and emotional loneliness.

Cyril always held a grudge about his poor upbringing and he nursed a deep, often violent anger at the way society had viewed him as a young man; the rejections, the refusal to serve him in shops owing to his illegitimacy, the hurtful laughter that followed him because of his weight. It left deep scars and the years of successful social climbing could never fully erase the hurt.

Then there was his mother, Eva, who he lived with until her death. Cyril never knew his father, though he claims he suspected who he was. But he must have known about his mother's alleged promiscuity. Never married, all three of her children were said to be born to different fathers. One former Liberal councillor explained she would regularly pinch the backsides of young Liberals even in her seventies. Rumours about her promiscuity were rife. Perhaps the politest description came from Cyril's friend and fellow Labour councillor, Eileen Kershaw, a confidante of Cyril's throughout the 1960s, who often heard Cyril's grandmother complain, 'Don't send Eva to the Co-op, she'll come back pregnant.'

Fiercely protective of her, Cyril doted on his mother and it was clear to anyone who knew him that she was the most important person in his life. To Cyril she was known as 'Ettie' and she was often by his side at political functions, secured positions at the council and hit the campaign trail with her son. Cyril's fellow MPs soon got used to him turning up at by-elections with his mother in tow. He even managed to get Rochdale Infirmary to name a ward after her. But the fact that he attended so many events with his mum on his arm made continual questions about his bachelor status inevitable.

'I haven't had a lot of time for courting women ... I've tended to be married to politics,' was his stock response when asked about this. The truth was much less banal. He was vigorously pursuing boys.

The police files sent to the Director of Public Prosecutions in the late 1960s make a compelling and disturbing case against Smith. He was a serial abuser. And the first victim of Cyril's that the police know of was groomed in December 1961.

In hours of TV footage of Cyril he frequently boasts of his great relationship with Rochdale's children. A 2003 ITV

Granada tribute for his seventy-fifth birthday sees Cyril speak happily of his time in local politics. The joy shines in his eyes as he fondly recalls how he toured the schools of Rochdale in 1966. Children loved meeting him, he says. 'It's like a fairy story for children. I visited every single school in Rochdale during that year.'

It wasn't the first year he'd spent visiting schools, though. As a councillor, he became governor of twenty-nine local schools and spent as much time as he could turning up in classrooms across the town for whatever spurious reason he could manufacture.

At the end of 1961, during one of Cyril's frequent visits to local schools, his roaming eye zeroed in on a fourteen-year-old boy. As the children enthusiastically sang 'Deck the Halls' during the school carol service, Cyril loitered alone at the back of the hall.

He patiently waited for the singing to finish then made his way to the front, clapping loudly. After congratulating the teacher on his pupils' successful performance, he made his way over to the boy who had caught his eye and commented on his fine voice. 'You've got a great talent there, lad,' he remarked. 'Don't let it go to waste.'

Cyril offered to pay for singing lessons for the boy and, with his parents' agreement, he set these up. Filled with pride at being shown such encouragement by Councillor Smith, a politician who everyone in the town knew, the boy eagerly began to attend regular singing lessons paid for by Cyril. Then, after a few lessons, Cyril invited the boy to drop by his office one night after his class.

The two chatted for a bit and Cyril listened carefully as

the boy proudly told him of the progress he was making. That's good, said Cyril, offering to help him improve even more. To really learn how to control your voice and achieve the optimum singing range, he explained, you needed to practise breathing exercises.

He instructed the boy to drop his trousers, so he could show him what he meant. Then he abused the boy in the privacy of his office.

Of the seven boys who gave police statements about the abuse Cyril Smith inflicted upon them in the 1960s, this young boy was the first. Performing medical examinations, helping with breathing exercises, Cyril's requests for boys to drop their trousers for spurious reasons established a pattern of abusive behaviour.

But after this first experience, he decided it would be too risky to try the same approach again. He needed a safer environment that put him less at risk of being caught. And in Cambridge House children's home he found the perfect vehicle.

As a nine-year-old, Cyril had dreamt of opening a children's home after watching Mickey Rooney star in *Boys Town* and at the start of the 1960s he got his chance. Set up by local politicians, including Cyril, and funded by the town's Rotary Club along with the council, Cambridge House, a 'hostel for working boys', on Castlemere Street opened in 1962. It was a big Victorian house with cold tiled floors and white walls. It had a clinical feel to it and was 'like something out of *Oliver Twist*', as one of the boys described it. Above the door, a Latin inscription read, '*Labor ipse voluptas*': Work itself is a pleasure. It offered affordable lodgings for teenage boys who came from difficult backgrounds. Some were orphans, others wished to escape alcoholic parents, most just had a tough upbringing. Some were even handpicked by Cyril, as he would urge parents undergoing difficulties at home to place their children with him.

Barry Fitton, who had been a resident at Cambridge House, recalled in an interview with the *Manchester Evening News* in late 2012 that Cyril had just turned up at his family home and suggested he move to Cambridge House. The offer of all the food he could want plus shelter was readily accepted by Barry's newly single mother.

Barry was another boy who was later sexually abused by Cyril.

His parents had just split up and the day after he arrived at Cambridge House, Barry was ushered off into a side room to be given a medical examination by Cyril. He was instructed to take his trousers down and Cyril began to grope his testicles. He was later reduced to tears as Cyril took his trousers and pants down, bent him over his knee and smacked him hard with his bare hands. Afterwards, he stroked his backside and fondled his buttocks.

From day one Cyril was the driving force behind Cambridge House. A live-in couple provided food for the boys and cleaned the hostel, but Cyril had keys to the building and came and went as he pleased. He generally gave the impression that he ran the place and was known to the boys as 'the fat man'.

It was the ideal place for a paedophile to operate. He could observe the boys freely, mingle with them at teatime and spot the more vulnerable ones. 'There were some boys he wouldn't go near,' one former resident told me. 'He gave the rough boys from Glasgow a wide berth.' The Glaswegians were down as apprentices for Whipp and Bourne, a local manufacturer specialising in marine switchgear. 'He knew they'd fight back. He picked on the smallest and shyest boys.'

To some of the boys he abused he offered a choice. Leave the hostel and become homeless or accept punishment. All of them reluctantly accepted Cyril's punishment. There were other times, though, when Cyril's temper gave them no choice. The threat of brutal violence always hung in the air. One boy was Ronald Neal, who arrived there in 1964. As one of ten children, Ronald's parents had separated and his mother had been left unable to cope. Her children were subsequently farmed out to different children's homes and Ronald ended up at a home in Outwood, Lancashire. Known as 'runaway Ron' because of his continual efforts to escape, the owner had contacted Cyril to ask for help. 'Bring him to me,' he said.

Straight away, Neal found it a cold and unwelcoming environment. Around a dozen boys stayed there, he says, sometimes more. 'There were no girls. I thought it strange at the time, because there were girls in the children's home I'd come from. But there were only boys there.'

At breakfast the boys would troop into the dining room and sit at a long refectory table. There was a choice of porridge or corn flakes – with water, never milk. Tea was always sandwiches. The boys were discouraged from talking to each other and ate in silence.

Neal had an allergy to meat. 'It made me physically sick,' he explains. To this day he won't go near it. But one evening at Cambridge House he came down from his room to a pile of ham sandwiches, with Cyril stood at the head of the table.

'I can't eat meat, it makes me ill,' he said.

'It's your tea, get it eaten,' snapped Cyril.

Neal stood there trembling, shaking his head. 'I can't,' he said. He was eleven years old and, though tall for his age, he weighed just five-and-a-half stone.

Cyril grabbed him and started to force the sandwich down his throat. Within seconds Neal was sick and vomit splattered Cyril's trousers and shoes. Cyril erupted. A cold fury shone in his eyes and he backhanded Neal across the face, smashing his head back against the wall. Two teeth fell to the floor and blood dribbled down his chin. His head was bleeding badly.

He had to go to hospital to have stitches in a cut on the back of his head. He told them what had happened and was advised to say nothing further. 'I was told that I should say I'd fallen,' he explains. 'They knew who ran Cambridge House and nobody wanted any trouble.'

It was years later before Neal first realised who had attacked him. 'I had no idea who he was. We just called him "the fat man". I'd moved on and was put with foster parents. That's where I first saw Cyril Smith on the front page of the local newspaper. I told my foster parents all about it and they said they believed me, but Cyril was an important person so it was best to drop it. People said that all my life. It was as though he was untouchable.'

Shocking as it is, Neal's story is one of the less distressing. To sit before grown men forty years later and listen to them recount their own terrifying ordeal with Cyril Smith is an experience no one can prepare for. There is anger, confusion and a deep sense of shame at what happened. Violence, groping, spanking and fondling as part of a perverted ritual are recalled from evenings that will never be erased from their memories. Some did try to fight back but they were no match for this 29-stone bully. One explained how the shame of what happened had led him to flee the hostel and sleep rough in alleyways and doorways, turning his back on everyone he knew. The casual abuse Cyril meted out changed these boys' lives. Their innocence was smashed in the ugliest possible way. As Cyril's legend continued to grow these stories of abuse and humiliation were remote footnotes, seemingly destined never to be heard.

Although most of the boys were too ashamed or too afraid to speak out, some of the boys were determined to make sure this side of Cyril was known and gave statements to the police. These affidavits show a chilling pattern of abuse: Cyril throwing his weight around, ordering perverted medical inspections and ritually humiliating boys. Terrified boys sat before police officers, warning them of how one of Rochdale's most powerful politicians was getting out of control.

By now Cyril's penchant for corporal punishment was becoming known across the town, so much so he would literally offer his services to give boys 'a bloody good hiding' if they stepped out of line. This disciplinarian populism resonated at the time and, according to Stephen Moore, who was to go on to become a Labour councillor in the 1970s, parents on Rochdale estates would often use Cyril's name to try and frighten badly behaved boys.

'He was a kind of bogeyman. Parents would say, "If you don't start behaving, we'll call for Cyril Smith." And sometimes they would,' he explained. 'Cyril would make his way round, tell the parents he was happy to help, then go upstairs and spank boys till they screamed. He saw it as a kind of public service.'

The fact that he could hide his lust for boys and pretend he was carrying out an important public duty, merely instilling discipline, must have made him feel untouchable. He was riding the crest of a populist wave and was seen as the kind of politician the town needed. In the post-war years civic figures like Cyril and T. Dan Smith in Newcastle were much admired. They came to symbolise upward mobility and a sense that working-class leaders were replacing figures from a pre-war patrician era.

One person who observed Cyril's rising star was Lyndon Price. He arrived in Rochdale in March 1965 to take up a job at the council as children's officer. At thirty he was the youngest in the country to hold the position. 'I can still remember getting off the bus now and seeing a bus heading for Jericho [a village in Lancashire] and wondering if I was in the right place,' he smiles, a faint Welsh lilt betraying his origins. It wasn't long before he began to notice Cyril's stranglehold on the town. 'He was very popular. Everything he did was reported in the local newspaper. He was almost on every page. They built him up to be a god.'

Keen to do a good job, it wasn't long before Price was put to the test, as rumours of Cyril's abuse of boys started to filter through to him. 'It was in November 1965. A social worker came to see me to say he was worried that boys in Cambridge House were being abused by Cyril Smith,' he says.

Aware that he had no powers of entry, as it wasn't a local authority hostel, Price went to see Rochdale's Chief Constable Patrick Ross to voice his concerns. 'He said inquiries would be made,' Price remembers. Then a few months later Ross told him that it had been decided no action would be taken.

This troubled Price. What was this strange kind of punishment that Smith was administering all about? And why was *he* punishing the boys and not the head of the house? Cyril wasn't in charge. Even then Price suspected it was of a sexual nature. 'I trusted Ross. He was honest,' he says. 'But I wondered if he'd been leaned on.' Deep down he suspected that Ross knew it would be very difficult to make a case against Cyril because he was too powerful.

'He would have rubbished the boys, had witnesses from all over the country saying what a great man he was who did all this work for charity, and he would have had our jobs, that's for sure,' Price says.

It's hard to understand from today's perspective the kind of power Cyril had back then, but Price offers a valuable insight.

'He had a network of people in high places and he could pull their strings and get what he wanted done,' he says. This was the benefit Cyril had as chairman of the establishment committee; his job was to appoint all the senior staff from the town clerk to head teachers. And you can be sure he would have pushed for this position over others because of the power it brought.

'Cyril appointed virtually every headmaster in Rochdale. In fact he appointed most people in senior positions. They were all Cyril's men. And he was very popular in the sense that it would need a lot of evidence to get people to believe anything contrary to what he told them.'

Cyril had become so synonymous with Rochdale that people defended him as a matter of civic pride. To criticise Cyril was almost unthinkable. You would be accused of knocking Rochdale.

Price never told anyone else about his doubts about Cyril. Not even his wife. After his experience with the police he feared it would get back to Cyril if he pursued it. But he was of the view that someone must have warned Cyril because he never got another complaint about boys from Cambridge House.

And he wasn't likely to either. Soon afterwards, the council's children's committee decided they could no longer keep funding Cambridge House. Hundreds of boys had been through the doors over the years, seeking respite from family problems and troubled homes. They had hoped for a better future, a stable home and to be kept out of harm's way. Cyril Smith was the last thing they needed.

Cyril wasn't losing any sleep over the trail of havoc he was leaving in his wake, though. At least not yet. He was busy climbing the political ladder and had more important things to occupy him.

In 1966, at the age of thirty-eight, Cyril fulfilled a boyhood ambition when he was elected mayor of Rochdale. It capped a remarkable journey from the time he'd stood on the town hall steps almost thirty years ago as an impoverished child from the backstreets of Rochdale, dreaming that one day he'd become mayor. It was, he said, the best year of his life. That year he was also awarded an MBE in the Queen's Birthday Honours. In the grainy black-and-white footage of the BBC *Man Alive* documentary, 'Santa Claus for a Year', made in the same year, Cyril stands resplendent in his mayoral chains of office, proudly gazing ahead with the thinnest trace of a smile on his lips as the Rochdale Youth Orchestra perform for him.

He's shown coming out the front door of his family home on Emma Street and getting into a limousine, framed by two mayoral lanterns, which stood outside his house for a year while he was mayor. He made his mother, Eva, lady mayoress.

'I remember him turning up at our house in that limousine,' recalls his fellow councillor Eileen Kershaw. 'The doors would fly open and Cyril and his mum would get out. The driver would walk ahead of them carrying above his head two of the biggest portions of fish and chips you'd ever seen. It was a strange sight.'

Narrated by the novelist and journalist Angela Huth, the BBC footage of Cyril's time as mayor gives an eerie insight into how Cyril kept his double life secret.

'He does everything to protect his image and succeeds,' she says. 'The local newspaper is sometimes known as "Cyril's scrapbook".'

Cyril is then shown sitting opposite two local journalists, drawing heavily on a cigarette. He says he's 'appalled' at how they handled a story in Saturday's paper about the local football club being denied indoor training facilities.

'It wasn't me,' says one of the journalists defensively.

'It's a story out of nothing,' he says sternly. 'They must have been struggling to put something on the front page. If they had phoned me up I would have tried to find them something.'

After Cyril leaves, the cameras turn to one of the reporters who gives a hint of the seeds of doubt that were starting to be sown.

'He's popular,' he says. 'I think he's done a great deal for the town. But people have hyped up this thing that it's Smith's town. People get the impression that he's the be-all and end-all. But that's not the case.'

Later on in the documentary Cyril's mother makes an appearance. As his mayoress, she would finish her shift as the town hall cleaner and change into her glad rags to be whisked away by limousine to perform civic duties at hundreds of engagements. It's a wonderful story. She says she's proud of her son and remembers how she laughed when he told her as a nine-year-old that he was going to be mayor one day.

'He started from scratch as an ordinary poor boy. We've never had anything,' she says, giving the impression that her son's success still hasn't sunk in. 'After the hard life we've had, and then to become the first citizen of the town, it is rather much, isn't it?'

It certainly was. Gracie Fields had once remarked that she was 'taught to respect God, the King and the mayor of Rochdale, in that order'. But as Cyril was basking in the glory of becoming Rochdale's first citizen and England's footballers were raising the World Cup trophy for the first and only time, 1966 was about to throw up another twist that would end up changing the course of national politics. Cyril Smith quit the Labour Party.

There had been tensions for a while among his Labour colleagues. Some didn't like Cyril's big-headedness. There was a growing resentment at the enormous publicity he generated for himself wherever he went. But matters came to a head over an argument about housing rents. With the council facing a £120,000 deficit on the housing account, difficult decisions had to be taken to balance the books. Putting the increase solely on the domestic rates bill was simply impractical. As chairman of the council, Cyril reasoned that they would have to increase council house rents as well. The way he saw it, there was no alternative. This made perfect sense, but he hadn't reckoned on how politically difficult a pill this would be for Labour councillors to swallow, knowing that council house tenants were traditionally core Labour voters.

Matters became further complicated when the Labour Minister of Housing and Local Government, Richard Crossman, called on all councils not to raise rents. Despite this intervention, Cyril still convinced his Labour colleagues to continue with the rent increase. It would be unfair to balance the books by raising the rates alone. Then, halfway through the council meeting at which this decision was to be ratified, a nervous cough attracted Cyril's attention and a scrap of paper was passed up to him on his mayoral platform.

As Cyril's eyes followed the hurriedly written scrawl before him, anger worked its way across his face. The Labour group had met informally before the council meeting, the note read, and had decided to vote against the rent increases. Suddenly the red mist descended and Cyril stood up. From this minute, he loudly announced across the chamber, I am no longer a member of the Labour Party.

It was a classic Cyril tantrum. And it made headlines. Mayors didn't usually change parties halfway through their term. But then few were as hot-headed and impetuous as Cyril.

According to Eileen Kershaw, Cyril probably regretted it almost immediately afterwards. 'He told me he sat by his phone all the next day waiting for it to ring and for him to be asked to come back,' she said. 'But the phone never rang.'

Eileen wrote a letter asking for Cyril to come back. 'I couldn't get one councillor to sign it. They just didn't want him back,' she says.

The man who took pride in his image as Mr Rochdale enjoyed great popularity with the public. But in his own party there was little respect among his colleagues. They were happy to get rid of him.

But Cyril did at least cause some damage by making sure Labour lost control of the council. When he left he took four other Labour councillors with him and set up an Independents group, which was to last for another four years. The fact that Labour no longer held control meant that Cyril could remain chair of a number of committees, including the education committee.

But a wedge had been driven between Cyril and the Labour Party. Relations had soured. Colleagues who he used to laugh and joke with now turned their backs when he approached. They had put up with his stunts and impetuous behaviour for too long. Now they'd had enough. Cyril's tantrums had made sure Labour lost power of the council and his former colleagues wouldn't forget this. When Labour regained power in 1972 they exacted revenge on Cyril in the most brutal way possible.

It would create decades of enmity between Cyril and the Labour Party, and he never forgave them.

'It was a time for taking stock,' he said of the period in his biography. His political career was uncertain and he wasn't sure whether Rochdale was ready to embrace a new Independent party. In the end it wasn't and his efforts to divert power from the big three – Labour, Conservative and Liberal – failed miserably.

But while he pondered how to recalibrate the local political compass, he was only too aware that his outburst had created a new set of problems. Cyril's temper had ensured he now had plenty more political enemies to deal with. But that wasn't the only problem he had to face.

Soon the rumours and allegations of abuse would finally be taken seriously.

It began when a former Cambridge House boy was arrested for trying to solicit minors for sexual purposes in Rochdale. He complained he'd only done what Cyril Smith had done. This time the police decided to investigate. They first sought to address allegations that boys were leaving Howarth Cross School at lunchtime and were being abused at a house nearby. Cyril was named by one of the boys.

The first Eileen Kershaw knew about it was when Cyril burst into her house one night with his mother in tow. He'd come round most nights after council meetings to talk politics and was usually in a jovial mood. But tonight was different. 'This young lad is making all sorts of wild allegations about me and has landed me in a lot of trouble,' he said breathlessly, his face pale.

Eileen pulled a chair up. What kind of allegations? She asked. 'Sex allegations,' responded Cyril. The police had a vendetta against him, he said. They wanted to bring him down and they were trying to turn boys against him.

Night after night he'd come and pour his heart out to Eileen. 'He never knew when to go home,' she said. 'He'd complain about this boy who'd accused him of abuse. He was making stories up and the police were egging him on. He'd wear us down with his woe. It was really eating away at him. But we believed him. He was very convincing.'

Not so convincing though that Eileen didn't confront another boy from Cambridge House that she knew. He'd gone on to open his own business in Rochdale and Eileen would see him from time to time. One day, when she saw him parked outside, she put her head in the driver's window and just came out with it. 'Did anything strange happen at Cambridge House? I mean, did Cyril do anything to the boys?'

He was silent. She waited for his response but it never came. He just stared ahead. 'He just wouldn't answer,' she says. Minutes passed. Then he drove off.

Cyril continued to come round almost every night. He'd slump in Eileen's chair and talk for hours about how the police were plotting against him. It was beginning to take its toll. He wasn't eating and he'd put his hand in his pocket and scoop handfuls of pills into his mouth. 'What are those?' she asked one night.

'Valium,' he said.

Other boys had now given statements to the police. The evidence was growing.

But Cyril wasn't planning to lie back and wait for the police to prosecute. He would beat these boys. He started by paying the police a visit demanding to know whether they'd prosecute him. 'He came round boasting one night,' recalls Eileen. 'He said he'd told them to sort it out and had frightened them.'

This was far from the truth and typical Cyril bravado. Cyril did indeed walk into Rochdale police station and ask to speak to investigating officers. But a police transcript from the interview that followed shows the police were less than frightened. They were more annoyed with Cyril for trying to interfere in the investigation and with witnesses.

Cyril was in fact doing just that. One of the boys who'd been abused, Kevin Griffiths, recalled that Cyril even turned up at his wedding and wheedled his way into the photos. 'There's nothing I haven't done for these boys,' he'd tell the police. 'I was like a father to them.'

His arguments were getting more convincing, and Eileen and her husband Jack would listen for nights on end to his valium-fogged lament. The police, the boys, they were just jealous of his success. It was all a conspiracy. After everything he'd done for this town, this was how they treated him.

Eileen listened. And listened. She'd been friends with Cyril for years. He knew her children. She'd never seen any hint of the side that the police were investigating. It just didn't add up. Was he really a child abuser?

Of course, she'd had her own run-ins with Cyril. He argued with everyone. When Eileen appeared on television talking about Rochdale's first day nursery that had opened on Ramsay Street, Cyril phoned the BBC to complain. 'His mum was against day nurseries, he made an idiot of himself,' she said. 'He just couldn't keep his nose out of things and he didn't like it when something was happening that he wasn't involved in. He constantly craved the limelight.'

Whenever the two of them had a fall out, Cyril's mum, a cleaner at the council, would come into Eileen's office the next day and attack her with the hoover. 'She literally would hoover all over my feet!'

But she counted Cyril as a friend. His heart was in the right place, she believed. And she didn't want to see him destroyed.

So one night, as they listened to Cyril complaining about the injustice of everything once again, she decided that enough was enough. She asked her husband to go and get the MP, Jack McCann, to see if he could help.

Jack had no car and lived in Eccles at the time. So her husband went to pick him up. At the end of the 1960s, Labour was in power and McCann was a Lord of the Treasury in Harold Wilson's government. McCann knew Cyril well. 'Cyril had pestered the life out of McCann to get him an MBE,' recalls Eileen.

That night McCann sat on the hearth at the Kershaws' house on Greenhill Avenue drinking coffee for hours as Cyril pleaded his case. For six hours he talked solidly. At three in the morning, Cyril necked a fistful of Valium and asked McCann to help him. McCann's face was glazing over. They were all exhausted. He thought for a moment, rubbed his eyes and finished the last of his coffee. He would contact the Director of Public Prosecutions and ask for a decision to be made one way or another, he said. This had to be settled once and for all. Cyril could not be seen as an object of pursuit. This wasn't justice. It was turning into a cruel sport.

'This has gone on long enough,' he said as he made his way to the door to be driven home by Eileen's husband. 'I'll get him to make a decision.'

Weeks passed and they heard nothing. Then Cyril rang Eileen's husband Jack at the school where he worked. By now Cyril had also gone into manufacturing and was involved in a small but growing spring-making business. After learning the ropes working at Ratcliffe's Springs (owned by Fred Ratcliffe), he'd launched his own venture. Spring making was a vital industry in the town as textile machinery depended on it. When Jack came to the phone, Cyril invited him to his office. He had something important to tell him.

An hour later, Jack pulled up at Smith's Springs and made his way into Cyril's office where he found Cyril at his desk with tears rolling down his face. 'It's over,' he said, wiping the tears from his eyes. His bottom lip wobbled. 'It's finished. They've decided there's no case to answer.'

Chapter 4

Revenge

Towards the end of the 1960s, Cyril's entrepreneurial efforts began to pay off. His spring-manufacturing business now employed seventy people and it looked as though a brighter future beckoned in business rather than in politics. This sometimes played on Cyril's mind, and he admitted to holding a few regrets about never becoming a bingo entrepreneur. He'd realised there were silly amounts of money to be made there. But his acrimonious departure from the Labour Party remained a powerful motivating force for him to remain in public life. He was shocked at how they hadn't wanted him back and for years he nursed a deep hatred towards his former colleagues. He wasn't going to rest until he'd had the last laugh. When, in the spring of 1972, Labour won control of the council they systematically set about stripping him of every position he held and removing him from committees. They purposely did all they could to humiliate him. He lost his education post, was removed from the youth committee, dismissed from the youth employment committee, sacked from the committee of Rochdale youth orchestra, booted off the committee of Rochdale youth theatre workshop and sacked from the boards of governors of twenty-nine Rochdale schools.

Despite the fact that his business was now thriving, he couldn't let attacks on his reputation go unanswered. Cyril Smith the businessman would always have to play second fiddle to Cyril Smith the politician. Politics was in his blood. And there were scores to settle. Even before the events of spring 1972, Cyril was resolved to enact revenge upon the Labour Party at all costs.

Lyndon Price, Rochdale Council's children's officer, remembers Cyril dropping into his office one day in 1968 and dumping a box of thousands of pens on his desk. 'Can you use these?' he asked. 'They're no use to me anymore.' Price peered into the box and saw 'Rochdale Independents Party' emblazoned across the pens. 'The party's over,' said Cyril as he marched down the corridor.

Cyril had decided to return to his roots and later that year he rejoined the Liberal Party, which had first inspired him to take up politics. It was eighteen years since he'd left the party and a very different Cyril Smith now collected his Liberal membership card. The youthful idealism of yesteryear had long since washed away. Cyril was now as tough as teak and ready for a new political challenge.

Now that he'd managed to evade the law and was certain that he wouldn't be charged with child abuse, he set about securing the nomination as Liberal parliamentary candidate for the 1970 general election. Not everyone within the party was happy about this prospect, though, and some members resigned as a result. But he managed to scrape home.

Cyril had returned at the right time and it was not difficult for him to take over Rochdale's Liberal Party. Since the 1950s, they had been in steep decline and a report from the Liberal Party archives shows just how moribund they were. Indicating that someone from the national party was sent to try and improve the Rochdale Liberal Party in the late 1960s, the report states that the town's long Liberal tradition 'can only be bleak in Rochdale as long as the present set-up exists'. The longer no prospective parliamentary candidate exists, the report concluded, 'the harder it will be for Liberalism to hold its place in Rochdale'.

Now that Cyril had been appointed the parliamentary candidate, he set about trying to reverse years of decline. He began campaigning as hard as he could, with much of his energies directed at venting his hatred of the Labour Party.

He was, of course, facing Jack McCann and, to those who knew how Jack had helped Cyril, there was astonishment at the personal attacks Cyril began to make.

As the campaign in Rochdale intensified for the 1970 general election Eileen Kershaw remembers seeing Cyril's big black automatic Mercedes slowly snaking its way round one of the many hills of Rochdale. Cyril's voice boomed out from the tannoy strapped to the roof.

'Vote Cyril Smith and get rid of your silent errand boy MP,' he urged passers-by heading home from work. For Kershaw this was a watershed moment. 'I stopped the car and said, "Cut it out, Cyril. There's no need for personal attacks. He's just done you a big favour."' Cyril slammed the car into reverse to drive away. In the passenger seat his mum glowered.

Deep down, Kershaw says, Cyril knew he couldn't beat McCann. 'McCann was a real gentleman. Cyril was very rough round the edges.' In 1970 he lost by over 5,000 votes.

It was the first major defeat Cyril had suffered and he didn't like it. I knew he would win, he said later of his battle with McCann. But that didn't soften the loss one bit. He hated losing. The smiles of his former Labour colleagues at the election count rubbed salt into his wounds. He knew what they were thinking. Mr Rochdale wasn't so powerful outside of the Labour Party, was he? He thought he was bigger than the party, didn't he? Maybe now he'll realise how foolish he was.

Or maybe not. Cyril still thought he was bigger than the Labour Party and had more guts and vision than every one of those obsequious lapdogs. But beating the Labour Party would take some doing. Liberals win seats in south-west England and sleepy coastal towns not in northern industrial areas. He would have to try a different approach.

This thought stuck with him as he returned to his business life. As he went through the order papers with his business partner Geoff Harrison, he contemplated how politics needed to change. He'd long ceased to fight elections on the basis of the rosette pinned to his lapel and he could see the public were tiring of party politics.

The general election of 1970 had been dubbed an 'unpopularity contest' with voters showing more interest in the England football team's campaign at the World Cup in Mexico. This wasn't lost on Cyril. With the country facing a decade of economic crisis, confident extroverts who could take the public with them were suddenly in demand. This was the role Cyril had been auditioning for all his life.

It wasn't long before he was to get another chance to secure the prize he wanted. One night Cyril's phone rang; it was the leader of the Liberal Party, Jeremy Thorpe. There could be a by-election for us in Rochdale soon, he announced. I'd like you to be our candidate. Jack McCann had cancer.

Cyril was hesitant at first. He'd think about it. But he didn't dwell on it for too long. The ignominy of the Labour Party stripping him of his various titles and positions hurt and a deep, cold-blooded anger now took hold of him. He withdrew into himself and spent every waking hour thinking about getting his own back. Even when he was asleep he dreamt about revenge.

Yes, he would fight the by-election and yes, he would have revenge. When Jack McCann passed away he knew there was no challenger with a local record like his. The seat was there for the taking. And he would teach Labour a lesson they'd never forget. They'd taken every political job Cyril had and now he was going to take the most important political job in the town from them. If they thought this was a safe Labour seat, they were wrong. He would see to that.

Politicians win elections competing as candidates for different political parties, pitting policies and manifestos against rival ideas on how the country should be run. This was peripheral stuff for Cyril. He planned to win the parliamentary seat of Rochdale with a very different strategy. He was going to convince voters to back him on the sheer strength of his personality and his record as a champion for Rochdale. 'Vote Cyril Smith – the Man' instructed the large plain posters that started to loom out from street corners and gable ends in Rochdale. There was no mention of the Liberal Party he was representing. He wasn't planning to debate political niceties; he was going to perform. And he was going to win hearts and minds in every community.

He began on Milkstone Road with his eye firmly on the 9,000 immigrant voters, mainly Pakistani, that lived in the area. The street today is noticeable for its many takeaways and restaurants. A rich aroma of Asian spice and food fills the air. There are Indian and Pakistani sweet emporiums, fabric shops, jewellery shops adorned with bindis, anklets and panjas, bridal shops and barbers. The streets hum with life and at the house of Mohammad Pasha, who runs the Pakistani Welfare Association, there are plenty of colourful memories to match.

Mr Pasha was a key figure in the 1972 by-election and remembers the day that Cyril came to see him. 'He came to my house and asked for our support,' he says, smiling as the memory comes back to him. 'He asked if I'd listen to him speak for a few minutes and said, "This is what I want to do for our town, if you don't like it then vote Labour."' In those few minutes, Cyril outlined a new settlement for Rochdale. Better community relations, a Member of Parliament that would hold surgeries and provide a much stronger voice for the Asian community. He wanted to democratise local powers and invite the Asian community to important meetings. And he'd make sure the bosses at the council and the head of police knew their views. Pasha listened and was impressed.

As a Labour supporter, he immediately called a meeting with his colleagues and four of them made the trip down to the local Labour Party headquarters on Oldham Road the next day.

Everyone was busy unpacking leaflets and no one showed any interest in the offer of help they brought. After a few uncomfortable moments trying to get someone's attention, a councillor finally gave them the time of day – but only to abruptly tell them they didn't need any help. 'We were told they didn't need our support. They had plenty of help already,' Pasha recalls. They were shown the door and the four of them left disappointed.

At the time racism was rife in Britain and there was a genuine fear running through the immigrant community in Rochdale. The last Labour government had pushed through a bill removing the right of Asians to enter the UK and trade unions were often involved in conflicts with migrant workers. London dockers had even taken part in demonstrations in support of Enoch Powell's 'rivers of blood' speech carrying placards that read, 'Back Britain, not Black Britain'.

There were huge divisions in the country. Powell was ultimately credited with helping Ted Heath win the general election for the Conservatives in 1970 and polls at the time suggested he was the most popular politician in the country. But his speech criticising Commonwealth immigration did enormous damage and the mood in the street hardened against immigrants. Guests at a West Indian christening party in Powell's constituency were stabbed in an ugly attack soon afterwards with a group of white youths chanting 'Powell' as blood was spilled.

Cyril, perceptive as ever, capitalised on the poor approach shown by Labour. It's not surprising that his willingness to engage with the immigrant community and promise of better community relations struck such a chord. Within the next few days Mr Pasha called Cyril and asked if he would have a meeting with them. At the meeting fifteen members of the Pakistani Welfare Association agreed to canvass for him and encourage the community to switch from Labour to vote Liberal. 'Lads,' Cyril smiled. 'You will remember this day. I will never let you down.'

It wasn't long before hundreds of 'Vote Cyril Smith – the Man' posters began to appear on the streets nearby. Cyril was winning hearts and minds all right, and taking thousands of voters with him.

He was as good as his word, too. He ran surgeries on Sunday mornings at the heart of the Asian community, often bringing the chief constable along, too. Jack McCann lived in Eccles and held his surgeries there. 'We never saw him,' said Pasha. They couldn't see enough of Cyril.

Cyril's style of politics reaped rewards. 'I support personalities not political parties,' Pasha explains. 'All political parties have their own agenda. It's who you trust on a personal level.'

Pasha and Cyril became close. He would translate Cyril's speeches and organise events for him. 'He was a great public speaker,' he says. 'When there was all this controversy about Pakistan getting nuclear weapons, Cyril came out straight away in favour of it. "Every country has a right to defend itself, Pakistan too," he argued. Cyril was the only politician I knew saying things like this. He said the *Satanic Verses* should be burned. He was outspoken and very courageous.'

It's fair to say Cyril went the extra mile in a number of

areas. In his mind he was councillor, mayor, Member of Parliament and champion of the people all rolled into one – not simply a parliamentarian. A kind of super local politician that could do anything. 'People would phone him at two in the morning to say someone was being deported,' Pasha explained. 'Cyril would phone the immigration officer and say, "Do not deport this person until I've spoken to the relevant officer in the morning." He stopped a lot of people being deported.'

Pasha is not alone in saying this. Khandaker Abdul Musabbir, who opened the Star of Bengal restaurant in 1976, one of the first Asian restaurants in Rochdale, similarly recalls how Cyril captured hearts and minds in his community. Cyril dined regularly there and Musabbir was a big supporter who was happy to campaign for him. 'He said to me, "I'm not an MP for the Liberal Party. I'm an MP for Rochdale." I always remember that,' he grins. 'I voted for him as a person, because I knew if we had a problem he would help us.'

Within a short space of time Cyril transformed politics in the Asian community and became a powerful voice. 'When we started the Jalalia Jame Mosque lots of white people tried to stop us getting planning permission,' Musabbir explains. 'Cyril stepped in and lobbied the council for us. He laid the first brick and gave us £50 towards our fighting fund.'

Cyril also had his hands full with plenty of immigration cases. 'I would take people to see him,' explains Musabbir. 'He helped all these people bring their family here.'

The Star of Bengal is still there today, albeit under different ownership. Now retired, Musabbir looks back at the period when Cyril came to prominence in the 1970s as a high-water mark for politics in the town. 'A lot of the community got behind Cyril in 1972,' he says. 'We knew he was on *our* side.'

It was in this community that Cyril unquestionably had the biggest influence. 'He broke down barriers,' said Pasha. 'White people were not approachable to us beforehand. Cyril changed that.'

Few would deny this, and it's clear that Cyril did do some good here. The climate of fear and racism in the 1970s was ugly and needed to be challenged. During the 1972 by-election, leaflets were regularly posted with the headline 'Enoch is right'. Community relations in Rochdale did improve and when race riots hit neighbouring towns in the summer of 2001, Rochdale avoided the troubles. Race relations, while never perfect, remain strong. The Oldham race riots in 2001 never came to Rochdale. And while the BNP won a number of council seats in Burnley the far right party has never come close in Rochdale.

But there are different views and questions have always been asked about the style of politics Cyril encouraged. Another of his champions during the by-election year was Karim Dad, also from the Pakistani Welfare Association. Dad was an enthusiastic member of the campaign, urging everyone to vote for Cyril, and a year later he became the Liberal candidate in the local elections for Wardleworth and Newbold. During these elections, which Cyril stood in and comfortably retained his council seat – despite now being an MP – Dad was arrested and charged with electoral fraud. He had been reported for collecting polling cards from residences people had left to return to Pakistan and arranging for teams of people to impersonate those residents. While on bail, he absconded to Pakistan and was never seen again. According to one of the officers involved in the investigation, Mike Smith, who was working for Greater Manchester Police CID at the time, the fraud was carried out on a 'massive' scale. While Cyril was not directly implicated in this fraud, Dad was a key part of Cyril's vote-winning strategy in the area and questions remain as to what Cyril knew.

Cyril's legacy regarding race relations is not universally seen as positive. Others believe he thrived off a feudal and tribal politics that was synonymous with corruption. Far from fostering community cohesion, he helped encourage a ghetto culture.

One person voicing such an opinion is the town's former Labour MP Lorna Fitzsimons. While she acknowledges Labour's failings when Cyril came to power, she dismisses the idea that Cyril delivered a better politics. 'He wanted to be an imperial leader and have his own tribe,' she says. 'He knew how to subjugate people and he carried on like a South Asian despot. He ruled with abject fear and patronage. You were either in the circle or out of the circle.'

These are strong words, and she doesn't hold back. When Cyril arranged for community leaders to have their photos taken with the chief of police, she argues, he was giving them power to carry on as though they were above the law. 'They'd show these pictures to people back home in Pakistan,' she says. 'Cyril was giving them a lot of power. He allowed a very bad kind of Asian politics to grow and be cultivated in Rochdale. Asian leaders would raid houses and break people's doors down and Cyril allowed them.'

One former Liberal Democrat, who was abused by Cyril, says Cyril skilfully worked the Asian community better than any politician before or after him. 'In that respect he was the George Galloway of his day,' he said. 'He focused on who was likely to vote and abandoned the people he should be standing up for. He adopted his language for his audience. He had a Pied Piper effect. Everyone was dancing to his tune.'

Labour had certainly left a vacuum for Cyril to exploit and he took full advantage. There was more than a touch of the despot about his style, too. He was not known for using soft power. Bludgeoning decisions through by sheer willpower was always favoured over consensual leadership.

Back on the campaign trail in 1972 it wasn't just voters he was winning over. Quite remarkably, he managed to convince the agent for the Labour candidate, Lawrence Cunliffe, to switch sides and become Cyril's agent during the campaign. Things were beginning to look bleak for Labour.

The MP for Nottingham West, Michael English, was among those sent to the by-election on orders from the Labour leader, Harold Wilson. He'd previously replaced Cyril as the youngest councillor in Rochdale when he'd been elected in 1953 at the age of twenty-two. Returning to Rochdale, he immediately sensed a big political shift. Wilson wanted to know whether Labour was going to retain the seat. Within hours of his arrival English knew one thing was certain. Cyril was going to win.

'You could feel it,' he says. 'Cyril had all the momentum going with him. The tabloid press were following him round.

He was pressing all the right buttons. It was a very populist campaign.'

When it came to 'people politics' Cyril knew how to work the town better than anyone else. And he played this card at every opportunity. Early on, the *Daily Mirror* indicated that Cyril would win and the sense of an underdog having victory within his grasp grew by the day. Cyril knew it; the town could feel it, and he threw himself into campaigning like a man possessed.

Watching Cyril canvass was an astonishing sight. There wasn't a door in Rochdale he hadn't knocked on. Streets where Gracie Fields had hauled a home-made maypole down and sang outside the pubs for money over half a century earlier were now the stomping ground for a new star. 'He'd thunder up the path, pound on the door and say, "You know me, I'm Cyril. Are you for me or against me?"' recalls Eileen Kershaw. To say he made an impression is an understatement. The strength of his personality alone could transform the most apathetic voter into an ardent supporter.

The 1972 by-election attracted considerable media attention and was a major turning point for the Liberal Party. It was also a turning point for politics. On the eve of the first golden age of TV, with three colour channels to choose from, Cyril was cooking up a calculated and astute form of populist politics that would put him at the vanguard of a new breed of politician. As reporters and cameramen crowded this towering figure on the campaign trail, he had them feeding out of the palm of his hand.

The arrival of colour TV towards the end of the 1960s and the re-launch of *The Sun* as a tabloid newspaper in 1969 gave birth to a new anti-establishment populism. A weakening of the 'old boy network' and an increase in social mobility allowed astute politicians like Cyril to peddle an increasingly seductive 'man of the people' persona that was seen to be much more in tune with modern Britain than yesterday's political elites. It was an incredibly effective political weapon and put Cyril in pole position to win the by-election.

'I knew I was going to crack it in the last fortnight,' grinned Cyril years later. Talking about the night of the count, he said, 'I knew before I had got to the town hall that I had won because I had a phone call from someone that said "you're in". Strictly illegal, of course.'

On 26 October 1972, Cyril Smith became the new Liberal MP for Rochdale with a huge swing in his favour. Lawrence Cunliffe trailed by over 5,000 votes. At Rochdale Town Hall when the result was announced, Cyril raised two giant hands in triumph. Delight shone in his eyes. He'd reached yet another peak in a relentlessly ambitious climb. TV cameras crowded round him and flash light bulbs popped as reporters jostled to get a word with the new MP. As activists cheered a stunning victory, Cyril momentarily looked at the dejected camp of Labour activists around his opponent. It was an image he'd conjured up thousands of times and now here it was in reality. He sucked in the smell of victory and let the sight of his despondent opponents indelibly print itself on his memory. He wouldn't forget this as long as he lived. He had crushed them and revenge tasted sweeter than he'd ever imagined. It would take twenty-five years before Labour regained the seat.

For a party that had just seven MPs his victory represented seismic change. The Liberals could normally only take rural Tory seats. Now they were winning northern industrial Labour seats.

In the years that followed, Cyril's by-election victory triggered a number of Liberal gains. 'When I became MP I was only the seventh Liberal MP and if you take Devon and Cornwall out, I was the only English MP. It was the turning point for the party,' he explained. 'They won four by-elections the year after. But they wouldn't have won any of them if I hadn't won. They never gave me the credit for that.' The Isle of Ely, Ripon, Sutton and Cheam, and Berwick delivered new Liberal MPs through stunning victories. With typical modesty, Cyril added that, 'My victory in Rochdale was the turning point for the Liberal Party in British history.' After a long spell in the wilderness, Cyril helped lead the Liberals back towards the political mainstream. He became the popular face of the Liberals and was a household name. Instantly recognisable, for many he was the politician that people who didn't care for politics knew. 'He was like nothing we'd ever seen before,' said *The Guardian*'s Simon Hoggart. 'He was a mountain of a man, working class with a real no-nonsense attitude. He really shook the place up.' He made his way into the public consciousness in a way few politicians could ever hope to. 'Ten years after he ceased to be a Liberal Member of Parliament,' the Liberal Democrat MEP Chris Davies later admitted, 'he was still the best-known Liberal politician.'

It had been a bitter contest, but among his Labour opponents there was grudging respect. Michael English admits that Cyril fully deserved to become a Member of Parliament and could easily have led his party. 'If he'd been to Cambridge or Oxford I honestly think he could have been leader of any political party.'

The result sent shockwaves through Westminster and quickly propelled Cyril to the attention of every lobby journalist. As the first working-class Liberal MP he was a rare species and soon in demand. In a party typified by Eton- and Oxford-educated, assiduously polite and effete types, Cyril came from a galaxy far away. He was as conspicuous as a bear at a dinner party.

Some may have been fazed by this attention. Not Cyril. He thrived on it. In fact, according to Lord Hoyle, formerly the MP for Nelson and Colne and Warrington North, this was a key reason why Cyril had rejoined the Liberals.

'He was a showman and it suited his act,' he explains. 'It was all a bit hammed up and he couldn't play this working-class jovial man of the people act in the Labour Party because there were too many working-class people who'd resent it. In the Liberal Party he was the only working-class guy there. You'd find him holding court with activists and MPs hanging on every word. He'd be saying, "Now this is how it is lad, let me tell you", and they'd be all ears. He just wouldn't get that attention in the Labour Party.'

Cyril was also part of a select club that instantly stood out. In those days politicians had props to define their character. Harold Wilson had his pipe; Jeremy Thorpe had his trilby hat and Edwardian three-piece suit. Cyril had a 29-stone girth. But in terms of making an instant connection with voters, Cyril was arguably the best performer in the House.

Cyril the showman soon set to work as the MP for Rochdale. He hired a train carriage to take his supporters to Westminster the day he took his seat in the House of Commons. But he didn't spend too much time there. He'd prefer to be seen wandering round Rochdale market in his slippers buying tripe. "Eh up, it's Cyril,' someone would shout. And Cyril would wink and begin his act, as he would time and time again.

Like all performers, Cyril fed ravenously on the attention he received. In Alistair Michie and Simon Hoggart's book *The Pact*, about the Lib–Lab government of 1977–8, Cyril is described as 'an extremely sensitive man who frequently sees insults where none is intended'. There was some truth in this, and Cyril was often thin-skinned to the point where he needed praise to perform.

A born extrovert in search of an audience, he became sharper, wittier and more manipulative as his star rose. A sign of his mastery with the electorate can be seen in TV footage of him campaigning in the streets of Rochdale in the early 1970s.

Munching biscuits and chatting easily to youngsters, he pulls out a gingerbread man. 'See that, that's Ted Heath,' he says. 'You're going to eat him up,' a voice responds from a giggling throng of youngsters. 'First thing I'm going to do is scalp him,' explains Cyril, taking the biscuit head off and feeding it to a young lad. As more people crowd round, Cyril holds the beheaded gingerbread man up. 'Now he's no head on, he's got no brains so he's Harold Wilson. We'll take the feet from under him,' he says, handing another part of the biscuit to another youngster. Then, finishing with a typical flourish, he says, 'We'll give you the best bit,' handing the middle to another youngster. 'This is the Liberal bit, the heart.'

But behind this northern bonhomie, there was a very shrewd, calculating side. 'He'd come from a very poor background,' explains Lord Hoyle, 'and I think he was amazed at how far he'd come. But it made him even more ambitious. There was a ruthlessness to Cyril that I've not seen in many politicians. Everything he did, he did to aid his progression. He didn't know how far he could go.'

This rapid progress was boosted when his brother Norman followed him into politics and did much to reinforce Cyril's local power base. Norman went on to enjoy a successful career as a local politician, but his first priority was always to protect his brother. He was awarded an MBE in 1988 for services to the local community, was also mayor in 1986, received the freedom of the borough in 2004 and was a councillor for thirty-four years. Throughout that time he was Cyril's line of defence and attack, frequently acting as his mouthpiece in the media and defending him when needed.

Cyril's power was growing by the day and, according to Hoyle, so was his boldness.

He certainly had an eye on how to make money. One time, he remembers, the pair of them sat in a TV studio with former MP Winston Spencer-Churchill, the grandson of the former Prime Minister, for a political programme for Granada.

'Just as we're about to go live, Cyril starts frowning and pulling faces. So the interviewer asks Cyril if everything is OK and he says, "There's just one thing you haven't told me and that's how much we're getting paid." The interviewer says he's sorry but there's no fee and Cyril says, "Well, if that's how it is I'm going," and gets up to leave. There's a minute to go before we go live and Cyril's trying to get us all to leave. The interviewer realises he has a potential disaster on his hands and asks Cyril if £250 would be acceptable. "That's fine," says Cyril, all smiles now, and sits back down again. He never missed a trick.'

There is an old saying that you gain power by giving it away. Cyril had no truck with this whatsoever. He was from the Napoleonic school of thought. 'Power is my mistress,' said Bonaparte. 'I have worked too hard at her conquest to allow anyone to take her away from me.' The French military commander and the Rochdale ruler had this much in common. Accumulating more power and defeating their enemies became a manic obsession.

Great Britain in the 1970s was trapped in a decade of decline. Against a backdrop of power cuts, strikes, failing industries, oil shocks and the three-day week, politicians stared greyly out of colour TV sets and offered little hope. On five separate occasions a state of emergency was declared, rubbish piled up in the streets and the maniacal, bug-eyed face of Johnny Rotten peered through the smoke at febrile concerts howling 'no future'. Families dutifully kept a ready supply of candles at hand.

A sense of impotence hung over the nation. Politics remained in the grip of ideologues and ditherers. Britain was treading water. The whiff of bankruptcy created a pressing need for strong leaders who could get things done and were ruled by common sense. This, along with his gargantuan size and common touch, was one of the reasons why Cyril was taken up by the establishment.

It's thought that Cyril was the main catalyst behind the Lib-Lab pact in the late 1970s that kept the then faltering Labour government on the road. But earlier in the decade, the Conservatives had invited the Liberals to form a coalition under which there was a very real prospect of Cyril being made a minister.

Initially, Cyril wasn't keen on the coalition, knowing that rank-and-file Liberals did not want to prop up a Tory government. But, equally, he liked the idea of a government of national unity and wanted to use electoral reform as a bargaining chip for any deal.

Whether he knew it or not, the momentum building around coalition talks would ultimately shore Cyril's position up, as he was now in the process of being vetted over the possibility of becoming a government minister.

Police files documenting the many allegations of child abuse committed by Cyril were suddenly disappearing. Tony Robinson, a Special Branch officer with Lancashire Police in the 1970s, confirmed that all files on Cyril were removed by MI5 officers from the safe at their police headquarters in Preston and taken to London. It wasn't just the lid of the box that had been slammed shut on Cyril's dark secrets. The box itself was now shipped away to permanent obscurity.

If Cyril was to ever become a government minister then scandals about child abuse could not become public knowledge. All evidence of this had to be hidden. Cyril potentially had a useful role to play. As governments and unions grew further apart, uncompromising militant trade unions were seen as the main reason for Britain's decline. The Tories were itching to tackle union power and people like Cyril were seen as a useful bulwark against the militant tendency.

Cyril had made his views known on the need for a government of national unity. He would have been ideal to keep what were perceived as militant enemies at bay. He could have played a part. And perhaps for that reason the establishment granted him a pardon. Cyril Smith became untouchable.

But the problem with cover-ups is that they rely on a master narrative. The view of the establishment or those who generally control the media takes precedent. The official version passes as the truth. The police, MI5, politicians and the media would protect Cyril by ignoring the rumours and not asking questions. They'd ensure he needn't worry about blue lights flashing outside and knocks at the door. But they couldn't control the whole narrative. In a small town like Rochdale no one could control the human grapevine and gossip rapidly spread.

Stories of Cyril's abuse persisted. Another side to the town's illustrious MP was told all around Rochdale. Few believed it, but it had currency and was starting to reach all kinds of people. 'I'd heard about Cyril's abuse of boys,' Dominic Carman, the son of the famous QC, George, and former Liberal Democrat parliamentary candidate, told me last year. 'I used to visit Rochdale in the 1970s and I heard people talking about it at the hotel bar on numerous occasions.' It speaks volumes that people were prepared to ignore these rumours at the time. There are numerous arrests nowadays relating to historic sex abuse going back to the 1970s because not nearly enough people were held accountable for this crime back then.

It certainly didn't help that the main political narrative in Rochdale was still controlled by Cyril. Expertly so. If he wasn't on the phone calling in favours, haranguing, cajoling and shouting the odds, then he was writing letter after letter. His letter-writing exploits were phenomenal. Everyone remembers getting letters from Cyril. He spoke at every public meeting going and few dared disagree with Cyril's view. He was one of the most innovative campaigners of his time. There was one compelling narrative in Rochdale that crowded out all others – and Cyril was telling it.

But Cyril wasn't the only one who could tell stories. You only have to wander over to Broadfield Park to be reminded of the town's heritage. There you'll find memorials to Lancashire writers such as Edwin Waugh, Margaret Lahee and Oliver Ormerod. In the nineteenth century, Rochdale was known for its great dialect writers who wrote remarkable stories and poems that have survived the test of time. The Lancashire dialect may be less common nowadays, but storytelling is in the town's blood. There's a folk culture that continues to thrive. People tell stories wherever you go.

And that's how I first heard about the dark secrets of Cyril Smith. Knocking on doors on a rainy day in Rochdale introducing myself to voters. 'I'm the Labour candidate and I want to know what issues are important to you,' I'd say to people. 'So you want to be MP for Rochdale?' one person said with a knowing smile. 'Come in for a cup of tea and let me tell you a story.'

Silent Voices #1: The Victims from Cambridge House

It was all I could do to clamber into bed and beg for sleep. I barely had the strength to undress. The only thought I clung to was for everything to be still. But behind my eyes a fever-bright delirium was on the march. As my breathing quickened my throat would tighten and nausea would surge through me. I tried to focus, concentrating on the gaudy designs on peeling wallpaper in this dimly lit room, anything to keep my mind off the churning in my stomach.

It was said that Leonardo da Vinci would gaze at the stains on walls and imagine vivid battles and landscapes. That day cheap, exuberant motifs gave way to a swarm of angry locusts bringing a load of plague and pestilence. I pulled the nylon sheets tightly over my head and felt the sweat roll into my eyes.

I'd told the housekeeper I wasn't fit to go to work today at the Avro factory at Greengate. She took one look at my ashen face, felt my fevered brow and told me to get to bed. She was still speaking as my stomach knotted and I bolted to my room.

'Councillor Smith will have to see you,' she half-shouted as I made my way up the stairs.

The remark barely registered at the time, so desperate was I to hurry back and lock the door behind me. I wondered why she hadn't called for a doctor. I knew that Smith was the owner of the place and something of a bigwig in local government. 'Mr Rochdale', some called him. Most of the lads here just called him 'the fat man'. Though never to his face. Chairman of the establishment committee and a man going places was Cyril Smith.

Lying in a cold sweat with a banging headache, I hoped he wouldn't visit this evening. What would he want? It was getting late. I'd yet to draw the curtains and a pale veil of light filled the room. A full moon was out. From down below I could hear strains of Petula Clark float up from the pub nearby.

Not a night had passed since I'd arrived at Cambridge House – a hostel for working boys, they called it – when I didn't wonder what I was doing here. Tonight was no different and the memory of my mother, whose death had brought me here, was more vivid than ever. When my mum and dad had split up I'd stayed with my mother. There was no choice. My dad was a drunk and, at fifteen, I wasn't ready to make my way in the world.

Two years later I had to do just that. When my mum died my childhood went up in smoke. Everything changed in a split second. I knew I was on my own now. But the sadness I felt quickly gave way to numbness. It was as though I'd known for a long time this day was coming. It comes to us all. That moment when childhood reference points dissolve and you slip your emotional moorings. You'll never discover new islands, my granddad once told me, unless you have the courage to lose sight of the shore. I'd lost sight all right. Everything behind me seemed long gone.

The truth is that I was starting to accept life at Cambridge House. I had a job, friends and some sort of purpose. The other lads in there were all right. The place was strict, but we had fun. Other boys would give their right arm to work for Avro. My mother had been proud of the fact I worked in the aircraft industry – Avro had made thousands of Lancaster Bombers. They were making 150 a month during the war and we were part of something special. Can you imagine working on Vulcan delta-winged jet bombers, 748 airliners as a teenager? It felt like we were building Britain.

Thousands of workers poured in through the gates every day into a huge brown hangar. Everyone walked tall, as though we were carried by the whiff of a heady pioneering spirit. We'd throw ourselves into work, gunning rivets in holes on bomb and undercarriage doors, outer and inner skins, trailing edge, ailerons and nacelles. You'd lose yourself for hours in a noisy symphony of rivet-guns.

That hypnotic pulse would come to me in dreams sometimes. It was the soundtrack of my new life. An enthralling pneumatic beat. Rat-a-tat-tat-tat-tat-tat. Rat-a-tat-tat. Rat-a-tat-tat-tat-tat. A hundred thousand rivets vibrating in close formation, punctuated only by the clanging of metal, the growling of engines and … a loud knock at the door.

There was a knock at the door.

I froze and listened to my breathing under the sheets.

'John, it's Councillor Smith. Are you decent?'

I heard a key turning in the door and I sprang out of bed. I'd got halfway to my clothes when the door swung open and he strode into the room.

'You're shaking,' he said, fixing me with hard, gimlet eyes.

'I ... I ... I'm not well, Councillor Smith.'

'So I've been told, come over here and let's examine you.'

As I made my way towards him, dressed only in pants and vest, I met his gaze and got a proper look at him in the light shining through the window. He was a colossus of a man, probably more than three times my size. I was nine stone wringing wet, a sparrow compared to this monster. He leaned back and tucked his thumbs in his braces to emphasise his grandness, all the time his eyes following me across the room, like a jaguar sizing up its prey. Then he shifted his huge bulk and started drumming his fingers on the dresser.

An unreadable expression crossed his face and in the folds of fat around his neck I could see rivulets of sweat.

'Take your clothes off.'

I didn't say anything. I just did it. I was shaking with fear and my stomach was churning like a washing machine.

He paced across the floor and pulled the curtains shut. The floorboards creaked noisily under his weight.

'Now stand there.'

He bent down and clasped me with huge hands like shovels. I could feel his breath like a flame-thrower on my thighs. Suddenly he grasped my testicles and fat, stubby fingers began to squeeze the life out of me.

I screamed.

Violence flashed in his eyes as he stood up, towering over me.

'Now, now, lad. I'll have none of your petulance. This is for your own good. I'm checking to see if there's anything wrong with you, see?'

My teeth were rattling and my hair was matted with sweat. I couldn't even look at him as he forced his way between my thighs again.

I don't know how long the ordeal lasted, but it felt like hours. When he rose there was a faint trace of a smile on his jowly features, which suddenly twisted into a disdainful sneer.

'There's nothing wrong with you, lad. You're swinging the lead, aren't you? Do you think this is a place for lads who want to bunk off work? It isn't, I'll tell you.'

'No,' I stammered. 'I've never had a day off in my life. I'm sick, look.'

My shaking hand beckoned towards a plastic basin by the side of the bed holding a small pool of vomit.

He gave me a look of disgust. 'So that's what the smell is.' Then he lunged towards me and in one brutal movement he dropped to his haunches and threw me over his knee. Then the violence began.

Thwack, thwack, thwack. Thwack, thwack. His monstrous hand rained down on my bottom, smacking me until I thought I'd pass out. He worked himself into a frenzy and every smack was a blur of throbbing pain, stinging more with each blow.

At first I cried out in pain, but that only made him hit me harder. Soon I was struggling to catch my breath. When he eventually finished I was a mess. Trembling, whimpering and quietly sobbing, I tried to turn my head but the back of his hand pressed down on my neck and he told me not to move.

'Rest, lad, rest. It had to be done.'

Above his heavy breathing I could smell his rancid body odour. It was like cabbage boiled in vinegar. As his breathing slowed, a continuous low sound rose in his chest like a purr of contentment. He was humming quietly to himself. Then he reached for a wet sponge by the sink and began to stroke my bottom, rough hands sliding over a minefield of welts. I gritted my teeth as the burning, stinging sensation intensified. Every once in a while he'd apply the sponge generously, letting cold water trickle down the back of my legs.

'There, there, lad,' he whispered. 'It had to be done, you know that, don't you?'

His humming was louder now, broken every now and then by strange squeals of pleasure. 'There, there,' he kept whispering, hot, stale breath bearing down on my neck.

When it was over he let me slide to the floor. As he stood before me, he cleared his throat and adjusted his braces. The floorboards creaked loudly again. He pulled a hand-kerchief out of his pockets and mopped his brow. 'You'll know better now,' he said, and made his way out. The door clicked shut.

For a while the only thought I entertained was death. My mum had found a way out and I wanted to follow. I wanted my small hands pressed in hers again and to feel safe. I dug my fingers into the shag pile rug and cried wave after wave of tears until my ducts were raw and there was nothing left.

I lay there motionless, as exhaustion worked its way through me, calming me until life returned to limbs and synapses fired with purpose.

There was no time to lose. I had to get out of there.

I dragged my clothes on quickly, drank deeply from the tap and caught sight of my reflection in the mirror. Red swollen eyes and a look of horror etched across a gaunt face stared back. I no longer recognised that person.

I quickly gathered my things and shoved them into a duffle bag. Outside, the pub was in full swing and music and laughter spilled out into the street. I recognised the bittersweet, ghostly croon of Roy Orbison. 'Dream Baby'. No one sang pained loneliness like Roy. His voice followed me as I ran through the streets and away from a place I never wanted to see again.

> Sweet dream baby
> Sweet dream baby
> Sweet dream baby
> How long must I dream?

I was picked up by a lorry driver on Kingsway just before the cross-Pennine road north. He agreed to take me as far as Wetherby and we thundered up the road into Yorkshire in silence.

It was in the early hours when he pulled over. 'You can sleep on the bunk here,' he offered, as he snapped the engine off. 'There's plenty of room.'

'No, you're OK. I need some fresh air. Thanks for the lift.'

I spent the rest of that night huddled in a bus shelter,

watching the rain on the window and thinking of everything I'd left behind.

I never set foot in the Avro factory again. Bus shelters, homeless hostels, strangers' settees, garages and churches became my home for the next two years. The winter of 1963 was the coldest in 200 years. Animals died in the fields and the sea froze in places. But that was nothing compared to the chill Cyril Smith had left with me.

It was a long time before I even stepped foot in the same county as Cyril Smith. It took me many years to recover from that brutal night. I was young with hopes and dreams. And he almost took everything from me.

I was in a roadside café in Wigan when I heard he'd died. 'Dream a Little Dream of Me' was playing through a tinny radio, Mama Cass was whistling away and steam was snaking from a mug of tea before me. The yellow Sky news ticker flashed up overhead. The former Liberal Democrat MP, Sir Cyril Smith, had died aged eighty-two. I dropped a sugar cube into the hot tea and ordered a bacon sandwich.

Sooner or later we all put a lid on our past. It's best left that way. Packed off to storage not to be disturbed. Now Cyril had been packed off to the hottest warehouse going and wouldn't be troubling me by popping up on Bananarama videos or episodes of *This Is Your Life*, I saw no reason to go prising that lid open.

Until the events of late 2012.

It started, I believe, by some MP making a speech in Parliament about Cyril Smith being a serial abuser. The first I heard of it was in the newspapers. They were full of it. Other victims spoke. Some went on television. Then the police said they had been convinced all along he was a paedophile and had tried to prosecute him. But the CPS had blocked it.

The lid flew off the box and the past came flooding back.

There was rage all right. A deep, roiling anger. So now I knew there were others. I'd always suspected as much. But this time I wanted to talk to someone about it. In all the years that had passed I'd never said a word to anyone. Not even my wife. I had dragged around this dirty secret for years and now I wanted to be free of it.

But who could I tell? I couldn't tell my wife. I just couldn't. One night, after sinking half a bottle of Jameson's, I emailed the MP who had spoken about Cyril's victims in Parliament. The MP for Rochdale, no less.

His aide responded and a few days later I pulled into Rochdale train station to greet a town I'd never wanted to return to. It had changed immeasurably since I'd last been there. For the worse. Boarded-up shops were everywhere. Recession-weary faces peered at me from taxi ranks. So this was Cyril's legacy.

I walked across town hesitantly, fearful of what memories this place would evoke. I'd walked these streets as a child, my small hand held safely in my mother's palm, eyes ablaze with wonder. Crowds of people, the shops, the noise, I loved it all. I didn't linger too long now; it felt dangerous to do so. So I quickened my gait and followed the road round the top of Yorkshire Street until I came face to face with a large sign denoting the MP's office.

I pressed the doorbell and waited.

Chapter 5

Showtime

Saturday matinees were the busiest day of the week at the Palace Cinema. Queues stretched all the way down Drake Street, as Rochdale's Bangladeshi, Pakistani and Kashmiri communities made their way past gloriously kitsch movie posters and piled into the 1,200-seat building on Great George Street to watch Bollywood films.

Mothers, fathers, grandparents and children squeezed into the velvet-upholstered fold-up seats to watch films like *Sholay*, *Muqaddar Ka Sikandar* and *Sanyasi*. Absorbed faces would stare at the big screen for hours, lost in a world of enchanting Hindi soundtracks and dramatic tales of love and revenge, the reverential silence only broken by the sight of ushers walking up the scarlet-carpeted aisles with neck-strap trays laden with ice creams.

And during the intermission, as the red velvet curtains drew across the screen and the lights went up, crowds in Rochdale would regularly witness one of the strangest sights in the history of British cinema.

Suddenly, from out of the stage wings a huge well-dressed figure emerged marching solemnly towards centre stage. A spotlight would fall upon him and he'd look up at a sea of blank faces. The sound of chatter died down. Children stared agog, lowering ice cream cones from their mouths. Whorls of smoke rose from ash-tipped cigarettes and a hush descended upon the auditorium. And then Cyril Smith spoke.

'Hello, everyone, I hope you're enjoying the film,' he'd thunder, making sure people in the back row could hear. 'I'm Cyril Smith and I'm here to tell you what I'm doing for you as your Liberal Member of Parliament, and why you should always vote Liberal.'

He'd carry on in this vein for a few minutes as the theatre listened in silence. Disbelieving eyes stared straight at him, almost hypnotised by this bizarre interlude. Then he'd tell them to 'enjoy the rest of the film' and march off stage right.

He'd do this most weeks and even now people in Rochdale still talk about these strange appearances by Cyril Smith during their Saturday film. It was remarkable politics and a measure of how Cyril was taking campaigning to a new level. There was no point treating politics as a dress rehearsal, he reasoned. You had to grab people's attention. Politics, as far as Cyril was concerned, was just another branch of the entertainment industry.

The American TV presenter and comedian Jay Leno memorably said that politics was show business for ugly people. Cyril demonstrated this to the letter. When he wasn't interrupting films at his local cinema he was popping up on as many television sets as possible. *Wogan*, *Swap Shop*, *Saturday Superstore*, *Noel's Telly Years*, *Blankety Blank*, *Heroes of Comedy* were just some of the programmes he appeared in. He made jokes with Keith Chegwin and went through the 'big red book' with Michael Aspel on *This Is Your Life*. At a time when grey men in suits with cut-glass accents dominated politics, Cyril defied convention. He did things others wouldn't dream of. If you think Boris Johnson riding a zip wire was strange, then imagine a 29-stone politician dancing around in a music video for the biggest girl band of the '80s, Bananarama. Or making a surreal appearance in *The Wizard of Oz*. Or mocking himself in a TV advert promoting a credit card by trying to touch his toes. It was pantomime, high farce and pitch-perfect populism rolled into one.

TV wasn't the only medium he was tightening his maverick grip on. For Fleet Street he was manna from heaven. Every journalist had Cyril's number. He was great copy and a fantastic source of stories, especially as he was frequently more than willing to criticise his own party. He was also one of the first politicians to understand the photo op. Happy to pose for all kinds of ridiculous pictures, you had Cyril wearing an 'I'm only here for the beer' hat, Cyril wearing an 'I skipped lunch' T-shirt, Cyril on a see-saw lifting up two bunny girls and Cyril clowning on deck chairs on a beach. The visual potency of these images meant that Cyril was one of the most instantly recognisable politicians in the country. He was years ahead of the rest. But others in his party certainly didn't appreciate it. Particularly the leadership. He was 'a bit of an ass' complained Jeremy Thorpe. 'He had an incapacity to say no to a camera,' grumbled David Steel.

The master of personality politics, Cyril was happy to blur the lines between politics and show business. The power of celebrity had enormous allure – and he could see how easily celebrities could secure access to young people. Mixing with the likes of Les Dawson, Ronnie Corbett, Bernard Manning, Jim Bowen and Jimmy Cricket, he retained a life-long fascination with their world. Northern nightclubs and working men's clubs were places that brought generations together over a cheap pint and a good night out. A combination of community spirit and glamour made them a unique institution. The cheers and roars of laughter that Cyril saw as the spotlight shone on the great variety show performers on stage were worlds apart from the sound of clocks ticking and MPs snoring in committee rooms. How could our politics be so dull, he wondered? The whole world is interested in British democracy; it's one of the oldest games in town. And yet we can barely put on a show that's capable of holding people's attention for longer than five minutes.

In the early 1970s, there were thousands of working men's clubs across the country with millions of members and many more on waiting lists eager to join. Working men's clubs were right at the heart of the community in a way that politics could only aspire to be. Would it ever be possible to bridge these two worlds? Cyril would certainly try.

Most politicians have an appetite for publicity. It's part of their job and helps improve their chances at the ballot box. But Cyril was in a league of his own. He craved publicity and began to engage with the public in the same way famous comedians did with their fans. He'd always offer them a glimpse of the show, a flash of humour and a little bit of celebrity stardust. As soon as his door closed behind him when he left his home a switch flicked inside. He was now in performance mode.

'He always loved to perform,' Eileen Kershaw remarked. 'He was a great dancer. When the band struck up at the town hall he'd drag me on to the floor. Waltzes, quick steps, he was a great mover. Light on his feet. You'd have to stretch your hand round his belly, mind. But he could dance.'

Cyril was also happy to be part of the joke about his weight. He'd long realised that obesity had its advantages. Fat people were funny and a tradition stretching from Fatty Arbuckle, Jackie Gleason, Oliver Hardy, Curly Howard and Lou Costello proved this. In George Orwell's 1939 comic novel, *Coming Up for Air*, the hero of his story observes that a fat man 'goes through his life on a sort of light comedy plane, though in the case of … anyone over twenty stone, it isn't so much light comedy as low farce.' Cyril was happy to borrow from this lineage and bring more than a smattering of 1970s showbiz to the grey world of politics.

A regular on the chat show circuit, he was well acquainted with all of the stars of the day and it wasn't long before he ran into someone he had more in common with than many would have guessed. Jimmy Savile. Just as Savile built his career around supposedly helping children, Cyril was doing the same.

He first met Savile at a medieval banquet in Worsley and they immediately hit it off. 'When I joined in the community singing,' Cyril recalled in his biography, 'Jimmy blurted out, "You've got a nice voice there, Cyril, you must come on my programme."'

Their friendship continued and in 1973 Cyril appeared on Savile's TV show *Clunk Click*, where children were bussed in to make up the audience. He took to the stage and treated (if that's the right word) millions to the incongruous sight of him singing. 'There's only one girl for me, she's a lassie from Lancashire, just a lassie from Lancashire, she's the lassie that I love dear,' he crooned, as the spotlight shone on his beaming, upturned face. Cyril was perfecting his own variety act. A few years later Savile appeared with Cyril in a Liberal Party political broadcast giving his backing to the party.

Like Savile, Cyril was building a remarkable public image that was to become an impenetrable shield behind which his extracurricular activities escaped any scrutiny. And like Savile, he also abused his position to get access to young boys. By now he'd founded the youth charity Rochdale Childer and was earning a reputation as a one-man charitable tour de force. 'He was our inspiration,' says Maureen Cooper, who runs the charity today. 'He gave his life to this town.' He raised thousands of pounds to help children in need and was seen as a tireless worker for good causes. Much of this energy focused on young people. There wasn't a school, youth club or youth theatre in Rochdale that Cyril hadn't managed to inveigle his way into. And it wasn't just children who couldn't get away from him, Cyril was everywhere. His raucous belly laugh was a familiar sound on teatime telly. And his jolly smile frequently leapt out of newspapers. This roly-poly barrel of fun was quickly becoming a national treasure. Whenever he ambled into view, pulled a daft face or cracked a feeble joke, people smiled. He was harmless; good fun was Cyril Smith. The image of this saintly northern jester doing anything untoward with young boys was unimaginable. It simply didn't compute.

Though rumours of child abuse still persisted, no one in the media took them seriously. 'It was a secret in plain view,' says *Observer* journalist Nick Cohen. 'Anyone who wanted to know knew. But everyone wanted to forget.'

Freud had a theory about this. He called it a 'negative hallucination', otherwise known as the art of not seeing: giving rise to a gap in reality so that when an unbearable reality presents itself a delusion appears to close the perceptual breach. It meant that the dark side of Cyril was forced out of view and could not be perceived. The unconscious knowledge of what would only be discovered later lay dormant and reality was repressed. In Cyril's case this was applying to a much wider audience.

And so Cyril's show carried on uninterrupted by the inconvenience of painful and ugly truths. What went on behind the curtain would stay secret. The glad-handing continued, the laughter never stopped, the drinks kept coming and Cyril's friends in the media grew by the year. His networks were incredible, people from all walks of life wanted to be associated with this smiling giant of northern politics. Among his closest friends was the former executive director of the Football Association, David Davies. Previously the BBC's political correspondent and a presenter on *North West Tonight*, Davies was so close to Cyril that he named him as godparent to one of his children.

Many journalists from that period have subsequently experienced a collective realisation that they were conned. Their hallucination has long since worn off and they are coming to terms with the early, frightening days of sobriety. In Manchester's Albert Square Chop House, the BBC veteran Jim Hancock is one such journalist. He aimlessly prods his corned beef hash cake with his fork and stares ruefully ahead. 'I should have got that story,' he says of Cyril's abuse of boys. 'But the problem was he was incredibly good value.'

Hancock agreed to discuss the period he reported on when Cyril was one of the most famous politicians in the land and his candour is admirable. A broadcaster in the north-west with over thirty years' experience, he admits that 'the media has a weakness for colourful characters' and says journalists couldn't help but notice that Cyril 'was loved by his public'. At a time when there were very few Liberal MPs around, Cyril was vital to safeguard BBC impartiality and achieve political balance. 'We used him in a lot of stories,' he says. There were strong similarities with Savile too. 'He had the same Savile chemistry. I mean, Savile was everywhere. On *Top of the Pops*, with the Queen, working in Leeds Hospital. You couldn't doubt his character. Then there was Cyril. Committed to charity. Rochdale Childer, man of the people. The idea that there's a different side to these people … you just can't see it. When these people are so celebrated, so famous … to make that leap is quite difficult.'

For anyone truly to grasp the nature of Cyril's double life, that leap was only going to get bigger and bigger. A chasm was opening between his public and secret life. During the 1970s Cyril's dizzying ascent to fame continued and he maintained a remarkable power base in Rochdale. Only his Newcastle namesake, the equally corrupt and charismatic T. Dan Smith, could claim to have the same level of local political influence. But T. Dan Smith ended up in prison. Cyril was feted all the way to the grave. As police files from the time later revealed, Cyril's influence was so extensive he had police in his pocket; social workers were terrified they would lose their jobs for raising concerns about Cyril's behaviour. He effectively controlled the town. If Cyril wanted something doing, it was done. No questions were asked.

For Hancock, it was a particularly febrile time where political shocks arrived on a daily basis. Two of the stories of the time included the MP John Stonehouse, a junior minister in Harold Wilson's government, leaving a pile of clothes on a Miami beach to give the impression he'd drowned, and Lord Lucan, who was suspected of murder and disappeared without trace in 1974.

And it was a time where strange views – at least by today's standards – prevailed. Simon Hoggart was a young writer at *The Guardian* during the 1970s and admitted to hearing of rumours that Cyril Smith abused boys.

'We heard the rumours at the bar,' he recalled. 'When you were having a pint people would say, "Do you know about Cyril Smith?" But paedophilia wasn't such an obsession then. It was distasteful, but we just thought poor sod, fat, unwanted. We pitied him. I didn't think, "I'll immediately go and out him."'

One of the more disturbing aspects of conversations like these is continually coming up against prehistoric views of child abuse. There was and sadly still is a strong notion of the morally corrupt nature of working-class culture in some circles. Sex abuse is all too frequently viewed as what happens to other people. It's what happens in a world not governed by decent middle-class values.

More worrying was that the same views that protected Cyril still persist in Rochdale today. Police and social workers still look down their noses at poor, abused girls on council estates and allow their abusers to carry on with impunity. This has carried on for years. Reports have confirmed that prejudiced views on the background of victims has prevented action being taken. Isn't it time that people in a position of power show some genuine shock at horrific abuse taking place under their nose?

This insouciance wasn't universally shared, though. Cyril's abuse may have escaped the mainstream media but a vibrant lesser-known press soon picked it up. The *Rochdale Alternative Press* was co-edited by John Walker and Dave Bartlett, two lecturers at the local college of further education, who had long been fascinated by Cyril's political grip on the town. Possessing one of the highest alternative magazine circulations in Europe, this local underground publication, inspired by political 'zines like *Mole Express* in Manchester, soon got wind of Cyril's activities at Cambridge House. When the rumours filtered through to Walker in 1979 he felt he had to investigate. 'We thought it was serious stuff and we risked a lot in deciding to publish it,' he said. 'My house was at risk, as Cyril threatened to sue, but we thought it had to come out. We certainly didn't think it was acceptable behaviour. We had a responsibility to out him.'

Their investigative efforts in the 1970s were part of a burgeoning alternative scene in Rochdale that began to fuel a growing dissent in the town. Britain's first graffiti artist Walter Kershaw was bringing fantastically vivid, huge murals to run down gable ends and giving condemned buildings a new life. There was also the M6 Theatre Company, started by four actors including Sue Johnston of *Royle Family* fame. And Cargo Studios, based in a converted warehouse in a backstreet not far from the town hall, where The Fall, Joy Division and The Teardrop Explodes, among others, would record.

It was perhaps because of this left-field cultural backdrop that the story they published of Cyril's abuse wasn't able to gain credibility with a wider media. It was deemed to be the work of left-wing agitators. Cyril issued a gagging writ – but never went to court – and the story never properly developed. It would take more than thirty years before the story eventually appeared in all the mainstream papers. With no sense of irony, Cyril fired off a letter to Walker's boss at the college he worked at in Rochdale arguing that Walker wasn't fit to be working with young people.

Back in London, much of the media weren't all that interested in what the Liberals were up to. While the Lib-Lab pact helped prop up Callaghan's Labour government in the late 1970s, Hoggart explained the perception of the Liberals wasn't comparable to how they're seen today.

'The Liberals now are a party of power,' he said. 'You go to their conference and there are councillors and mayors there who have to balance real budgets. Back then there were just a lot of people in earth shoes, beards and T-shirts waving "site value rating now" placards.'

On whether others in his party knew of Cyril's behaviour, Hoggart was unsure. Even if they did, after the scandal of their leader, Jeremy Thorpe, being accused of having an affair with a rent boy and then trying to kill him, they would have wanted to keep the lid firmly fastened on any other scandalous behaviour.

'There were too few of them to have scandals,' he said. 'The Liberal Party was a small, tiny world. You could almost fit them in a telephone box. If there had been another scandal it would have made a very big wound.'

The shambolic and slow response by the Lib Dems to the allegations of groping by Lord Rennard, made six years ago, suggests little has changed. The first party political instinct when allegations like this emerge is always to throw them into the long grass. When they subsequently re-emerge some years later, there is often panic, recriminations and threats of legal action. The overall effect is deeply unedifying and frustrating. The Liberals, in particular, have shown over the years that they are not capable of shedding much light on the substance of serious allegations of misconduct made against their members.

Attempts to close down the Cyril Smith scandal ensured it never saw the front pages. It never made the first bong of *News at Ten*. It never hit the airwaves. It lived in whispers in the bars of Rochdale and Westminster. But it could never really see the light of day. The most conspicuous man in politics was allowed to carry on abusing boys with impunity. Cloaked in a veil of respectability, the image of a professional northerner who talked about his dear mum made his terrible deeds invisible to the world.

Cyril only had to wink at reporters and they grinned and nodded back. His smile remained firmly intact. And he never lost the spring in his step. He'd bound into a room like Tigger. 'There's no damn business like show business,' said Billie Holiday. 'You have to smile to keep from throwing up.'

And smile he did, as Rochdale became a happy hunting ground for his sordid activities. Boys' teeth were knocked out and their bodies treated as playthings to satisfy his depraved cravings. From school to school and youth club to youth club he prowled until one day he stumbled across Knowl View.

Knowl View opened in 1969 and closed in 1994. It had fifty beds and was a residential school for children with learning difficulties. Cyril was at the opening ceremony and was there at the end, pushing for the school to be taken outside local authority control. Today, it's the site of penthouse apartments with Juliet balconies providing Pennine views. Every last trace of what happened there has been carefully erased.

Martin Digan was a social worker who started work at the school in the late 1970s. It represented quite a change for him at the time; he'd moved from the affluent, semi-rural village of Mobberley, Cheshire, where he had worked for Manchester Educational Department, to the Metropolitan Borough of Rochdale. But it was a change he was looking forward to. For many years he was oblivious to what was happening at the school – until he was promoted to head of care and began to realise that things weren't quite right.

The boys made complaints about abuse and the police were called in. But nothing happened. Cyril Smith was a governor there and had his own set of keys. Digan would see him sauntering around the school, with a key chain dangling from his pocket, eyeing up young boys. It didn't seem right.

Frequently, he was joined by the Conservative councillor, Harry Wild, whose presence Digan found particularly menacing. A former territorial army officer, Wild was taller than Cyril and the two of them were close with a shared interest in boys. 'He looked like a really unpleasant drill sergeant,' he says. 'He was about six foot five and was always standing behind Cyril on his left shoulder, as though he was his minder. He used to wear this really long Crombie coat that went down to his ankles, black polished boots and a shirt and tie. I remember he had really cold eyes.'

Wild had caused something of a stir when, as a Conservative councillor, he came out and supported Cyril during the 1972 by-election. Years later, in 1997, he was heavily criticised and accused by prison guards of assault following inappropriate advances to young male prisoners while on a visit to Buckley Hall Prison.

Wild was chairman of the board of governors at Knowl View and he, too, had a set of keys. The two of them would pace up and down the school for no reason, just looking at the boys. The way Digan saw it, they looked like they were cruising and he became more and more uneasy about their presence at the school. 'They would arrive and start walking through the units when the boys were showering,' he said. 'I could see it was wrong so I complained on about four or five occasions. I said we needed to have notice when officials were going to arrive at the school because the boys couldn't be in a state of undress. It got me into trouble and it just carried on.'

Digan was threatened with disciplinary action by the headmaster and warned not to say anything about Cyril

Smith again. If he made any more complaints he was told he faced dismissal.

He was not alone in this respect. Officials all over town, in schools, the police and social services, had suspicions about Cyril's interest in boys but they knew he was untouchable. For Digan, though, matters were to come to a head one night in 1994. From that day on, he was prepared to confront Cyril and Wild and face the consequences.

'I will never forget that day,' he says. 'One of the boys came up to me and told me he'd just been sexually assaulted. He was shaking. I sat with him and listened and it was horrifying. I knew he was telling the truth. He wasn't even eleven years old. I asked who did this and he started to describe the man. It was clearly Wild. The Crombie, the boots, it couldn't have been anyone else.'

Digan felt his chest tighten. Consumed with anger, he called the police and said there had been a serious incident at the school. The blue lights were flashing outside in minutes. They searched the place but could find no evidence of a break-in. Digan spent the time comforting the boy and assuring him he was safe, all the while thinking, how could this have happened?

He knew Wild and Cyril had keys but they didn't have the alarm code. He wanted to know where they got in at night. Over the next few days he combed the building, looking for signs of entry. He paced up and down the hall trying every door until he came across a door that was left ajar. It was the door to the headmaster's office. Was this how Wild and Cyril were getting into the school? The headmaster hardly ever slept on the property. It would be an easy way to enter at night.

He pushed the door open and looked inside. It was silent. He flicked the light, walked inside and looked around the room. He found it as he would expect. Neat, tidy and orderly with no sign of any disturbance. Then, just as he was about to leave, he caught sight of a file of papers spread out on the desk under an adjustable lamp. Without thinking he picked up one of the papers and began to read. He saw the name of the boy who'd complained to him about abuse a few days earlier. His eyes widened and his heart started thumping. Words leapt out at him and he felt sick. He quickly gathered up all the papers and took them to his room. That night he read through the whole report and started to weep.

The document in question was a report by the local health authority that had been presented to the council's director of education. It warned that boys aged eight to sixteen at Knowl View were at risk of AIDS. In matter-of-fact language, the report described the extreme sexual abuse that young boys had been subjected to. Boys were beaten and raped continually by men as far away as Sheffield who had travelled to Rochdale to take part.

Digan knew every one of the boys involved. They were under his care. 'It was my responsibility to look after these children,' he says. 'I can't explain how I felt when I found out what was happening. I was sick. Something inside me just died that night. I was destroyed. These boys were sold to paedophile gangs. I know the boys that have died since then have committed suicide. They had done nothing wrong. They were like lambs to the slaughter.'

He spent the rest of the night making numerous photocopies of the files. His hands were shaking as he did it. Then he put the original copy back on the headmaster's desk and went home to tell his wife.

She told him he had no choice. He would have to do something about it. The public had to know what was going on. The council's director of education, Diana Cavanagh, had already instructed the author of the report not to 'undertake any independent action' or circulate the report any further. The problem was being addressed, she claimed. But Digan knew otherwise. He couldn't let the council bury this. He would have to go public and face the consequences.

'At the time we didn't know what being a whistleblower would mean,' he admits. He soon found out. He ended up losing almost everything. His job, his career, his home. 'I was persecuted by the council. It was a nightmare.'

The file was eventually made public by Digan but Cyril Smith and Harry Wild's names were not mentioned. The resulting bad publicity was enough to force the school to close, but not before Cyril had done all he could to destroy Digan.

Soon after, Digan was tipped off by a journalist. Apparently Cyril was calling for the police to raid Digan's property to find files taken from Knowl View. 'I'd already distributed the material far and wide by then,' says Digan, 'and I had to move home.' But worse was to follow.

'I started to get phone calls threatening my children at school,' he says. The callers were paedophiles and Digan is adamant that Cyril was behind it all. 'They'd say things like, "We know where your children go to school. We're going to pick them up and take them on a ride they'll never forget."'

Digan spoke to anyone who might be able to help. But

no one wanted to listen. One weekend he even walked miles in the rain to see his local Catholic priest at St Vincent de Paul church in Norden for advice. 'I took the files with me and told him there was terrible abuse going on at Knowl View. I thought he'd be horrified, but he didn't want to know,' says Digan. Visibly irritated by the mention of child abuse, Canon Mortimer Stanley told Digan to leave and not repeat 'any of this nonsense' again. 'He literally threw me out,' he said.

It has now emerged that Stanley, who has not admitted to any alleged offences, is being investigated by police for sexual abuse of children over a twenty-year period.

In 2000, the *Manchester Evening News* reported that Harry Wild was being investigated for alleged abuse of boys at Knowl View. In their front-page story, Wild condemned the boys at the school as 'low grade with problems' and accused them of making 'mischievous claims'. Charges were never made but the investigation came at a bad time for Wild. He was in line to become the next High Sheriff of Greater Manchester, a role whose main duties were to 'protect and assist in upholding the dignity and the wellbeing of Her Majesty's judges'. As a result of the investigation, and on the recommendation of the police, he never became High Sheriff.

Almost twenty years later Digan is still trying to get people to listen and his sense of loss is painfully clear. The pain is etched in his face. From priests to the police, everyone has let him down. Time has not healed. He is still getting letters from Rochdale Council's solicitors now demanding copies of their report to be returned. The report he retrieved that night has lost none of its power to shock. It makes grim reading. A generation of boys had their lives destroyed and what lessons have been learned? Worryingly, Digan points out that some of the people working there at the time, who knew what was happening, are still working with children.

Looking at all the evidence it's hard not to conclude that paedophile gangs have been operating in Rochdale for many years. Digan, like others, is of the view they were encouraged and protected by Cyril Smith.

As revelations about Cyril continued to emerge, the files retrieved by Digan that night were soon winging their way to the chief constable of Greater Manchester Police. Not long afterwards, the police announced they had reopened investigations into allegations of historical sex abuse at Knowl View School. Let us hope justice finally catches up with those that were responsible and are still alive.

In the three years I've been Rochdale's MP I've dealt with many abuse cases. But the list of abused children at Knowl View provided by Digan will forever stay in my memory – and it continues to trouble me. It reads like a roll call of shame; a secret history of children who were denied a future. Digan tells me what happened to these boys. Some committed suicide, some died of drugs, some ended up in prison. It's heartbreaking.

One who did survive to tell the tale is Chris Marshall. He was abused by Cyril Smith at Knowl View when he was just eight years old. Hearing his story was unbearable. Now in his forties, Chris is a tough man. From Knowl View he joined the Foreign Legion. But the day he visits my office he breaks down and loses his fight to hold back the tears.

'I was dragged from my bed in the middle of the night and taken downstairs to a room where Cyril Smith was waiting,' he says, his voice faltering as the tears well up in his eyes. 'I was told to give him oral sex. I knew it was wrong. I just wanted to go home. I've spent years trying to forget it but it won't go away.'

And that's the feeling I'm left with listening to these gut-wrenching tales. The pain has endured much longer than Cyril's shallow legacy and now it demands to be heard. The bright lights of celebrity long kept Cyril's secret life in the shadows, but the misery he'd caused was never going to stay in the dark forever.

Cyril had promised so much. He came into politics to try and give people who didn't have a voice hope. But, though he did this for a while, ultimately he dismissed them and treated them as though they didn't matter. The philosophy that fired Cyril's ambition as a young mover and shaker in Rochdale was overtaken and trampled to dust by cynical ambition. The bashful and blenching boy wracked by self-doubt became a gargantuan joke overblown with self-importance. His politics were shot. He ruled by fear and frivolity. Officials in the town were too scared to speak out against him and the media were too busy slapping him on the back and laughing with him. 'Over here, Cyril,' they'd shout. 'That's right. Smile for the camera. Perfect.'

And Cyril never looked back. This was his town. He'd put it on the map, people would say. He was Mr Rochdale. And so it owed him. He'd take what he needed and do what he wanted. That was only fair, wasn't it? These lads didn't matter. They'd never amount to anything. Who wanted to hear their voice? History, let's not forget, is written by winners. And whatever he was, Cyril could always look in the mirror at night, smile and know one thing. He was a winner.

When the diggers came to tear Knowl View School down Cyril's days in Parliament were over. He'd stood down as MP in 1992 and Liz Lynne held the seat for the Liberals. The irony that Cyril's replacement was an actress didn't go unnoticed. The show must go on, he thought. But now someone else would have to sing the tune. Cyril was off to live the high life as a guest lecturer on the *QE2* cruise liner. He'd sit on deck with an ice cream and feel the blazing sun warm him, watching the trail of spume left in the ship's wake. An azure blue sea stretched out for miles in front of him. This was how it should be, he thought. As the years passed, he enjoyed his triumph. His was a winner's story, he'd remind himself. Who wanted to hear about victims? They were insignificant. As far as Cyril was concerned no one would ever hear their stories.

But there were people who knew what happened.

'The real tragedy of Knowl View is what happened to these boys,' says Digan. 'Their lives got a lot worse as a result.' Some joined the army to try and blot out what they'd experienced. Some got involved in crime and drugs. Others became abusers themselves. And for some the pain was just too much.

Digan remembers one boy in particular. 'He just couldn't be on his own. It tormented him.' He lived in one of the tower blocks known locally as the 'Seven Sisters' flats and he'd climb on to the roof and stand on the edge looking down at the matchbox cars below. Tears would pour down his cheeks as he stood there, twenty storeys up with the wind whistling round his ears and blowing through his hair, deliberating whether to jump. Digan was petrified that one night he'd do it. But he didn't need to. He took his life through drugs instead. A massive overdose.

He wasn't yet twenty.

Silent Voices #2: 'I Got Away'

The all-nighters at the Twisted Wheel club in Manchester were legendary. Hard rhythm and blues, rare soul and American imports: it was the best music you'd hear anywhere in the north of England. On a Saturday night there was nowhere else for any self-respecting Mod to be. Scooters would make the pilgrimage from all over, Rochdale, Stockport, Wigan, they'd form a glorious phalanx and converge into Manchester, turning heads down every road. It was an amazing sight. The acts that played at the club were something else. The Spencer Davis Group, Ben E. King, Edwin Starr, Stevie Wonder … it was all about the music. And, of course, the fashion. Pageboy style, back-combing, Caesar cuts, Italian mohair three-button suits, polo shirts, desert boots: these guys looked the business. And so did the women. Twiggy-style makeup, go-go boots, Peggy Moffitt's signature look. The place reeked of attitude and it was there I experienced some of the best nights of my life.

We'd stumble out of the club at around 7 a.m. blinking in the morning light, pull up our parkas and ride back to Rochdale still high on speed. Sometimes we'd smoke a bit of dope to come down. The exhilaration coursed through our veins. We were young and indestructible. Or so we thought.

My parents hated me staying out. They worried constantly. I'd get back to our house and they'd be sat downstairs in their dressing gowns waiting. My dad was an ex-war hero and he'd start screaming in my face about how I was causing my mum to worry. A few hours earlier I would have been dancing with an amazing girl in an op-art dress to the sound of Jimmy Ruffin. Talk about a comedown.

I don't know how long it went on like this. But the weekends were what I looked forward to the most. I was sixteen at the time and worked for a local manufacturing company making car parts; things like petrol caps and brake shoes. It was a good job and I enjoyed it. But then I got in trouble with the police and things changed.

It was only a few wraps of speed they found on me outside the club, but it was enough to get me sent off to Foston Hall detention centre in Derbyshire. I was there for three months, and it was tough. They said it was going to be a 'short, sharp shock' and it was exactly that. There were some pretty fierce lads there and you had to watch yourself. When I got out things were different with my parents. I could see the look of disappointment in their eyes. They were ashamed of me. I'd let the family down and it drove a real wedge between us. I went out with my mates as soon as possible and I remember racing up St Mary's Gate on the back of a scooter with the wind blowing through my hair and the smell of freedom in my nostrils again. We drove out to Hollingworth Lake and smoked fat joints as we watched Canada geese flying over the boats while the sun went down.

Me and my parents just didn't see eye to eye anymore. I couldn't tell them there was a revolution going on because they wouldn't understand. The world was changing and they were standing still. I was fascinated by the world of Emmett Grogan at the time and my mind was full of wild possibilities. Grogan founded the Diggers, a radical community action group in San Francisco. He was at the heart of the Haight-Ashbury counterculture explosion in the 1960s that spawned the summer of love, street theatre, direct action and art happenings. The Diggers would give out free food to the hungry and they opened stores that gave away their stock for free. They came up with all these incredible slogans that were everywhere at the time. 'Do your own thing', 'Today is the first day of the rest of your life' and 'Take a cop to dinner' were just a few I remember.

My world was expanding at a rapid rate and my parents' view of the world was just so narrow. It was getting harder and harder living under the same roof and I knew something would have to give. We'd eat in silence around the breakfast table and the tension was unbearable. I knew they were unhappy with how I was living my life but I didn't know they were about to take drastic action to try and get me back on the straight and narrow.

And that's when I met Cyril Smith.

I came home one night from work and turned the keys in the door and there he was sitting on the settee with my parents on either side of him.

I shut the door and just stared. He was enormous. Acres of flesh packed into a pinstriped suit. His cold eyes glared. Surely this guy couldn't be a police officer, I thought. No one could be that fat in the police.

'Sit down,' my dad said. 'I want you to meet Cyril Smith.'
For once I did as I was told.

'Cyril is a politician. He's the mayor of Rochdale and is very important,' my dad announced. 'We've told him all about the problems we're having and he's here to have a word with you. We're going to leave you to have a little chat, OK?'

I nodded and my mum and dad left the room, closing the door.

For a moment we just stared at each other, not saying a word. His eyes bored into me, as though he was about to leap off the couch and eat me alive. I sat back and thought how ridiculous he looked. Like a big fat cartoon villain. What was he going to do?

'I don't like your attitude,' he suddenly snapped, his lips peeling back into a snarl. 'Things are going to have to change.'

I was about to respond when he stood up and loomed over me. For the first time I felt anxious. I could feel the threat of violence and this guy was huge.

'I ... errr, don't think ...'

'I'll have none of your backchat,' he growled, and lunged forward, lifting me off my feet and throwing me over his knee. I was only about nine-and-a-half stone and he easily overpowered me. He pulled my trousers and pants down and started to ferociously paddle my backside, smacking me as though his life depended on it. His forearm had pinned my head over his knee so I couldn't move. I just lay there as he hammered my flesh with his bare hands like a man possessed.

Aligning himself with children's charities helped Cyril gain access to boys.

Although he was never going to occupy 10 Downing Street, Cyril built his own northern powerbase.

At over twenty-nine stone, Cyril was said to be the heaviest MP ever.

Typically fooling for the cameras, but British Transport Police eventually caught him on camera approaching boys at Euston Station.

Cyril cultivated a homely, man-of-the-people northern image.

Cyril and Mohammad Pasha, who ran the Pakistani Welfare Association.
'I support personalities not political parties,' he said.

David Steel meets Mohammad Pasha (left of Steel) at an event with Cyril and his brother, Norman
Smith, who was mayor of Rochdale at the time.

Former Lancashire mill owner Edmund Gartside (right of Cyril) helped write Cyril's maiden speech when he became MP.

Cyril had a big impact on Asian politics in Rochdale – he defended Pakistan's right to nuclear weapons and said Salman Rushdie's book *The Satanic Verses* should be burned. 'Cyril was the only politician I knew saying things like this,' said Pasha.

Pictured at a Liberal campaign event for the Manchester Central by-election of 1979, Cyril was accused by the host of 'lewd and crude' behaviour. He was thrown out by her former police officer husband after he groped a fourteen-year-old campaign volunteer. A complaint was made to David Steel's office about Cyril's behaviour, although Steel says he was never notified of the incident.

Martin Digan, the whistleblower who exposed the scandal of child abuse at Knowl View School. He is still haunted by the scale of abuse he discovered at the residential school for children with learning difficulties where Cyril was a governor and had his own set of keys.

The first issue of the *Rochdale Alternative Press* had a cartoon of a huge Cyril Smith-shaped blimp clinging onto Rochdale Town Hall.

Cyril's clown-like persona and cheeky grin hid a bullying and ruthless streak.

Even in her later years, Gracie Fields was a massive star and Cyril was jealous of the attention she commanded.

After what seemed like an eternity he threw me to the floor and stood above me. I bit my lip and screwed my eyes shut for a second while I lay with my face to the floor trying to forget about the pain. I never made a noise. He wasn't going to get the satisfaction of knowing he'd hurt me. My butt was on fire and I could feel the welts forming but I pulled my trousers up, sat up and stared insolently back at him. 'Is that it?' I asked.

He was still panting but a nasty little smile began to form on his face as he knelt down next to me and pushed his face close to mine.

'It's going to stop,' he whispered. 'This is going to stop or I'll kill you.'

He prodded my forehead with a chubby index finger and pushed me to the floor to make his point. I just lay there watching him as the words sank in. This guy was a psycho, I thought. He adjusted his tie in the mirror above the fireplace and left the room.

I pulled myself together and sat there for a few minutes listening to him talking to my parents in the kitchen. 'If you let me take him in hand,' I heard him say, 'then he won't do it anymore. Not after I've finished with him.'

This was going to be a challenge, I realised. But I wasn't going to let a fat cartoon character turn me into a stiff shirt. Cyril could do his worst but he wouldn't be taking me in hand.

All week I couldn't get Cyril out of my head. I knew politicians were strange people, but I'd never heard of them turning up at people's houses and tanning the backsides of strangers. I didn't want this man in my life at all.

That was all about to change, though, and it wouldn't be long before I had to see him every day.

Even though I'd been away for three months in a detention centre, my boss had kept me on. He'd told me I was lucky to keep my job but he was going to give me one last chance. 'We all make mistakes,' he said. I didn't know what I'd done to deserve a second chance but I gratefully seized it.

Not long afterwards he sidled up to my workbench and asked what I was doing at the weekend.

'The usual,' I said, not looking up from my work. 'Going to the Twisted Wheel with mates.'

He gave a nervous little cough and I put my tools down and looked up.

'I was thinking that maybe we could go camping together in the Lake District,' he said.

There was an awkward silence.

'Err, that's not really my thing, sorry.'

'If you don't like camping we could get a caravan, if you like?'

'I'd rather not, thanks.'

I glanced around the room to see if anyone else could hear our conversation, but the radio was on and everyone seemed engrossed in their work.

'Sure, I understand,' he replied, and I saw a look of embarrassment flash across his face. 'Get back to your work.'

He strode off and slammed his office door and I didn't think anything more of it.

But later that day, when he called me into his office, I found out that rejecting his camping invitation had serious consequences.

'You know we've been very good with you, haven't we?' he asked, as I sat down.

'Yes,' I nodded.

'All that business with the police, drugs, your visit to the detention centre. I've been very understanding, haven't I?'

I didn't say a word.

'Well, it turns out that we are in breach of company rules and I'm afraid we can't keep anyone here with a criminal record. We're going to have to let you go.'

I couldn't look him in the eyes. I stared at my boots and didn't say a word. I knew what this was about. I'd turned down his advances and wouldn't let him have his wicked way with me. Homosexuality was still illegal at the time and we both knew it. This was my punishment for turning him down. I needed this job, but there was no way I was going camping with him.

'OK,' I finally said. 'You're the boss.'

'You won't be out of a job, though,' he smiled. 'I've seen to that. There's a friend of mine who runs a spring manu-facturing company across town and he takes on lads with criminal records. He helps get them back on the straight and narrow, if you know what I mean. I've called him this morning and he said he can give you a job at his factory. His name's Cyril Smith.'

I didn't know what to say. I couldn't turn it down. I needed a job. But now I was going to have to work for the fat psycho.

My mum and dad seemed happy about the arrangement. But I wasn't. I became an apprentice toolmaker at Smith's Springs and I worked under Cyril's watchful eye every day.

He'd set the business up a few years earlier and it seemed to be doing well. Cyril had gone from production controller in Fred Ratcliffe's spring-making factory across town to setting up his own venture. The rumour was he'd stolen the order book and taken the business with him.

I remember my first day there. After I'd been shown the ropes by Cyril's business partner Geoff, Cyril came up to me and put his arm round me. 'I'm going to be like your dad,' he said. 'I'll look after you now.' I shuddered.

And so began the strangest time I've ever known. All week I worked for Cyril and at the weekends he'd be round our house beating the living daylights out of me. I started to smoke more dope and became withdrawn. How had this come about? What was I doing with my life? I worked for an enormous fat man who'd wink at me all day and tell me he was going to be my dad, then when the weekend came round he'd be knocking on our door itching to get my trousers off and start spanking my backside. I sometimes wondered if it was all a bad dream.

But despite Cyril's beatings, it didn't stop me going out. I still went to the Twisted Wheel most Saturdays and I'd lose myself for hours, smoking dope, dancing to the music and getting high on life. These were my people, I thought. This was where it was really at. If I had to tolerate Cyril's fanatical spankings every week then so be it. It was a small price to pay.

Cyril tried everything to intimidate me. He'd circle me sometimes, walking round the carpet like a madman, glaring at me for five minutes or so before he pounced and threw me over his knee. He told me all the important people he knew. He was always doing this, trying to convince people of his power. I remember he'd taken us to the mayor's parlour for our works do that year and all the other lads who worked for him were really impressed. He boasted of his relationship with the chief constable. Why was he telling me this, I wondered? Did he think he could scare me? I wasn't impressed. I asked him once why he had such a fixation with taking my pants down and smacking my backside. Did my parents know he was doing this? He backhanded me and told me I had an attitude problem.

After a few months, I think Cyril started to realise he wasn't going to win this battle. My parents knew it wasn't working, too. One week I stayed out all weekend and only came back on Monday morning to get washed and changed before going to work. Cyril wasn't going to batter me into submission. He'd picked on the wrong guy.

That week he got Geoff to sack me. Cyril didn't have the guts to do it himself. He told my parents I was a lost cause and there was no hope for me.

It was the best day of my life.

I got another job soon afterwards in engineering and things started to look up. My relationship with my parents began to heal, too. I never told them what Cyril had done to me, though I suspect they had known what was really going on. They may even have been complicit in it.

I was more than relieved to have escaped Cyril's clutches, but I soon came into contact with other boys who hadn't. Because I'd spent three months in a detention centre I still had to report regularly to a probation officer and every few weeks I'd make my way over to the probation services office on Drake Street in Rochdale. That's where I met other boys who told me that Cyril had seriously sexually abused them.

We'd all sit in the corridor waiting to be seen and the conversation would quickly turn to Cyril. As I listened to their stories, I started to realise I'd got off lightly. These were damaged kids, you could see the deep sadness in their eyes, hear the loss in their voice. They had no confidence and came from broken homes. Some had been in care, others had not seen their parents in years. Most had stayed in the Cambridge House boys' hostel that Cyril had opened. That's where he'd abused them. Their stories sent shivers down my spine. I asked one lad why he'd put up with it. I had nowhere else to go, he said. He couldn't bear the thought of sleeping on the streets.

There were other boys I'd bump into in town who told me Cyril had abused them, too. I remember one lad in particular who worked in the cinema as an usher. He had a hollow look in his eyes as though his future had been ripped out of him. All he had left was a deep sense of loss. I wonder what happened to these lads. Where did they go?

Once I no longer had to meet the probation officer any more, that world began to recede and I moved on to different things. The 1960s had given way to a different era. In 1978 Emmett Grogan died of a heroin overdose. The dreams of the '60s were starting to fade.

I worked hard, got married, had children and ended up leaving Rochdale altogether to go and work in Australia.

I returned to Rochdale many years later and no longer thought about Cyril. Then one day in 1990 the police knocked on my door. They were investigating claims that

Cyril Smith had abused young boys. My wife was out at the time so I invited them in. It was just as well she was out. I'd never told her or anyone in my family about Cyril.

I had no idea how they'd got hold of me, perhaps some of the lads who I met at the probation office had mentioned my name. But I told them what'd happened in the 1960s and gave them a statement. Cyril was still the town's MP and I hoped it wasn't too late for his past to catch up with him.

I never heard anything more from the police and it wasn't until his crimes were publicly exposed after his death in 2012 that I realised there'd been a number of investigations into Cyril that had gone nowhere.

Why would someone protect him? Who was preventing justice taking its course? It just didn't make any sense.

When you get older there are some things that you bury and try not to think about. The past is gone and it's better to move on. But the past can catch up with you and I ended up doing a lot of soul-searching about Cyril Smith. When everyone else had gone to bed in our house I was still awake downstairs thinking about the time Cyril landed in my life.

I blamed myself for what had happened. I should have stopped him. I could handle myself as a teenager and I should have hit him. What he was doing was wrong and I should have done everything I could to stop it. It was only the fear of losing my job that made me go along with it.

But when I look back now, I know he was grooming me. He was trying to break me so he could take things further, like he had with other boys. He always used to look in my eyes after he'd smacked my backside and I guess he could see the sense of defiance shining back at him. He tried hard to extinguish that but he couldn't. If he'd succeeded I've no doubt he would have seriously sexually abused me. I thought back to what he'd said to me at the time. The threat that he would kill me, the talk of how close he was to the chief constable. I'd laughed it off. But how would other, less assured boys have reacted? They'd have been terrified. That was his aim. Finding vulnerable young boys, striking fear into them and breaking them.

What saved me in the end was my parents and upbringing. I came from a solid, middle-class home and although I'd gone off the rails I had enough self-respect and confidence instilled in me to stand up to Cyril. After me, he'd moved on to easier meat.

I had escaped and I thanked my lucky stars. But I couldn't stop wondering what happened to those that hadn't managed to. The lost generation that Cyril captured. Where did those poor boys go?

I tried to talk to my mum about it one time, before she got Alzheimer's disease. She just shook her head and I could see the tears forming in her eyes. I put my arm round her and didn't say any more. She knew it was a mistake but I guess they were just at their wits' end and didn't know what else to do. I didn't blame my parents. How could they have known what a real monster he was?

But plenty of people did know what a real monster Cyril was. He wasn't acting on his own. There were others, too. We used to laugh when we saw groups of men coming in to Rochdale off the train because we all knew what they were up to. The dirty mac brigade, we called them.

Cyril couldn't have abused all these boys on his own. He had a team of people behind him. They were all in on it.

It took the police long enough to knock on my door. I hope there's still time for Cyril's cronies to get a knock on their door.

Chapter 6

The National Stage

When Cyril became an MP in 1972 and arrived at his new place of work, like many before him he succumbed to a momentary sense of awestruck wonder. As someone who'd struggled against poverty and prejudice, to be welcomed into the Palace of Westminster represented an astonishing journey. Grand neo-gothic architecture, beautifully ornate interiors and nearly a thousand years of constitutional history now stood before him.

But his awe soon gave way to irritation and annoyance at the excessive flummery and outdated traditions at the heart of British democracy. The Palace of Westminster, he observed, was more suited to eighteenth-century gentry than the MPs of the twentieth century. In the cloakroom he was shown to a hook where he could hang his sword from if he ever chose to bring it to the House of Commons. This somewhat bizarre sense of tradition, coupled with the stench of snobbery that filled the place, made him feel as though he'd gone back in time to a medieval kingdom.

That sense of awkwardness never left him and Cyril struggled to fit in around the House of Commons. Some people adjust to their new surroundings; Cyril didn't. He simply didn't see himself as a grand parliamentarian pontificating from the green benches and idling away the hours over afternoon tea in historic rooms with wonderful views. He didn't travel well. Despite having strong links with the Pakistani and Bangladesh communities in Rochdale he'd never travelled to their countries either. He was more at home pottering around Rochdale in his slippers.

Cyril struggled to fully grasp the value of Parliament. It's hard to recall him ever saying a positive word about it. He could and should have seen it more as a place to achieve positive social change. Yet this recognition barely flickered. Instead, he dismissed it as 'the longest running farce in the West End' and 'a charade'. In later years, he came to almost give up on the place, staying away for months on end. By the mid-1980s he was even considering standing down, as letters in the Liberal Party archives suggest. In 1984 Richard Wainwright MP wrote to John Spiller, the secretary general of the Liberal Party, expressing concern that Cyril might quit Parliament at the 1987 general election and urging him to get a parliamentary candidate in place as soon as possible. 'I wonder,' he warned, 'whether, if Cyril, to my great regret, is determined not to stand again.'

He didn't make much of the responsibilities he was given by his party, either. First as a whip and then as social security and employment spokesperson he failed to make much impact. While his colleagues, like David Steel and Jeremy Thorpe, were helping introduce major social reforms like the Abortion Act or fiercely opposing apartheid in South Africa, Cyril was refuting growing public concerns about the dangers of asbestos and warning about anarchists and totalitarian socialists infiltrating the National Union of Journalists. It was hardly inspirational stuff. His barnstorming, passionate oratory was rarely seen in the House of Commons. Trade unions, education, industry, housing and immigration were subjects that drew him into the Chamber, but despite the odd flash of rhetorical steel there's little to match the great public speeches he saved for Rochdale. It seemed that public meetings, the council chamber, journalists and TV cameras got the best out of Cyril.

But while he never developed a love of Parliament he did recognise from time to time that it had its uses. And he did recognise government. On occasion, says a Liberal Democrat government minister, Cyril helped make changes to legislation before it was passed. He worked constructively with the government on trade union legislation, for example.

Long before Cyril arrived in Parliament, however, he'd been making journeys there to try and make sure Rochdale voices were heard.

Edmund Gartside was a Lancashire mill owner in the 1960s and remembers Cyril helping him in 1966 during the year he was mayor. He'd founded a committee of Lancashire mayors and led a delegation to London to meet with a trade minister in Harold Wilson's government. Gartside was among those in attendance as they went to lobby for the textile industry. Their chief concern was that large amounts of cheap imports – from places like Turkey and Pakistan – were flooding the UK market and making it hard for the British textile industry to compete. They needed help. Other countries were getting cotton subsidies, why wouldn't the British government do the same?

'We'd had a mini revival in the 1950s but seen steady decline since,' Gartside admits. 'The cotton industry was a big employer in Rochdale at the time – and across Lancashire, too. We warned that we were looking at huge job losses. Around 120,000 jobs would go across Lancashire unless significant action was taken.'

But their words were ignored and the minister was unmoved. An industry that at its peak in 1912 produced eight billion yards of cloth now saw an uncertain future. 'It had been a huge industry. At one point Oldham had more mills than the whole of America,' reflects Gartside.

When Cyril became Rochdale's MP, he went to see Gartside to ask for help in writing his maiden speech. At 4.30 p.m. on 2 November 1972, Cyril stood up in the House of Commons and delivered a passionate plea for government help for the cotton industry.

'My constituents greatly fear the effect that exports, particularly from Turkey and Greece, will have on our ability to sell home-spun yarn,' he announced. 'We cannot easily compete against countries which subsidise their yarn exports, as does Turkey, for example, to the tune of 15 per cent. I am therefore pleading for some control of yarn imports. If this is not done anything from 5,000 to 30,000 jobs in the spinning industry are likely to be lost.'

It wasn't done and jobs were lost.

An All-Party Parliamentary Group for the textile industry was set up and Cyril became the secretary. Other Lancashire MPs including Barbara Castle sat on it and it continued to fight for a better deal from government for the British textile industry.

But it never came and Cyril lost interest. 'He didn't come to many meetings,' admits Gartside. 'After a while he stopped. I think he thought there weren't that many votes in it anymore. He lost interest in the textile industry and that disillusioned me.'

Unbeknown to Gartside at the time, Cyril's attention had shifted to another industry in the town, where there was more money and more votes, but also a massive health risk. His lobbying energies were now being employed to help the asbestos industry.

Gartside would soldier on, though, without Cyril's or the government's help. In 1997 he ran the largest cotton-spinning mill left in Lancashire, employing 1,000 people. 'Governments have been completely indifferent to this industry,' he told me. 'They haven't helped.' Did Cyril's sudden loss of interest in the textile industry still rankle? 'It stuck in my throat,' he says. 'But I'd lost faith in politicians by then.'

However, despite Cyril's half-hearted approach to Parliament the Liberals recognised his significance. His visits to constituencies always created a frisson of excitement and his campaigning skills were duly recognised. After only two years in Parliament, the Liberals decided to deploy Cyril as the 1974 general election approached.

He appeared in their general election TV broadcast, famously telling millions it was time to 'get rid of all this hypocritical rubbish' and calling for the restoration of Christian-based moral values. He featured heavily in election tours and the Liberals' media campaign. Many Liberal press releases from the time are full of typical Cyril attacks on Labour and the Tories. One, for example, has Cyril attacking 'nonsense' policies dreamt up by 'Tory campaign managers seated in comfortable offices in Westminster and backed by smooth advertising executives from Mayfair'. Another has Cyril reunited with a pub landlord who he claims saved him from drowning when he was a boy. There were all sorts of stories, speeches and attacks from Cyril in the campaign and it established a pattern that would be repeated during every election. This was where Cyril shone. Out campaigning, in front of the cameras and telling it straight. He was in his element.

No one could doubt his charisma, big personality and maverick appeal. But questions continued to hang over his political judgement.

Among many of his peers, the overriding feeling associated with Cyril was distrust. That's not to say he didn't have friends, though. He was a prodigious networker who also reached out to those in other parties. The Conservative, Sir David Trippier, a former Minister for the Environment and Countryside who now operates under the title of the Provincial Grand Master following his appointment as the highest-ranking freemason in east Lancashire, struck up a friendship with Cyril very early on. Rochdale-born Trippier explains in his biography that his friendship with Cyril stemmed from his mother's relationship with Cyril's mother. During the war his mother had always made sure that she had enough meat for Cyril and his brother and sister. Cyril never forgot Trippier's mother's kindness and was the first person to welcome Trippier when he was elected to Parliament in 1979.

But among many of his colleagues no such kindness was shown. He was seen as impetuous, cantankerous and someone who leaked to the press. Ironically, it was this nature that ultimately paved the way for a unique constitutional event, the first pact since the Second World War.

In early 1977, following a by-election defeat the Labour government were left with no overall majority and faced a motion of no confidence. The Prime Minister, Jim Callaghan, was in trouble and the last person he would have envisaged riding to his rescue was Cyril Smith.

What Callaghan didn't know was that for some time now Cyril had been urging his leader David Steel to approach the government to open talks. Labour no longer had a clear majority in the House of Commons and a pact would give the Liberals some opportunity to wield power, argued Cyril. Steel was reluctant to make such overtures, feeling it would diminish his status as leader if he were seen to be offering help to the government. So Cyril rashly decided to go ahead anyway and try and initiate talks himself.

On 3 March 1977, a surprised Callaghan received an official approach from Cyril regarding the possibility of a pact to prevent a general election from being called, which Callaghan stood little chance of winning. Much to Cyril's annoyance, and in line with convention, the Prime Minister was not about to meet a Liberal politician – and one who was renowned for leaking to the press – to discuss such an important matter and so he suggested a meeting between Cyril and Cledwyn Hughes, the chairman of the Parliamentary Labour Party.

Cyril took this as a snub and leaked news of it to the

Daily Mirror. Callaghan was certainly not going to fob him off with some underling, he thought. In the meantime, Steel had come to the conclusion that his party wasn't in any fit state to fight a general election, as the Liberals were still recovering from seeing their previous leader, Jeremy Thorpe, forced to step down by a sex scandal. There had been two general elections in 1974 and the party was hardly awash with cash either. The prospect of an immediate general election did not suit him at all and it had to be delayed. 'It would have been torture,' Steel admits in his biography. He would meet with Hughes, he decided, and so began the Lib–Lab Pact.

A deal was struck in which the Labour Party accepted some Liberal policy proposals in exchange for the Liberal Party voting with the government on any subsequent motion of no confidence. However, many believed that Steel had failed to drive a hard bargain and the Liberals ultimately got very little out of the deal.

Cyril's reputation as a headstrong politician who was forever changing horses was further cemented when he changed his position to vigorously oppose the pact he'd initially fought to bring about. The Labour government was too unpopular, he'd decided, and the Liberals continuing association with it was doing enormous damage. What's more, he'd begun to notice how it was affecting his prospects in Rochdale. He needed Tory votes to keep his seat and they weren't likely to support him if his party was propping up a Labour government. If his party renewed the pact, he warned, they would be 'slaughtered' at the next general election.

But Cyril's view wasn't unanimous. Other Liberals felt they had to stay the course and stick with the pact as an immediate general election would be catastrophic. Cyril stepped up his campaign to end the pact, leaking a letter to the *Daily Mail* from Jo Grimond, the party's former leader, in which he expressed grave doubts about the pact and urged the Liberals to keep hold of their freedom. It was extremely damaging and Cyril's colleagues were furious.

As Alistair Michie and Simon Hoggart acknowledge in their book on the inside story of the pact, Liberal MPs met the following day, when Cyril was away, and had 'a pleasantly bitchy session' about Cyril's many shortcomings.

It was descending into a farce and the thirteen Liberal MPs propping up the government were locked in a bitter battle that was only ever going to have one outcome. The country was still reeling from the International Monetary Fund crisis, which had seen the Chancellor forced to ask for a £2.3 billion bailout after unemployment and inflation had reached exceptional levels, and now the government was lurching from one crisis to the next.

There was even an argument over whether there would be sufficient electricity to support the Queen's Silver Jubilee celebrations. The power saving campaign run by Tony Benn's Department of Energy was said to be against floodlighting major public buildings along the Thames. In the end, the Prime Minister had to intervene. 'Bloody nonsense', retorted Callaghan, ordering Benn to 'let them light up' and ensure the Silver Jubilee celebrations went ahead as planned. It was a difficult year and, as Steel acknowledged at the time, his party 'lived permanently on the brink of disaster'.

At the Liberal Party conference in Brighton that year Cyril told hordes of activists that he was not instinctively an anti-coalitionist, but he was 'anti-coalition unless you have enough MPs to guarantee your identity within that coalition and an electoral system which gives a fair chance of survival…' As applause rang out the message was clear to everyone. The Liberal Party's identity was dissolving and the longer it stayed in the pact the more their chances of survival diminished. The mood was changing and Cyril was leading the revolt among activists. Steel was slowly being pushed into a corner. Many would argue he'd performed miracles keeping it together so long. Some thirty-three years later as Cyril lay on his death bed in the summer of 2010, his body now wasted away by cancer, he warned his Liberal Democrat colleagues that history could repeat itself. 'This coalition could be the death of us,' he whispered.

By May 1978 an announcement was made signalling the end of the pact. Some months earlier, when Liberal MPs had finally come to the conclusion that they had to end the pact, Cyril could barely contain his glee. 'I haven't been so happy after a party meeting for years,' he grinned. He could now go back to Rochdale and tell Tory-inclined voters that he'd put a stop to the pact and sent Callaghan packing. And the result? They'd smile, shake his hand and continue voting for him to 'keep Labour out of Rochdale'.

Cyril had started to carve out a position for himself as the conscience of the Liberal Party. He was frequently critical of his party's leadership and would act as though he were fighting for its soul. As ever with Cyril, he would ham this up and the grassroots membership applauded him for doing this. However, it antagonised his parliamentary colleagues and resentments started to fester. You could see their point. He'd initially supported the Lib–Lab Pact but when the going got tough he turned against it. He had a nose for shallow populism and his switching between parties didn't exactly impress some. At one point it has been suggested that he even approached Ted Heath to try and form a new centrist party. But behind Cyril's impetuous outbursts often lay an impeccable sense of timing. At the launch of the Social Democratic Party–Liberal Alliance in 1981, for example, he publicly announced that it 'should be strangled at birth'. The pact marked a difficult period in government and was widely viewed as an experiment more than anything else. It did achieve some successes, but the media hated it. Ironically, for the man who helped bring about its inception but became one of its most vocal critics, it could well have brought him considerable personal benefit.

When Tony Robinson, a Special Branch officer with Lancashire Police in the 1970s, revealed in 2012 how police files on Cyril had been requested by MI5, he explained that he had known immediately why they'd wanted them. MI5 had a unit that monitored MPs and reported to the Cabinet Office. At the time of the Lib–Lab Pact Liberal MPs would have been checked out to determine whether they were suitable for high office. 'The fact that the security service wanted the file brought to my notice obviously indicated that he was about to be vetted,' said Robinson. Within the files were affidavits from young boys detailing their abuse at the hands of Cyril. There was plenty of compelling evidence suggesting he was not fit for high office.

Why Cyril was ultimately afforded protection by both Special Branch officers and MI5 is baffling. This became a complex jigsaw puzzle that was slowly starting to piece together, revealing a worrying picture. Many pieces were still missing though, including the eventual discovery of why a criminal file on Cyril's activities had ended up in a safe in Hutton, Lancashire. But as more evidence came to light a bigger picture emerged.

For millions of people, Cyril's image was clear enough. It was the laughing, straight-talking, bluff-speaking northerner they'd hear on the radio or see on television or in the paper. The lasting impression was of a colourful, outspoken politician with common sense. Cyril knew this and that's how he controlled his image. To see the real picture, of course, you had to flip the board and look at the wiring underneath.

In his diaries, Tony Benn called him an absolute cynic and opportunist who was always 'trying to seize the leadership'. A sense of the frustration felt by his colleagues is shared by former Liberal MP Michael Meadowcroft, who said, 'his tendency to shoot first and qualify later was exasperating'.

The biographies of Liberal leaders at the time indicate that his colleagues tolerated him. Cyril is barely mentioned in their biographies and it seems most of his peers went through the motions of having a positive relationship with him. They knew he had a strong relationship with the media and that he had to be kept onside to avoid him briefing against them to journalists. But they tried to keep him at arm's length and were always wary of him. It's hard to see how he could have enjoyed a positive relationship with Steel after he publicly dismissed him as an effete politician that 'couldn't make a bang with a firework in both hands'. His relationship with Thorpe wasn't much better. Cyril's politics were diametrically opposed to Thorpe's. Thorpe opposed capital punishment, for example, while Cyril championed it. And Thorpe advocated legalised abortion while Cyril was against it. During the height of the 1970s energy crisis, and with Britain reduced to a three-day working week, Thorpe went abroad to try and sort out his increasingly fraught personal life. Cyril took the opportunity to write an open letter that he circulated to the media calling on Thorpe to show some leadership. It was hardly a surprise that his party viewed him with great suspicion.

Yet throughout the 1970s and into the 1980s, Cyril was always capable of throwing his weight around and exerting influence on the direction his party took. In many of the major events and crises for the Liberals during this period, he would charge straight into the fray, wanting to have his say and shape the outcome he wanted. Some activists liked this; they saw him as the conscience of the party. But senior Liberal figures generally viewed him as an irritant. Whether it was the Thorpe affair when he was chief whip, the end of the Lib–Lab Pact, the birth of the SDP–Liberal Alliance or new rules for electing the Liberal leader, which Cyril devised, he proved his influence time after time. People in his party didn't always necessarily like Cyril. Hoggart famously noted that Thorpe found him 'distasteful'. But they could not ignore him.

And neither could other people away from politics, who had been keeping a close eye on him. Up until now Cyril had only come to the attention of regional police officers. But as the 1970s progressed, both MI5 and Special Branch officers from the Metropolitan Police Service began to take a growing interest in him.

Silent Voices #3: 'Stick with Me, You'll Be the Next MP'

I first met Cyril Smith in 1979. Within minutes of meeting him, the impact he made was astonishing. I was sixteen years old and hungry for new experiences, anything to break away from the council estate torpor that was draining the life from me.

It was a frosty day in January and I remember rushing upstairs to see what was going on in the street outside. My brother was playing ELO's 'Mr Blue Sky' at full volume and I shouted at him to turn it down. A loud voice was booming out over a tannoy and from my window I watched a big black Mercedes crawling round our estate with an entourage in tow pushing what looked to be leaflets through letterboxes. Now the tannoy had stopped, I could hear the song 'Nice One Cyril' being played. When the car came to a halt, I saw the sign on the car. 'You're behind Cyril Smith', it read. The door swung open and a huge figure hit the tarmac. He strode purposefully across the road and I watched him start to talk to our neighbours. Then he knocked on our door.

I sometimes wonder what would have happened if I hadn't answered that door. If I hadn't thundered downstairs to get there ahead of my brother how different would my life have turned out?

I was working in a textile mill at the time and the boredom I felt was inescapable. I'd never known my real mother and my dad was in prison. It was the best place for him. I only had to look at the scars on my arms from cigarette burns for a reminder of why he had no place in my life. I'd lived with my grandmother for a while before going into a children's home. I was put up for adoption at an early age and lived with my adopted parents on a horrible, boring estate. Growing up as a teenager in the 1970s was interminably dull and I was at the cutting edge of tedium.

I'd play kerby in the street for hours looking up at contrails stretching across grey slate skies, wishing I was on a plane too, jetting away to somewhere else. Sometimes I'd spend the whole day holed up in my bedroom reading books. I was learning about the history of the trade union movement, workers' rights and how the common man had been screwed for centuries. I was searching for something, but I didn't really know what. And when I finally opened the door and stared at this smiling hulk of a man, I saw a trace of it in his eyes. As he held out a giant hand in front of me, something flickered across his face. Excitement, risk, purpose. I knew he didn't live by the same rules as the rest of us.

'Is your mum in, lad?' Cyril asked.

'No, there's just me and my brother. She's at work. You're our MP, aren't you?'

'Yes, I'm Cyril Smith. Are you interested in politics, lad?'

'Yes, I am.'

His face lit up.

'Then perhaps I've got a new recruit. Why don't you come and join us?'

I just stood there, open-mouthed. Was it that easy? Is this how you got involved in politics?

He waved to his colleagues, who were waiting patiently at the gate. 'We've got a new recruit here, lads,' he shouted as he gestured for them to move on to the next house without him. Then he started to tell me all about the Young Liberals and how he'd been one once. 'Come and see me next week,' he said, handing me a leaflet with his office address on. 'There's an important general election coming up and I could do with some help. We can't let Labour take Rochdale, can we?'

I said I would and he winked and made his way down the path. I stood at the door watching him for a moment, mesmerised. The way he walked captivated me. He didn't walk like other people. He walked like he could walk through a brick wall, like he owned everything and nothing could stop him.

I joined the Liberals as soon as I could and the following week I made my way down to Drake Street to join their campaign. It was a hubbub of activity and his secretary made me welcome and told me to join the team and get stuck in. We stuffed envelopes and took turns on the phone bank speaking to voters. I saw Cyril at the back of the room and he gave me a wink.

I started to do this regularly and suddenly got caught up in the excitement of a general election campaign. I joined Cyril on the doorstep campaigning for every vote and went to the town hall for the count where I watched Cyril win by a majority of more than 5,000. The cheers nearly shook the building as Cyril was returned as the town's MP for the fourth time. It was the night that Margaret Thatcher became Prime Minister and there was a huge feeling of change in the air. We all knew a new era beckoned. Cyril thanked everyone for their help and told me to come down to his office again the following week. 'We keep going all year round,' he grinned. I had begun to feel part of something exciting and a newfound purpose was starting to shape my life. I was hooked.

It wasn't long before I was a close member of his team and I started to spend more and more time down at his office. I watched with awe at how he did casework and tended to people's problems. He'd listen attentively as someone told him how they needed a bigger council house for their family, for example, then he'd pick the phone up and the council would leap to attention and sort out whatever he wanted. He seemed to have complete control over the public sector in Rochdale. In those days MPs had real power. Then, he'd take his grateful constituent over to his secretary and get her to write up a letter saying how remarkable Cyril was. They'd gladly put their name to it and Cyril would post it off to the local paper. He did this all the time.

If you became a friend of Cyril's he'd make sure he looked after you. 'You want to be a magistrate?' he'd ask. 'Leave it to me.' He was well in with the freemasons, too. He could always get something done by calling a contact. Everyone wanted to know Cyril. They all thought he'd provide a foot in the door to somewhere. When Cyril picked up the phone he always got straight through to whoever he wanted. I remember him calling the chief executive of the council once to ask him to get someone's drains unblocked. That's how he operated.

You couldn't help but admire his style. When a politician comes on TV nowadays and is interviewed you can see the calculated look in their eyes as they prevaricate and dither in their response. With Cyril it was different. You could see conviction in his eyes. He had a directness about him that people liked. He just came straight out and told it how it was.

Sometimes I'd walk with him to the post office to send his letters. He'd always sellotape them first. MI5 steamed them to get at their contents, he said. He'd stop and talk to everyone as well. He knew all the police officers and lawyers in Rochdale.

By this time Cyril began to insist that he gave me a lift home instead of me getting the bus. And that's when he started to show a different side.

I remember the first time he pulled up on our street to drop me off. A group of lads playing British bulldog just stopped and stared as I got out of his car. A few months earlier I would have been playing bulldog with them or kerby. When they asked if I wanted to play one night after Cyril had dropped me off I said no. 'I'm into politics now.' They looked back blankly, as though a chasm had opened between us. It was as if they didn't know me anymore. My world had changed completely.

In 1980 Cyril took me to the Liberal conference in Blackpool at the Winter Gardens. We stayed in the Imperial Hotel and I loved it. It's a stunning place. Winston

Churchill and the Queen have stayed here, he told me as we checked in. I stood in the lobby and sucked in the majesty of the place. If I closed my eyes I could almost smell one of Churchill's cigars and imagine him standing next to me. Cyril knew I was completely overawed. He could see the starstruck look of wonder in my eyes. He just laughed and tousled my hair in that rough, affectionate way of his. I'd never seen anything like it.

Then one day Cyril asked me to come for a drive with him late at night. 'Let me get my mum to bed first,' he said, and then he picked me up and we headed over the tops. Cyril was dressed in his pyjamas and slippers and we drove in silence for a while. I watched the lights of Rochdale recede as we flew down the lanes and past the Owd Betts pub on Edenfield Road. The moon glistened above Knowl Hill in the distance and we both listened to the hum of the engine as we left Rochdale behind. We were somewhere in the south Pennines when he pulled up by a stone wall in a remote spot. I remember looking at his huge clenched fist on the handbrake on the dashboard. I could see the whites of his knuckles. An owl's hoot broke the silence and Cyril leaned towards me.

'You know I'm not going to be the MP forever,' he said. 'I've been in politics a long time. If you stick with me, I'll make sure you're the next MP for Rochdale. I'll show you the ropes, I'll groom you. It can be yours if you want it.' His face was an inch away from mine now and I could smell his stale breath. The leather seats squeaked as his weight shifted towards me. As he spoke, his hand slid down my inside leg and he began to pull me towards him.

I know now I should have screamed and punched him in the face. I should have got out of that car and never turned back. But I didn't. I sat there frozen as he groped me and his hands slid all over my body. He moaned and groaned and buried his face into my neck. I didn't say a word. I just stared at the crescent moon on the hill outside. My heart was pounding like a ticking bomb.

I lost count of how many times he did this to me and I could tell by the look in his face that he knew he had complete control over me. It was true; I had hardly any confidence and my self-esteem was on the floor. I'd never had a girlfriend before and Cyril's world was exciting and unpredictable. Every day was different. I wanted to spend time with him but I knew his behaviour was wrong. Very wrong. He pushed the boundaries every time and the shame stuck with me for years. I still wince when I think about it now.

In the years that followed, Cyril repeatedly used me to satisfy his perverse cravings. He treated me like a sex object. I got used to seeing dark clouds of lust scud across his eyes and he would regularly create opportunities for us to be alone together. At one point he even groped me in Parliament. He'd taken me there a few times and introduced me to all kinds of people. I remember meeting Michael Foot and watching the pair of them laughing hysterically at things that weren't in the slightest bit funny. I wondered if you had to be mad to get into that place. In his office he was all over me – with the door open, too. Politicians walked past but no one said anything. It was as though different laws applied to people here.

I was trapped in a circus. Boredom and a longing for a different life had driven me to him and now I was too weak to escape. Cyril's world was one I never could have imagined and he took me everywhere with him. My world of battleship grey had now gone technicolour.

You couldn't help but notice Cyril's fame. He was known wherever he went. He'd walk round Rochdale market in his slippers and he'd be treated like a demigod. They loved his eccentricity and he had a great backstory. He made the most of it, too. He'd always tell people how his mother scrubbed the steps of Rochdale Town Hall for a living. People looked up when he entered a room and then you'd hear it. A ripple of appreciative noise, almost like a trilling sound. You could feel a frisson in the crowd. He had a powerful aura. Man of the people, the face of the Liberal Party, a champion for the north, a rebel with a cause. He meant something to everyone. But to me he was an outlaw. He lived on the run and took what he could. Most of the time he didn't care what people thought. He'd take me to fancy dinners with the great and the good and sometimes he'd wear a suit and slippers. He'd wear a shabby old tie and his flies would be jammed at half-mast. He just didn't care. He had nothing to prove to them. He didn't particularly care about convention. He was above all that; a bit regal if you like. I sat next to him once in my best suit at some posh function and he pushed his knife and fork aside and started to eat with his fingers. The pearl necklaces and dinner suits started to look at him askance, but it didn't bother him at all. I think he did it deliberately.

Later that night Sir Robin Day came up to him and started to make conversation. Cyril began to tell him some ridiculous Rochdale yarn and Day hung on every word. When he went to light a cigar Cyril winked at me, as if to say, 'Look at this fool. Like putty in my hand.' The royal family aside, he hated the establishment. He thought it was rotten. But he still wanted their seal of approval. It was all a bizarre game.

I began to realise that Cyril could only belong in a minority party like the Liberals. He couldn't fit in anywhere else. He knew the Liberals had no chance of being elected to government but he didn't care. He wanted the independence and there was no way his party could control him. He broke every rule going, he didn't toe the party line and he used to brief against his party leader all the time. The only thing he seemed to care about was his image and the legend he was creating.

He saw me reading the *Rochdale Alternative Press* once. 'You know, when you're famous,' he told me, 'there are always people who want to have a go at you. But it's not true what they say. What we have is different.'

I just looked at him and put the magazine down. I didn't say a word.

We drove a lot. We were always going somewhere in a hurry. His big black Mercedes was like something the SS would drive. I can still hear the noise of the engine now as we hurtled down the motorway, the wipers noisily swishing through the rain with his agent Rodney Stott driving. Cyril treated Rodney like an idiot. He was always ordering him about. He showed no respect. Rodney was twiddling the dial, trying to find better reception before landing on a familiar song. The pounding intro suddenly gave way to Jeff

Lynne's voice. 'Mr Blue Sky'. I mouthed the words in the back. 'For so long, so long, where did we go wrong?'

We headed to Pebble Mill Studios in Birmingham where Cyril took part in Radio 4's *Any Questions*. Rodney and I waited in the car while he marched off into the BBC building. We always waited in the car. He never let us come with him on visits like this. We waited for hours. But we didn't mind. We were with Cyril.

I remember one time driving over to Yorkshire to do an advert for a supermarket chain. They had Cyril sat down eating a pie, I seem to remember, and he'd gobble a mouthful and grin at the cameras. 'It gets Cyril's vote', was the catch line. He was doing stuff like this all the time now. He'd never say no to any request that put him on the telly. He loved the fame.

As we sat in the car again, Rodney whistling a tune and twirling his key chain, I began to think seriously for the first time whether I should get away from Cyril. Perhaps I was finding my confidence at last.

I was tired of being used and abused by him. His rudeness was beginning to get to me as well. He was charm personified at first. Kind, funny, full of surprises. But I knew a different side to him. He could be boorish, grumpy and show a real nasty edge. He had no manners either. I remember watching him shove a whole pie in his mouth once. He was scoffing away, trying to force more into his mouth, and he caught sight of me watching him. I once excused this behaviour as eccentric. Now I could see it was just disgusting. He started to shout at me while he was eating, but I couldn't hear what he was saying. Transfixed by this ghastly sight, I was showered by pieces of pie flying from his mouth. It was revolting.

I was also beginning to worry about Cyril's populist stance. He always played to the gallery and behaved as though cameras were following him round and he was starring in a film of his own life. But there were plenty of times when popular opinion had to be challenged and Cyril would not do it.

I remember meeting Stefan Kiszko's mother Charlotte a couple of times through Cyril. She came to see him begging for his help. Her son had wrongly been convicted of the murder of Lesley Molseed and there seemed to be something very wrong about this case. Her tears were genuine and her story was heartbreaking. Cyril listened, but I don't think he cared.

One MP later described it as the 'worst miscarriage of justice of all time', but Cyril wouldn't take it on. Years later Kiszko was proved innocent and released, but no thanks to Cyril. Kiszko arrived back in Rochdale three months before Cyril stood down as the town's MP in 1992. He died a year later. His mum died shortly afterwards a heart-broken woman. Cyril didn't say much, which was unlike him. I think he was embarrassed by the whole situation. And so he should have been. He had adopted the rather illiberal position of calling for Kiszko to be hanged. He played to the gallery and wouldn't dare go against popular opinion. He knew the public was baying for blood over the horrific murder of an eleven-year-old girl and they had a man in prison for it. As far as he was concerned that was 'job done'.

Elections occupied Cyril's mind a lot of the time. He'd often steeple his hands beneath his chin, sit back and let Machiavellian thoughts furrow his brow. There was a scheming look that never really left him when he was on his own. He told me early on you had to win the Asian vote to become Rochdale's MP. 'Every bugger else sits on their backside watching *Coronation Street* but those Asians vote,' he said. He was always thinking of how to gain an advantage over his rivals and he used to drag me in to all sorts of wheezes to wear down the opposition.

One day, on the eve of local elections, he placed an advert in the *Manchester Evening News* for a brand new car at a ridiculously cheap price. He put Rochdale Labour Club's phone number at the bottom of the advert. 'That'll keep them busy,' he chuckled. Sure enough, it did. Their phone never stopped ringing. Cyril thought it was so funny he even told a journalist about it and mentioned my name. He warned me that I might get a call and said I should say nothing. He was laughing all the while he was telling me. He thought it was hilarious. There was nothing he loved more than outsmarting the Labour Party and he wanted them to know that he'd had one over them again. He was right, I did get a call. A local broadcast journalist turned up at my door to ask me about it. 'Cyril Smith has advised me to say nothing,' I stammered. I was eighteen and being interviewed on Piccadilly Radio. It felt exhilarating, but I knew it was wrong and I was being used. I sat in my bedroom that night listening to music and wondering what I was doing with my life. 'It's time to leave the capsule if you dare,' sang David Bowie. How right he was.

It's fair to say I didn't have much self-esteem when I

met Cyril. But he'd taken what little self-respect I had and trampled all over it. He'd made dignity a foreign word to me. Sometimes I looked in the mirror and felt sick at what I saw. I began to dream of killing him.

It wasn't long after when we had our first argument. I was leading a local campaign at the time to 'Buy British' to save our textile industry. Cyril bounded into the club one night and said he'd got hold of a new Skoda car and was doing a raffle to raise funds for the Liberals. I snapped. 'I'm trying to get people to buy British, Cyril, and you're here peddling Czechoslovakian cars.'

'Now, now lad, I think we need a talk,' said Cyril quietly. He could see I was angry and didn't want to make a scene. There were around fifty people present. But I was having none of it. 'You should be supporting British manufacturing,' I said, and stormed out.

When I got home that night there was a message on my phone from Cyril. It was four minutes of solid abuse. 'You're a disgrace, after everything I've done for you,' he shouted down the line. I played it to a journalist from the local paper and he ran a story on it. I think they described it as a 'four-minute tongue lashing from Cyril Smith'.

The problem with Cyril was that he'd become intoxicated with power. He was reckless, he took risks, but he knew he'd get away with it. Nothing else mattered apart from him. He used all the people close to him. He used everyone in the town. People loved him. I could see that. They wanted a hero and they had no one else to go to. But he betrayed them all. They just couldn't see what he was doing to them, but I'm afraid I could.

Everyone has a breaking point, but Cyril didn't understand this. And I'd reached breaking point a long time ago.

In the months that followed I fought back. I could see Cyril for who he really was. Nobody ever really sees anyone except through their own flaws, said Tennessee Williams. Our own failings condition our vision of those in relation to us. He was right. I'd seen Cyril through the eyes of a weak, scared teenage lad. But I was no longer a boy and I had learned to stand up for myself.

The last time I saw Cyril was in 1982 and he knew his power over me had long gone. I'd resigned once from the Liberals and he said he wouldn't accept it. But he had no choice now. He was a fat, middle-aged, lonely man who liked abusing boys. He caught my eyes for a second then turned his back on me. He knew I'd seen through him.

I lived on my own now, having fallen out with my adopted parents, and I had plenty of time to reflect on being abused by the town's MP. I drank from a well of ugly, bitter bile and was consumed by rage.

I kept my own company for months and it seemed that was how it should be. Then, one day, I jumped on a bus back to Milnrow from Rochdale and caught sight of my future wife. Our eyes met across the bus and she smiled back. She was stunning and I couldn't stop staring. It was as though a beam of sunlight had burst through the darkest cloud. A lifeline had been thrown to me and I grabbed it with both hands. She came over and sat by me and asked if I wanted to go out with her to the Eagle pub that night. By 1985 we were married and leaving Rochdale and Cyril Smith behind for good.

I lived hundreds of miles away and Cyril couldn't hurt me anymore. Or so I thought.

One day my brother called me with serious news. 'I've got mesothelioma,' he said. 'I think my time's up.' We both knew how he'd got it. He'd worked at Turner Brothers asbestos mill in Rochdale during the 1970s. There was no protection from the asbestos dust.

The doctor had told him not to research it but I did and found half a dozen articles about Cyril Smith. The bastard had 1,300 shares in Turner Brothers and helped cover up the dangers of asbestos. He asked asbestos bosses to write speeches for him that he read out in parliamentary debates and boldly declared that the public at large were not at risk from asbestos. 'It is necessary to say that time and time again.' Once more, this phony man of the people had failed to stand up for workers and was more interested in lining his pockets and cosying up to the boss classes. It was Cyril all over.

When the story was reported on BBC *North West Tonight* in 2008, a much older and meaner-looking Cyril stared into the cameras and said he was unrepentant. Asked about the health risks to workers that he prevented from being made public, not a trace of compassion could be seen on his face. 'Nobody made them work there,' he shot back, 'they could have left.'

My brother died a terrible, painful and undignified death. The cancer took half his back away. It was horrible to have to watch him die this way. Cyril had found his way into my life when I first opened the door to him in 1979. It was as though he'd sunk his claws into me there and then and never let go. He'd left me with thirty years of shame and now my brother was dead because of him.

When Cyril died I couldn't watch the sickening simpering politicians on TV. You'd think this man had found a solution to world poverty the way they fawned over him and talked of his legacy. What legacy?

Cyril Smith was cremated when he died. If he'd been buried I would have torn his gravestone down. I phoned the chief executive of Rochdale Council and told him if they built a statue in memory of him I'd personally get a digger and demolish it. Hate is a powerful emotion and it's one I fight with constantly. I don't want to be owned by it, but I can't forgive Cyril. The sense of shame stubbornly clings on, too; it stays with you and gnaws away at your insides. Why did I allow Cyril to do what he did? How on earth can a fifty-year-old politician get away with molesting sixteen-year-old boys? How many more were there like me? I was just a kid, my friends tell me. I didn't know what was happening.

I look at my own children now and a shiver runs down my spine. I never want them to know any of this. I've burned every one of the letters Cyril sent to me and I'm pleased that his political legacy is crumbling. What he built up was always going to collapse sooner or later. But there's a different legacy he left that will be much harder to shift. It's one of pain and shame. It's lodged deep in every one of Cyril's victims like a cancer that can't be removed. The best you can hope for is that it won't spread. You learn to contain it, but it never leaves you.

You know the thing that's stayed with me the most, though? It's his laugh. Utterly mirthless, loud and hollow. Sometimes I can still hear it now.

Chapter 7

Killer Dust

The executive lift chimed as it reached the top floor. The doors opened and a large man stepped out. He walked down the corridor alone, the sound of his heavy footsteps beating a dull rhythm on the polished parquet wooden flooring. 'Hello Cyril,' a friendly worker's voice called after him from the office he passed, but he didn't answer. Through the window manicured lawns and rose bushes stretched out before him. But he wasn't there to appreciate the views. Staring straight ahead, his jaw jutting stubbornly to the director's office he marched towards, he only looked up once to acknowledge the portraits on the walls. John, Robert and Samuel Turner. A dynasty of shrewd and determined mill owners. Reformers, too. They had perfected a highly profitable industrial system of production that controlled everything from mining to processing to distribution. Two-and-a-half pence of raw asbestos from their mines became £10 of finished product when it left the factory gate. These are my kind of people, he thought.

When he reached the door his hand hovered above the knob engraved with the company logo. It was shaking. He pulled it back and took a deep breath, smoothed his hair and adjusted his braces. The Turners were part of a Nonconformist, reform-minded liberal town establishment. Married into the Royds family of local bankers, landowners and freemasons, they had taken a strange new material seen in a nearby mill and developed it into a magic fireproof cloth. Their Rochdale factory was the first, then largest asbestos textile factory in the world – and also the headquarters to its multinational empire until 1948.

He extended his hand once more. His shoes could have done with a bit more polish. Wingtip loafers with leather-fringed falls. He'd only bought them a few days ago and they already needed cleaning. He straightened his tie, used his fingernail to remove some food from between his teeth and knocked twice.

'Come in,' a voice from inside boomed.

He turned the doorknob.

'Cyrrrilll!' the men sat round the table exclaimed with welcoming smiles. 'So glad to see you again.'

Cyril eased his bulk into a seat around the boardroom table and smiled back. His eyes swept the wood-panelled walls, the candelabra-style light fixtures and, of course, the beautifully polished floor. You could see your reflection in it. No carpets were allowed in this part of the building, he'd been told. As befitting a place with the best air-conditioning system in the country, there wasn't one speck of dust in the management area.

A large serious-looking portrait of Samuel Turner in velvet court dress dominated the wall opposite. The pioneer at the heart of this empire, he was the man who'd made

Turner & Newall the biggest asbestos conglomerate in the world. And he was a great Liberal too.

'Drink, Cyril?'

A Baccarat decanter of Salignac Napoleon cognac appeared in front of him.

Cyril winked. 'Don't mind if I do, thanks.'

A box of Joya de Nicaragua Antaño cigars was handed round and he jammed one between his teeth, careful to savour the odours of the cognac for a few moments before he lit his cigar and inhaled deeply.

'What are we toasting?' he beamed, exhaling a plume of smoke and holding his glass up.

'Business and friendship.'

'To business and friendship.'

Their glasses chinked in unison. Contented smiles spread over well-fed faces and the men sat around the table eased back in their leather chairs and puffed thoughtfully on their cigars. The smoke billowed above.

'Is this the first time you've been here?' the man at the head of the table asked.

'No,' said Cyril.

He looked up and grinned. He puffed on his cigar for a second then stood up.

'I came here once before, many years ago,' he said. 'I was just as impressed with your factory then as I am now. But I came not as the town's MP looking to establish a good relationship with the most important employer in the borough. I came as a hungry and unknown teenager in search of work. I applied for a lowly job at your place and you turned me down.'

He paused for effect and took another puff on his cigar.

'I still have no idea why I was rejected.'

There was silence around the table. Cyril could sense the discomfort and he took pleasure at the awkwardness his story had caused.

'There must have been a mistake,' a voice piped up. 'We would never turn away a man of your obvious abilities. After all, someone with your talents would be an asset to any company.'

'That's what I thought,' interrupted Cyril.

'Yes,' the voice continued, 'I am sure it was a simple error. If you say it was a lowly job you applied for then it is possible we thought you were over-qualified for the job. I'm sure there's a simple explanation.'

Cyril smiled and sat down. 'I'm sure there is,' he said. 'But that's in the past.'

'Hear, hear,' another voice boomed out. 'The fact is you're with us now and we're very happy to have you on board. It's important that we have a good relationship with the new MP and we expect you to be here for many years to come. You have an important role to play, Cyril. You know as well as we do how important T&N is for Rochdale.'

He nodded at one of his colleagues, who leapt to his feet and quickly replenished the empty brandy glasses around the table.

'A toast,' he said, as the men round the table stood up together.

'To Cyril.'

'To Cyril,' they all bellowed and poured the expensive cognac down their throats.

Cyril drained the last of his glass and felt the cognac burn its way into the guts of his stomach. A cold, knowing rictus spread across the faces at the table. He glanced at the wall opposite and even Samuel Turner himself appeared to be smiling.

They were his kind of people, he reminded himself. He was one of them now. The deal had been done.

To understand the relationship that Cyril forged with asbestos bosses in the early 1970s as the newly elected MP for Rochdale, it's necessary to wind the clock back to the 1920s. Then, when Cyril was making his entry into the world, T&N was a burgeoning multinational asbestos empire that had just been listed on the London Stock Exchange. T&N had factories across the north of England and its HQ was based in Rochdale.

They'd witnessed many changes in the intervening years, as T&N cemented itself as a powerhouse manufacturing company with mines in southern Africa and Canada. But one thing remained constant. The asbestos giants had a dirty secret that needed to be kept under wraps. Inhaling asbestos dust could kill. Back then, as was the case when Cyril started a special friendship in the early 1970s, political muscle and skilful communicators were needed to make sure this secret stayed hidden.

In the 1920s the Turner family dominated Rochdale in a way that Cyril would certainly have approved. They *were* the local establishment and laid strong political foundations. When Turners' social club on Julia Street was demolished, a time capsule was found among the foundation stones with a newspaper dating back to 1884. Among the other contents in the capsule included the rules of the Spotland Liberal Association and the memorandum and articles of association of the Spotland Liberal Club Building Company Ltd. The Turners had a strong and lasting association with the Liberal Party. Three directors of the company were Liberal mayors of Rochdale and Sir Samuel Turner was to exert a particularly powerful influence. A Liberal alderman and former mayor of Rochdale, who came from the same philanthropist tradition as other Nonconformist mill-owning families in the area, Turner pushed mayoral charity to new heights. He purchased the Mount Falinge estate and then donated the eighteen-acre Falinge Park to the town in 1906. He was part of a new aristocracy of wealthy mill owners making untold riches from an exceedingly profitable product. But in the Turners' case, the product they were selling was poisoning their workers, the town and the people who used their products.

Dubbed the 'magic mineral', asbestos mining started on a large scale at the end of the nineteenth century and had become a booming global industry by the 1920s. Resistant to heat and chemicals, it was used widely in building materials and household products, often as fireproofing. Asbestos could be found in the handles of kettles, saucepans and irons to stop fingers being burned. It was in tablemats, oven gloves, aprons and tiles. T&N became the first company in the UK to weave it into cloth. It was found in Lancashire steam boilers feeding lagged pipes round countless factories, steam locomotives and shipping. It was in cement products, insulating boards and in the ceiling and floor cavities. Cheap, indestructible, flexible and a perfect insulating and fireproofing agent, asbestos was everywhere. By the 1960s new markets were emerging. A regeneration boom created system-built schools, hospitals and tower blocks all filled with asbestos products. There seemed to be no end to its potential usage and the profits to be made from selling it just kept growing and growing.

But the dangers of asbestos soon become apparent. In the early 1900s asbestos manufacturing towns started to show a large number of early deaths and lung problems. One of the reasons the dangers had been masked was that symptoms of serious and often fatal health conditions did not become apparent until fifteen to thirty years after exposure. By 1924 the first diagnosis of asbestosis was made in the UK. Nellie Kershaw started work at just twelve years of age in a cotton mill and was working at Garsides asbestos mill before she'd reached her thirteenth birthday. Towards the end of the First World War, she began a new job at the famous Turners asbestos site as a rover, spinning asbestos fibre into a yarn. In 1922 she became too sick to work and was diagnosed by her local doctor as suffering from 'asbestos poisoning'. Because this was an occupational illness she was ineligible for sickness benefit from a local scheme to which she had contributed and her husband Frank, who was now looking after the couple's two children, pleaded with her employers for assistance. They refused to offer any help and she died in poverty on 24 March 1924. To this day she lies in an unmarked 'paupers' grave in Rochdale cemetery. She was just thirty-three years old.

Her death threatened the profitability of the Rochdale asbestos giants and their solicitors aggressively swung into action. They wrote to her doctor demanding to know what he'd said about her asbestos poisoning and then wrote to the Medical Insurance Board repudiating the term 'asbestos poisoning'. They refused to accept any liability and denied that asbestos could cause any such illness. Asbestos was a growing industry and they couldn't afford a worker's death to undermine the confidence of this booming market. Their medical and legal experts vigorously fought their corner and the battle lines were drawn for a titanic struggle to achieve justice for workers that would last over half a century.

But while the Turner family was doing all it could to cover up the dangers of asbestos, they were unable to stop Kershaw's death raising awareness of the health risks that asbestos posed. An examination of her lungs at the coroner's request saw her cause of death stated as 'fibrosis of the lungs due to the inhalation of mineral particles'. It was the first case ever to be recognised as 'asbestosis' and the term 'asbestosis' was used for the first time in a report on her case in the *British Medical Journal* that year.

As the 1920s came to an end politicians moved to amend the Factory and Workshop Act and introduce asbestos industry regulations. The UK government had also commissioned a report by the chief inspector of factories that was to become known as the Merewether and Price report of 1930. It represented a turning point and showed that chronic exposure to high levels of asbestos could lead to asbestosis, which put people at risk of lung cancer and mesothelioma.

New regulations came into force in 1932 requiring industry to suppress dust and introduce periodic medical examinations. It wouldn't save thousands of British workers meeting their death from asbestos-related diseases, and many factories went on to flout the regulations. But a truth had now been established: that asbestos dust was dangerous and could kill. There were many cases to prove this. Like Nellie Kershaw, workers were dying painful deaths at a young age, suffocating from scarred lungs that were unable to pass oxygen to the blood. It was an excruciatingly painful way to die and sufferers would fight for every breath.

The report did not fully grasp the true, lasting danger that asbestos posed but it was a starting point. Industry was asked to make changes, but by reducing the exposure to asbestos it only stopped workers dying at a young age. It could not prevent the longer latency disease, lung cancer, taking their lives.

The Turners were worried. In 1937, director Robert H. Turner wrote: 'All asbestos fibre dust is a danger to lungs. If we can produce evidence from this country that the industry is not responsible for any asbestosis claims, we may be able to avoid tiresome regulations and the introduction of dangerous occupational talk.' The battle to cover up the true threat of asbestos had only just begun.

The 1932 regulations also failed to take into account the exposure to asbestos of people working outside the factories with asbestos products. Shipyard workers, boilermakers, insulators and plumbers were all greatly exposed to the killer dust and the law was doing nothing to protect them. It wasn't until 1969 that Parliament made regulations to start protecting people in the workplace from the dangers of being exposed to asbestos.

By the 1970s, T&N were employing the US public relations giant Hill and Knowlton to protect their image and go on the offensive. Hill and Knowlton had plenty of experience in supporting the US tobacco industry and denying links between smoking and cancer, so they were well prepared for the battle. 'Their job,' the board's minutes noted, 'will be to combat and, if possible, to forestall adverse publicity.' It would take until 1999 before asbestos was banned in the UK and there were millions more in profits to be made before the inevitable happened.

Working-class people were still dying horrific deaths, clutching their sides in agony and gasping for air, as asbestos cancer slowly squeezed the life out of them. The death toll was increasing, but the asbestos bosses in Rochdale remained hell-bent on defending one of the most profitable industries going. By the early 1970s they were importing 190,000 tonnes of asbestos a year and in 1974, in a display of the huge influence the company wielded, the chairman of T&N was elected the new president of the Confederation of British Industry. Throughout the 1970s the factory enjoyed royal visits and, at one point, a visit from representatives of the Pakistan government. The Turners even had their own private security force made up of ex-soldiers. But despite their power and influence, T&N was under threat like never before and they needed to take the fight to their detractors.

A sophisticated propaganda operation was devised with a strong political thrust. A politician was needed to take the Turners' message to parliament – and Cyril Smith fit the bill perfectly.

Right from the beginning he was a fiercely vocal champion for T&N but by the time the 1980s dawned, public health concerns were mounting. In a now famous 1981 parliamentary debate, Cyril showed just how determined he was to go out and bat for the asbestos industry. 'There is no danger to the public at large from asbestos,' he told the House, as Labour's move to have the sale of asbestos products banned throughout the Common Market was defeated. Ignoring the likes of Nellie Kershaw, he went on to boast of T&N's 'long and proud history of deep interest in the safety of the workers in the industry'.

He was stretching credulity to its limits and his speech became an exercise in blatant propaganda. T&N, he argued, 'has never been afraid to discuss with anyone the safety aspects of the products and the raw material'. It was a bravura performance. Accusing the Labour Party of using the debate to scaremonger, he emphasised that it was necessary to repeat that 'the public at large are not at risk from asbestos'. Members of Parliament should be praising the asbestos industry in the UK, he argued, 'for leading the world in safety techniques and concern'.

He carried on in this way in successive debates on asbestos, becoming bolder each time. In 1983, to loud cries of 'shame' from MPs in the chamber, he declared an interest in asbestos by announcing he owned 1,300 shares in T&N. He also used Parliament to aggressively attack the growing health lobby against asbestos.

At a time when TV was having an enormous impact on social issues, the 1982 documentary *Alice – A Fight for Life* was to play a huge role in raising awareness of the links between asbestos and cancer. Following the last days of 47-year-old Calderdale local Alice Jefferson, who had developed mesothelioma after working for just nine months at an asbestos plant in West Yorkshire, the programme, broadcast at prime time, provided an incredibly moving account of the tragedy and injustice of asbestos-related cancer. It also shone a powerful light on the dangers in Rochdale, detailing the deaths of several of Cyril's constituents who'd suffered painful deaths from the asbestos cancer, mesothelioma. 'For fifty years, Turners has been Britain's showpiece asbestos factory,' the narrator observed. 'Since the 1920s every investigation into asbestos disease has depended upon the evidence from here.' The implication was clear: T&N was suppressing the truth. Scientists had suggested that one in ten employees at T&N could die as a result of working there, the narrator concluded. It immediately pushed asbestos higher up the political agenda and Cyril didn't like it.

He came out fighting. The headline on the front page of the local newspaper read 'Sue 'Em Says Cyril', with an article suggesting Yorkshire Television had made deliberate mistakes. He then stood up in Parliament and said that the programme had 'told blatant lies' about T&N. Rather than sticking to the facts, he said, Yorkshire TV had chosen to 'blatantly sensationalise a human situation which gives no joy to anyone'. He went on to accuse the programme makers of creating 'hysterical pressure' on the government to act 'for political rather than industrial reasons'.

Although possessing one of the worst Westminster attendance records for an MP, Cyril was proving to be exceedingly useful to T&N both in Parliament and back in Rochdale. Cyril's vocal offensive, calling for libel action against the documentary makers and broadcasters, had dominated the local newspaper pages. His confident anger in defending T&N had given the company breathing space locally and made the regional news editors doubt the worth of taking the story further.

The early 1980s had already been bad for the T&N share price and it dipped further after *Alice*. However, once again, Cyril came to the rescue. In a scene reminiscent of a Victor Kiam Remington razor TV advert of the time, Cyril proclaimed that he was so confident of the future of T&N he had instructed his stockbroker to buy further shares in the company. In hindsight, Cyril's direct involvement in lobbying for T&N and defending its share price might be seen as a scandalous example of insider trading. But this was far from the minds of many in 1983 – especially those families who had lost loved ones and had seen the documentary about asbestos cancer affecting their town.

Any pretence on Cyril's part that he was simply sticking up for jobs or held the health concerns of his constituents in mind when he weighed up the arguments for and against asbestos was subsequently disproved with the emergence of shocking documents in Cyril's eightieth year. The truth had been hidden for a long time, but now the facts were laid bare. He wasn't sticking up for workers. He was helping the owners make more money. There was damning evidence that he was in the pocket of asbestos bosses and acting as a lobbyist for them.

In 2008 I was passed a series of documents by researchers to prove this. An American lawyer acting for Chase Manhattan Bank had managed to secure a discovery order from a New York court to access the entire T&N archive of over a million pages. Retrieved from the company archives were many letters from Cyril to company directors. They gave a chilling insight into the close relationship between Cyril and T&N.

The first letter I looked at, dated 5 August 1981 and written on House of Commons notepaper, got straight to the point.

'I understand that the debate on asbestos will be on Friday 23 October,' began Cyril, writing to Sidney Marks, a T&N director. 'Could you please, within the next eight weeks, let me have the speech you would like to make (were you able to!) in that debate? In particular, points of disagreement with EEC documentation, points to urge, etc.'

Five days later Marks responded, thanking Cyril for his letter and confirming he would 'forward in good time a proposed draft test for your speech along the lines you have suggested…' A day later, another letter from Marks was sent containing Cyril's draft speech. It was headed in block capitals: 'SUGGESTED SPEECH BY MR. CYRIL SMITH IN THE FORTHCOMING DEBATE IN THE HOUSE OF COMMONS ON EEC DIRECTIVE ON ASBESTOS-CONTAINING MATERIALS.'

There were handwritten notes in the margins by T&N health and safety manager Reg Sykes noting technical references and suggesting areas that might need to be amended.

On 24 August, Cyril responded to Sidney Marks thanking him for the speech. 'I want to read it ten times before I come to see you,' he explained, suggesting that some time in the week commencing 12 October would be a good time for the two of them to go through it.

More interestingly, he then went on to instruct, in very clear terms, Marks to send a brief overview of the issues to the neighbouring Labour MP for Heywood and Royton, Joel Barnett, but not to send him his speech. The words 'do not' and 'my speech' are underlined by Cyril. In the event, Barnett did not speak in the debate.

A few weeks before the parliamentary debate, another letter from Cyril was sent to Marks explaining that he had organised four seats in the public gallery for Marks and his colleagues to come and watch the debate on asbestos. He added that he would be delighted if they could join him on the night before the debate for dinner in Parliament.

Within ten minutes of reading through these documents a clear picture emerged. Cyril was bending over backwards to help T&N bosses. He was wining and dining them in Parliament, securing seats for them in the public gallery and getting his speeches written by them. The concerns of dying workers, suffering from the terrible effects of asbestos poisoning, did not even enter his mind.

I passed the documents to the associate editor of the *Daily Mirror*, Kevin Maguire. He promised to visit Cyril and confront him about this relationship. Meanwhile, Cyril was making no attempts to deny the relationship. 'If you've got the documents it's all true,' he told Ed Howker of the *New Statesman* for an article he wrote, headlined 'Asbestos – the lies that killed'.

True to his word, Maguire journeyed up to Rochdale and went to visit Cyril at his house on Emma Street. Cyril was unrepentant.

'Of course the speech was extremely useful to me because it made it sound as if I could speak intelligently on a subject I knew little about,' he told Maguire, before going on to reiterate his old argument that asbestos was no danger to anyone.

'It's not like, how can I put it, like flu and contagious,' he bizarrely claimed, arguing that 4,000 deaths was 'relatively low'. For Cyril the only injustice was that he had to answer questions about this. He said he was the victim of a left-wing plot. 'They think they've got Cyril Smith on toast,' he fumed.

When the article appeared I shook my head in disbelief as I read Cyril's ridiculous defence of his actions. How could someone who'd come from such a poor background and was seen by thousands of people in his constituency as the voice of the underdog, a champion of the people, have gone on to betray working people in such a spectacular way? He had sold them down the river for a bundle of shares and the fact that he was so unrepentant about it while people were dying all around him made it all the more sickening.

Cyril's mastery of public relations had now deserted him. Rather than accepting he'd made a terrible error of judgement, as was also the case with Stefan Kiszko, he decided to aggressively defend himself to the media. Cyril Smith never apologised. That wasn't his style. He'd never backed down before and he certainly wasn't going to start now. It was a watershed moment. His carefully crafted image as a man of the people was starting to be dismantled brick by brick. His halo had fallen and in the autumn of 2008 I watched him give an appalling interview on BBC *North West Tonight*.

People suffering from mesothelioma in Rochdale couldn't hide their disappointment. One of these was Derek Phillips. 'I always used to rate Cyril Smith. He called a spade a spade,' he told the journalist Stuart Flinders. 'He should have been coming out on the side of people that were poorly.'

From the face of a disillusioned constituent the camera quickly shifted to Cyril's obdurate features and a dramatic shift in tone. 'There never was any danger and there isn't now,' he angrily insisted. 'There's no danger to the public at large. You weren't in danger, I wasn't in danger.' This was like Cyril of old. You could hear the passion in his voice. But it was an angry, empty passion and he only sounded bitter and ignorant. When Flinders interrupted to say that people who lived near the factory believed they were in danger, Cyril was dismissive, telling him that was incorrect and accusing Flinders of 'overstating that case'.

It ended with Cyril telling thousands of people in their living rooms across the north-west that, 'there were people who worked there who knew they were in danger, but no one made them work there, they could have left'. It would have been hard for him to sound more heartless if he tried.

Locally, the correspondence showing Cyril's links to asbestos bosses achieved significant press coverage and it did him a lot of damage. It started to make staunch supporters of Cyril question whether he really was all he claimed to be. His mythical image was beginning to melt away.

Within his own party his iron grip was slipping, and Cyril's dismissal of the dangers of asbestos and blindness to the damage it was causing in the community had already angered some. The worm was turning.

Four years previously, in 2004, a new chapter in the fight to prevent more victims of asbestos began through the local campaign group, Save Spodden Valley. It was organised after the site of the former T&N companies, now an almost empty shell, after asbestos processing ended in the mid-1990s and a partial demolition took place in 2001, was sold to MMC Estates, a property developer. A planning application was promptly submitted to build 650 homes, as well as a children's day-care centre and a business park on the site. Despite asbestos fibres being clearly visible on the ground, asbestos dumping sites everywhere and asbestos dust all over the woodland area, the developers claimed there was 'an absence of asbestos contamination'. The reverse was true. The site was riddled with it.

When trees started to be mysteriously chopped down in the middle of the night, as though preparing the ground for immediate development, the local community moved quickly to oppose it. Jason Addy was a legal researcher who had lost family members and friends to asbestos cancer. When people started knocking on his door asking him what was going on, he began asking awkward questions to find out. The Save Spodden Valley campaign was born. 'Women in the street were knocking on doors waking people up, asking what was going on,' he recalls. 'We all had concerns. From an impromptu group of people talking in the street, we saw the community was so distrustful of what was going on and we knew we had to do something.'

Assiduously non-political, Addy sought to win support from all political parties in Rochdale over the unsuitability of the site for a housing development. 'We were able to prove it was contaminated with asbestos. It was unsafe for urban development,' he said. But not all local politicians were overly concerned with the risk to public health and one of the biggest barriers to achieving a lasting consensus remained Cyril Smith.

At first Addy was puzzled as to why Cyril was keeping silent on the issue. 'I knew he must have a view on it as it was happening right on his doorstep,' he said. 'I soon found out that he was calling local politicians to his house and telling them that this development had to go ahead. He didn't want questions asked about the public health dangers of asbestos. It was as though he feared this could expose his links years before.'

Hundreds of people attended the local meetings and attempts to rush through a hazardous planning application hardened the resolve of the community. Too many lives had been lost. There was no appetite for a dangerous development.

There was now also an emerging group of Liberal councillors who didn't fly the flag for Cyril. They were respectful of his achievements, but didn't particularly like him trying to carry on controlling the town in his dotage. Cyril had long since retired. He was the past, they thought, and it was time to look to the future.

One of these councillors was Elwyn Watkins. He had grown up not far from the T&N factory and was only too aware of the dangers of asbestos. As a child he remembers playing in asbestos dust. 'Anyone who grew up in Spotland had a relationship with asbestos,' he says. 'We all knew about it. You either knew people who worked there, or who had caught mesothelioma or asbestosis. T&N employed thousands of people at one time.' He'd seen local people die of asbestos cancer and wasn't prepared to stand for any more cover-ups. Right from the beginning, the Save Spodden Valley campaign had his full support and this made a confrontation with Cyril inevitable.

As the Liberal Democrat parliamentary candidate in neighbouring Oldham, Elwyn made national headlines in 2010 for his decision to mount a sensational legal challenge against the former Labour minister, Phil Woolas. For the first time in almost a century he managed to get a Westminster election declared void because of criminal wrongdoing by an opponent, in this case through Woolas's team issuing leaflets containing untrue statements about him.

But what most political commentators didn't know is that Watkins went into his titanic legal challenge with Woolas already battle-hardened from a fight within his own party with Cyril Smith.

When I met him to discuss the difficulties that Cyril caused him while he was a Liberal councillor in Rochdale, he made no attempt to hide his contempt for the former giant of his party.

'Cyril Smith was a monster,' he says firmly. 'He destroyed the lives of many people and you can't defend that. That's not to say Cyril didn't help people in other areas ... but you can never justify what happened because of that.'

Like all young Liberals in Rochdale in the 1970s, Watkins had grown up in Cyril's shadow. It was impossible to escape his influence, he says. Cyril was known by everyone. Watkins went to the same school Cyril had been to and grew up in the same area. His view of Cyril now, he admits, is very different to how he'd seen him as a young man.

In 1977, as a fourteen-year-old, he joined the Liberals and

put up a poster in his window. It didn't take long before Cyril knocked on his door. 'I told him I'd just joined the party and he asked if I'd like to come down to London.' Soon afterwards, Cyril arranged for him to come and stay at the National Liberal Club and spend some time in Parliament. 'He got me in to see PMQs with Callaghan and Thatcher. Cyril was my hero at the time and I became part of Cyril's gang,' he says. 'He was a national figure that everyone loved. If you walked down a street with him all the kids would come out and want to talk to him.'

He was also very good at his job, he adds. 'He worked incredibly hard for people. If you needed re-housing or anything from your MP, he would say, "Come round to the house and I'll sort you out." He was a good constituency MP. He knew how to get things done.'

But he didn't always bank on democracy getting in his way. As a young Liberal Watkins started to get on the wrong side of Cyril by blocking some of the plans he presented to the local party as a done deal. He recalls two occasions that stand out. The first was a pact that Cyril had orchestrated with the Tories in the late 1970s that agreed the Liberals would field candidates in certain wards and not put up a candidate in other areas. The plan was to keep Labour out and it was assumed by Cyril that everyone in the local party would agree with the deal he'd struck. However, he hadn't reckoned on Watkins and a growing number of young Liberals wanting to have their say. 'I said this should surely be decided by the constituency party not by Cyril just announcing it,' Watkins explains. The subsequent vote saw Cyril completely overruled. 'He was not happy about it.'

After this, Cyril presented another done deal to the party when the council was under no overall control. 'He just turned up and said I've negotiated this deal with Norman (his brother, who was a councillor) and we're going to get half the seats with the Tories and we'll get this committee and they'll get that committee,' he says. Again, Watkins stopped him in his tracks and said any talk of a coalition should be discussed with the local party. 'He lost that vote as well.'

Understandably, Cyril was furious and Watkins was knocked off Cyril's Christmas card list. In Cyril's world you were either for or against him. Watkins was now in the latter camp. 'Cyril controlled the agendas, he controlled the issues, he controlled the strategy and he would make sure that people were committed to him,' he says.

Among a younger generation, Cyril's modus operandi was no longer infallible. A new group of politicians were prepared to challenge him. When he wanted support at a vote, Watkins explains, he would phone people and say, 'I do hope I can personally count on you for this.' He always made it personal. They were unlikely to say no. 'Who's going to confront him and say I'm not doing that for you?' There was a good measure of fear and veiled threats in his approach, and it tended to work on nearly every occasion.

But it wasn't all one-way bullying traffic; there were definitely perks to being seen as one of Cyril's team. 'If you were in Cyril's gang you got looked after,' Watkins explains. 'He would make sure your mum was OK in Rochdale Infirmary, for example. He would make sure the consultant had done a proper job. He would make that phone call. It was too simplistic to just say he bullied people. There was certainly some sweetness and light as well.'

There certainly wasn't much sweetness and light on offer once you pushed Cyril's limits, however, as Watkins found out. Anyone who challenged his asbestos-championing narrative was certainly going to have a difficult time. The truth was staring people in the face and, while many accepted Cyril's assurances, others could not go along with such obvious propaganda.

'Cyril had so much respect in the area that the community would have taken the attitude that if Cyril says it's safe then it must be safe,' admits Watkins. 'But there was a new generation of people coming through who were not prepared to say, "Well, they know best."'

Cyril understood this and he summoned Watkins to come and see him at Emma Street. He made it clear he was unhappy at his position on the T&N site and Watkins had to decide which side he was on. At the time Watkins was heavily involved in grassroots campaigning with the Save Spodden Valley group, which was establishing a cross-party consensus regarding health issues at the T&N site. This didn't go down well with Cyril. As far as he was concerned, Elwyn was either for him or against him. 'I said I would decide issues based on what I thought was right. I wasn't prepared to compromise on safety,' Watkins explains. Cyril nodded and showed him the door.

The niceties were over and Cyril began to step up his campaign to rubbish those who stood against development at the site.

He made sure Liberal councillors and allies infiltrated the

Save Spodden Valley campaign group to report back to him. He arranged for letters to be sent to the local newspaper in favour of the development. It became so ludicrous that some Liberal Democrats close to Cyril suggested, in conversations with local campaigners, that asbestos was so safe 'you could sprinkle it on your cornflakes'. Watkins suddenly found his motives questioned by his Liberal colleagues. Then Cyril turned up to a meeting in Rochdale with Simon Hughes, the president of the Liberal Democrats at the time, to support candidates for the local elections. Cyril told other councillors it was time to vote Watkins out. Moves were made to deselect him as a councillor, which he narrowly survived. By now Cyril's contempt for Watkins was obvious to all. He even turned up with his brother to the council township meeting, which Watkins chaired, to try and publicly break him.

Around 200 people were in attendance at the open-forum meeting in the town hall. Cyril stood patiently until he had his chance. Then the septuagenarian godfather of Liberal politics in Rochdale exploded. He attacked Watkins as an 'incompetent, pathetic, useless' councillor. There was a stunned silence in the public gallery. These were extraordinary scenes.

Looking back, Watkins acknowledges it was a bruising time but ultimately it was a fight Cyril lost. The battle to declare the former T&N site permanently unsafe for urban development and seal all possible sources of asbestos dust continues to this day.

Watkins didn't attend Cyril's funeral and he's adamant that the failings of Rochdale's former MP need to be confronted before the town can move on. He reflects on Cyril's great election victories as a period of wasted opportunities that culminated in a lot of unnecessary pain and deaths.

'The crucial thing for me is why, when Cyril got elected in 1972, did he not say there are lots of people dying from asbestos?' he asks. 'He should have said we have to clean all this up and sort it out. The health of my constituents is paramount. T&N was one of the wealthiest companies in the UK. But why was he supporting them when it was so dangerous?' For anyone who knew about asbestos at that time, he adds, it should have been Cyril's big campaign to clean things up. 'Our town has been responsible for the deaths of thousands of people across the UK. It's a scandal.'

Jobs could have been retained, he argues. There is always a market for insulating agents and T&N had the wealth and resources to research a new, safer means of doing this. The fact they failed to modernise and explore a safer model was the reason they went bust.

'If you look at how many lives have been lost as a result of people keeping their mouths shut and not being prepared to seek the truth you're talking about tens of thousands of people that have been affected. That was on Cyril's watch. By the 1970s it was very clear how dangerous this material was.'

A stone's throw away from Rochdale Town Hall an International Asbestos Memorial stands in the memorial gardens as a permanent reminder of those few who failed to look after their own. 'Asbestos: once a magic mineral but always a killer dust', reads the plaque on the memorial stone.

According to government figures, around 4,500 people die in the UK from asbestos-related diseases each year.

T&N was known as 'the asbestos giant' and had about a 75 per cent share of the UK market. Their products and decisions have caused countless disease and deaths to former employees as well as those who came into contact with dust from their asbestos products.

In the House of Commons, where Cyril's voice once boomed across the green benches telling people asbestos posed no danger to the public, a different voice is heard nowadays. In recognition of the fact that Britain is expected to see a peak in mesothelioma cases in the coming years, a £350 million compensation pot for some victims was announced in late 2013 and ministers were rightly contrite. 'Victims of this terrible disease ... have been failed by successive governments and the insurance industry for decades,' said the Work and Pensions minister, Mike Penning.

His words will be little comfort to those whose lives were tragically cut short by asbestos in Rochdale. But they do ensure one thing. The years of cover-up and denial that Cyril presided over were finally at an end.

Chapter 8

Lancing the Boil

In politics you see a lot of anger. If people are angry about something in their community then politicians are the people most likely to bear the brunt of it. So it's something you get used to. Most of it dissipates quickly and rarely do you see genuine, deep emotional anger. But when you do, you don't forget it. And you never get used to it.

I came to see a lot of that where Cyril was concerned. There are still some people who passionately hate him even though he's no longer alive. That kind of hatred is strong. It endures. From my office in Rochdale I don't have to walk very far to find it and the words of one nearby small businessman began to act as a daily reminder that it was time Rochdale came to terms with Cyril's crimes.

Because he was one of the town's more prominent small businessmen, when Cyril died he was called by the local newspaper and asked if he'd like to pay tribute to the town's former MP. 'I don't think you'd want to print my views on Cyril,' he said curtly, and hung up.

I soon came to find out why.

'My brother was abused by Cyril and he tried to commit

suicide as a result,' he told me one day. 'I absolutely hate the bastard.'

When Cyril died, he explained, someone from the council had come to see him and asked if he would close his business on the day of Cyril's funeral as a mark of respect. The funeral cortege would be making its way down his street and the council was asking other businesses to do the same. 'I told him to get stuffed,' he said. 'I'll be drinking champagne on the day of his funeral and I'll be open for business.'

I shudder when I think back to a speech Cyril gave in 1985 in the House of Commons. We need to appoint a minister for youth with responsibilities for young people, he bellowed across the chamber, no doubt having one person in mind who would be ideal for the job.

Details of abuse had begun to filter through to me almost casually. I'd spent the first few years of my time in Rochdale marvelling at Cyril's political achievements. The only thing I heard about now was his foul deeds. Someone who had previously occupied a high place in my mind now made my stomach turn.

I remember one morning talking to our office cleaner who just came out straight away and asked if I knew about Cyril. I'd heard the rumours, I admitted. 'He was a wrong 'un,' he said, shaking his head. 'I used to play for a football team in Spotland as a teenager and Cyril sponsored and presented our awards every year. He'd grope all the boys as he was presenting their medals. It was awful. So we complained about it to the coach and told him we didn't want to come to the awards night anymore. He told everyone they'd have to put up with it because Cyril was the sponsor and he paid for the do.'

The matter-of-fact way in how he related this tale disturbed me. It was just another everyday story of Cyril abusing boys. Because he'd got away with this behaviour for so long it almost seemed to have lost its shock value.

This thought played on my mind when the Rochdale grooming scandal broke in May 2012 and nine men were jailed for horrific abuse committed against teenage girls in the town. It made headlines all round the world and was the subject of heated debate in every pub in the town. When the father of one of the victims called me to tell me how his daughter's cries for help had been ignored by the authorities I started to make my own enquiries. I spoke to the director of children's services, Cheryl Eastwood, straight away and was staggered by her attitude. She implied that young girls who were being systematically raped were making lifestyle choices and said that this kind of abuse was 'a new phenomenon' on which they hadn't received guidance. You don't need guidance from central government to know that when someone is reporting being raped that it's seriously wrong, I told her. Not long afterwards she left her post and subsequently appeared before MPs in front of an incredulous Home Affairs Select Committee. The chair, Keith Vaz, could barely contain his exasperation at her lack of interest in the case.

'When you found out this was so widespread did you ever meet one of the victims?' he asked her. 'I haven't met any victims,' she replied calmly. Vaz furrowed his brow and asked for assurances that she wouldn't be working in this field again. It was astonishing stuff.

The former chief executive of the council, Roger Ellis,

was also summoned to appear before the same Select Committee. He too was on his way out and his performance was even worse than Eastwood's. He claimed to know nothing about this type of sexual abuse in Rochdale despite being chief executive for twelve years. He had served on the local safeguarding board. He'd been the chief executive when the council set up a working group in 2007 to look into child sex exploitation, which identified fifty girls who were at risk or who were experiencing sexual abuse. But still he claimed to know little. He had no idea who was to blame and was at a loss on numerous questions. You could almost feel the anger in the room as one MP after another took him to task. Vaz concluded by saying his evidence was 'deeply disappointing'.

It made for depressing viewing. I couldn't believe the staggering complacency being shown by senior officers at the council towards such a terrible crime. They just didn't get it and neither did some councillors. There would be far more interest in potholes than child protection. We'd suffered from a horrendous child abuse epidemic for years and it was being passed off as a minor problem or administrative oversight.

A few weeks earlier a police officer had told me fellow officers had suggested the victims on council estates should have been drowned at birth. This attitude was subsequently confirmed in the Serious Case Review. It also emerged during the Rochdale grooming trial that when one of the girls had reported her abuse to a police officer, the officer had yawned.

I ended up meeting this girl, now a young woman, and her story deeply troubled me. If you saw her in the street you'd never know what she'd experienced. She looked just like any other teenager, full of life and, you would think, still relatively innocent. How wrong you'd be. She'd been through hell and her story was like nothing I'd ever heard. I had children of my own and I hadn't anticipated dealing with problems like this when I was elected MP. It was extremely upsetting.

Everyone who came into contact with a victim of grooming was affected. National journalists quickly poured into Rochdale and even though they had years of experience in confronting the worst aspects of humanity they were still affected by it. I remember one journalist struggling to fight back the tears as she interviewed the father of a victim. I could see how it affected Penny Marshall from ITV News and she'd filmed Bosnian Serb atrocities in the early 1990s. Everyone, it appeared, could see what a horrendous case this was except the council. There were even councillors – one Labour and one Liberal Democrat – who'd written letters of support for the perpetrators of these awful crimes to assist them in court.

We had truly reached a sorry pass. I began to wonder if years of child abuse being covered up in Rochdale had normalised this crime. We had become institutionally blind. The cover-up of abuse at Cambridge House and at Knowl View, the failed police investigations, all had ensured that the necessary public cry of outrage that needed to be heard was silenced. And without that manifestation of public anger and scandal it became accepted. People in Rochdale had become blinded to one of the most heinous crimes imaginable. They'd been conditioned into thinking this was what happened. For every case of abuse there was a perfectly reasonable explanation.

For the young victims at Cambridge House in the early 1960s it was because they were bad boys from troublesome backgrounds who needed disciplining.

For the young girls who were victims of grooming gangs in the 2000s it was because they were bad girls from troublesome backgrounds that were making lifestyle choices.

The blame was always on the victim. Never on the abuser. That way, the abusers were allowed to carry on with impunity and the people responsible for their protection could simply shrug and say, 'Move along, nothing to see here.' It was always just a case of poor people misbehaving.

This had gone on for way too long and it was time the pattern of injustice was stopped.

Even though I'd met with a good number of victims, heard incredibly powerful and convincing tales of abuse by Cyril, I still knew I was only scratching the surface. Cyril wasn't the only abuser in Rochdale and he was influential enough to ensure that other abusers were allowed to hang on to his coat-tails and carry on undetected by the authorities. The problem that the town had to face up to, I believed, was that paedophile gangs had been operating here for years.

There were just too many coincidences. A council HIV prevention officer, Phil Shepherd, had already reported that men as far away as Sheffield were travelling to Rochdale to abuse boys at Knowl View School. Who was organising this? Why were gangs of men from another county coming to abuse boys in Rochdale at a school where Cyril was chairman of governors? I was struck by the story of one of Cyril's teenage victims, whose boss had asked him to go camping with him. When he rejected his advances he was told he'd have to leave. The consequent phone call to Cyril Smith to arrange for him to continue his employment at Smith's Springs was more than odd. From what I was hearing, a lot of phone calls were made from various people in the town to put Cyril in touch with young boys. I remember phoning one of Cyril's old accomplices at the time to discuss this. The voice on the other end of the phone sounded stricken with fear. 'I don't want to talk about it,' he said. 'I'd rather not co-operate.' I am sure Cyril didn't abuse boys solely on his own. There would have been others involved. My worry now was how many of these were still alive and did any of them still have influence? Who knew what was happening and had chosen to remain silent?

I'd heard plenty of whispers about MI5's role in keeping Cyril Smith out of trouble, but no one is prepared to go on record about it. A former Labour MP started to tell me about it once when I visited him, but after a few sentences he went silent. 'No good will come of this,' he said nervously. 'It's best left how it is.' And then he shut the door on me. Another police officer I tracked down to his pub in Cheshire went white when I mentioned Cyril's name. 'I can't talk about that time,' he said, and again the door closed. It was hard not to conclude that powerful forces were still at work.

There was clearly a network and I have no doubt that Cyril maintained a huge influence even in his later years. Elwyn Watkins later told me his theory of how this network operated and it confirmed my own view.

'You have to ask why he was so involved,' he says of Cyril's continued involvement in local politics right up to his death. 'There is always the dread when you get involved in child abuse that someone will knock on your door eventually or someone will start asking questions. If you have influence over the council, even if you're not in control or in power, people still think, "I don't want to come up against him because he'll cause me real hurt." So I'm clear that he kept this network of control and bullying in order to make sure that people were never able to ask questions.'

Over the years, he added, he'd seen too many people in Rochdale lose their jobs, retire or move somewhere else all because they came into conflict with Cyril. Elwyn's comments made me question just how many people he'd held power over in my own party – and indeed in the local Conservative Party. I'd been warned years ago by a Labour MP to steer clear of Cyril and leave him alone and I wondered why we'd given him such an easy ride. It was as though there was an unspoken rule: you don't criticise Cyril. Give him a wide berth.

I wasn't interested in secretive political pacts and I didn't believe in a politics governed by fear. Whatever consensus had been agreed where Cyril was concerned had to be broken. I wondered whether this protective behaviour among politicians really did go on. Did fellow politicians turn a blind eye to appalling abuse? The very thought of it seemed absurd. But I was beginning to think this had to be the case.

After I'd revealed Cyril to be an abuser in Parliament, the Labour MP, Chris Bryant, wrote eloquently about it in

The Independent. The problem with politicians' willingness to protect their own was what Winston Churchill had called 'the persistent freemasonry of the House of Commons'. The case of Cyril Smith perfectly encapsulated this, he argued. He was able to get away with destroying young men's lives with the connivance not just of his own party but of political opponents too.

'What was it?' Bryant asked. 'Squeamishness, embarrassment, a naïve refusal to see what was going on, the deliberate turning of a blind eye or a conspiracy?'

The same thoughts ran through my head in the autumn of 2012, as I began to look for an opportunity in Parliament to raise my concerns about Cyril's history of abuse. Unintentionally, I'd been following Cyril for some time now. Wherever I went in the town people told me stories about him that made me wince. I'd learn something new about him most weeks. It wasn't just about abuse either. I heard plenty of stories about planning applications, party funding and electoral tricks, too. Eileen Kershaw had told me that when Cyril collected postal votes he'd go through them to see if they'd voted for him or not. She watched in horror once as he went through a huge bundle, throwing postal vote after postal vote onto the fire. 'What are you doing?' she asked. 'These buggers are against me,' Cyril responded, carrying on as though what he was doing was perfectly reasonable. How long had the town been run like this?

If we didn't face up to the past, I reasoned, then anyone who knew about these activities, and there were plenty of people all over the town, would think you could get away with it. Cyril had got away with it, but I wanted everyone who'd assisted him to know they'd done wrong. How could anyone possibly think there was a place in politics for this kind of behaviour?

Others had been in a similar position years ago and I spoke to them before I made my mind up. David Bartlett was the joint editor of the *Rochdale Alternative Press* in the 1970s and a lecturer in sociology at the local college. When he'd first come into contact with boys that told him they'd been abused by Cyril Smith he had struggled to believe it.

'He was just so popular at the time and was seen as someone who'd done an awful lot of good for the town,' he said. Nevertheless, he came to realise it was true and knew the story had to come out. 'We were terrified at the time. There was a huge risk of libel action.'

But they did publish and, aside from *Private Eye*, no one else touched the story. It was all a load of nonsense made up by crazy lefties, said Cyril, and the media believed him. He never sued though. The irony, Bartlett notes, is that the year they published their story, 1979, Cyril achieved an increased majority at the general election.

Cyril put on a brave front when the story appeared, dismissing it as scurrilous smears from his political opponents. In the ruthless cauldron of Rochdale politics people were used to all sorts of malicious rumours flying around. So, in many respects, it wasn't surprising that the public believed Cyril's side of the story. His public image was so far at odds with this kind of behaviour that it was hard to begin to contemplate him being involved in child abuse.

Cyril was worried, though. One political activist during the period told me that just before the general election

Cyril had called a meeting of Liberal activists at a school in Norden. 'I've given my life to this town,' he said tearfully. 'There's nothing I haven't done for these people.' It sounded like a valedictory speech.

He needn't have worried. 'In Cyril we trust' was still the unofficial motto of the town. His huge profile and saintly image acted as a kind of awesome force field preventing any real scrutiny of his secret life. What struck me about Cyril's double life was that he'd successfully created the environment where the truth simply *could not* be heard. It was a trick very few people could pull off with such panache. Only Jimmy Savile is comparable.

I don't think any politician nowadays could do the same. Those deferential days are over. But I'm sure some celebrities in other fields could manage it.

Around the time I was thinking about publicly raising my concerns about Cyril I also came into contact with the journalist Paul Waugh, the editor of PoliticsHome.com. Paul, originally from Rochdale, told me he'd been approached by two victims of Cyril Smith from Cambridge House and he was looking to run a story on new abuse claims. The victims were prepared to be named and he believed it was time for a fresh look at the rumours that had persistently clung to Cyril for years. I agreed. The environment that Cyril had created where the truth couldn't be heard no longer existed. The victims had waited long enough for their stories to be heard and the town had hidden this shame for far too long. It was time Cyril's legacy was seen for what it was. Then the town could move on and stop cleaving to his poisonous brand of politics.

A few days later, I finally found the opportunity to broach the subject. A backbench debate had been secured for Tuesday 13 November on child sexual exploitation.

I remember working on my speech in my London office and pacing the floor nervously. I knew I would be attacked for raising this subject. The Liberal Democrats would come after me and I would be accused of making serious accusations against someone who could not defend himself. I wished he were still alive. He would have put up an almighty fight, I was sure of that. But, this time, he would lose. Times had changed. Surely the establishment could not keep protecting Cyril?

When I was eventually called to speak by the Deputy Speaker, I began with the recent grooming scandal and was critical of my own Labour council for trying to cover up the failings of their social services department by attempting to lay the blame at the feet of private children's homes in Rochdale. Only one victim had actually stayed in a children's home and I was deeply suspicious of why the council kept trying to shift the blame away from social workers and senior officers, who I knew were responsible for failing these girls.

Then I changed tack.

'If we are to ensure that victims of child abuse are sufficiently empowered to claw back some of the dignity that has been taken from them, we must be open about the widespread abuse of power in our borough. That is why it is necessary to turn to Sir Cyril Smith.'

I then read from a victim statement that had been given to Lancashire Police in 1970 documenting his abuse at the hands of Cyril and said it was time that these stories were heard. These were young boys who were humiliated, terrified and reduced to quivering wrecks by a 29-stone bully imposing himself on them. What happened to them? How can they ever forget what happened to them?

I concluded by expressing my hope that Britain was now reaching a tipping point where victims are taken seriously and given a voice. That hope is as strong now as when I first uttered those words and I remember sitting back with a sense of relief washing over me.

At first there was little reaction. A Liberal Democrat MP followed my speech and said nothing about Cyril. A Labour MP congratulated me on attacking my own Labour council. He said we should do more of this! That wasn't what I had in mind.

But in the hours and days that followed, Cyril's abuse started to creep up the news agenda. The town's former Liberal Democrat MP, Paul Rowen, went on television to attack me. Cyril's brother Norman called me a coward.

But then more victims came forward. And the Liberal Democrat attacks went silent. Within a few days I'd been in touch with half a dozen more people who said Cyril had abused them. Former police officers called, emails poured into my office and a much bigger picture of Cyril's abuse started to emerge. I spoke to former residents of Cambridge House, former pupils at Knowl View, victims that had worked at Cyril's spring-manufacturing business, former Liberals that had been abused by Cyril and everyone from dog handlers, CID officers, detectives and police trainers from all round the country who knew about Cyril's abuse.

'I have just been listening to your report on child abuse in Rochdale ... and as I write this email I have tears of relief running down my face that we are going to be listened to. Thank you for taking the stand in Parliament and the stand in Rochdale where we both know some of the people will not believe what has been spoken,' emailed one victim soon afterwards. His story was later to make the Channel 4 *Dispatches* documentary on Cyril. I wanted all victims to have their say and let the world know what had happened.

After raising the issue at Prime Minister's Questions, the press coverage really started to grow. Soon everyone in the land knew about Cyril. People who had once defended him in Rochdale now began to denounce him. Eileen Kershaw told the *Sunday Times* that she felt physically sick because she'd believed him. She now wanted to dig him up and 'cut off his dick'. Unfortunately he'd been cremated. The blue plaque that had been erected in honour of Cyril outside Rochdale Town Hall a year before was removed.

It was a frenetic time and my phone never stopped ringing. We worked late into the night. Looking back it's the conversations with victims that stand out. Years of pent-up pain, frustration and anger were evident in their voices. They'd been airbrushed out of history. They were invisible people, whose voices were not supposed to be heard. One man who was abused by Cyril at Cambridge House told me that Cyril had lined up the boys outside for a photo once for the local newspaper. He'd put his arms around them, beamed and their startled faces were recorded for posterity. I tried to find this photo, as I wanted to see the faces of boys that had been terrorised by Cyril, but the local newspaper had lost it when they moved their offices. Another clue to Cyril's secret life had been lost.

This book is not so much Cyril's story, as their story. I knew they had to be heard. It's often said that history is written by the victors but this time it was going to be written by victims. I listened intently to every last detail of their stories. Forget the razzmatazz of the chat show circuit, *This Is Your Life* and Bananarama videos. This was the real story of Cyril and Rochdale politics. 'Power, that is what politics is about,' Cyril had once said. For him it was about an abuse of power and I was seeing for myself what his real legacy was.

Of course, there were mixed feelings in the town. Sending sacred cows to slaughter is never going to be universally welcomed. There is one house that I still knock on now when I'm out canvassing and the man who answers it always says the same. 'I'd still vote for Cyril Smith if he were alive now.' There are restaurants I go to where I know the owners won't hear a bad word said against him. A picture of Sir Cyril continues to hang on the inner walls of the town hall and across town there's the Sir Cyril Smith Business Centre. Denial runs deep.

Even the police still showed signs of apprehension in coming to terms with Cyril's abuse. When I went on the BBC's *Sunday Politics* show to talk about Cyril's victims I received a call from the police late that night. They were unhappy that I'd used the word 'rape' in connection with Cyril's abuse. At the time I was talking about Cyril forcing a young boy to give him oral sex at Knowl View School and the Deputy Children's Commissioner, Sue Berolowitz, had advised me to use this word. Under the Sexual Offences Act, which came into force in 2004, non-consensual oral sex was now classed as rape. However, because the offence happened prior to this Act, the police insisted I was guided by the 1956 Sexual Offences Act and used the phrase 'indecent assault' to describe non-consensual oral sex. It seemed odd but they were worried it would upset Cyril's family.

By and large, however, people have welcomed the truth coming out. It is painful for some but necessary. Most weeks I'll end up in a conversation with someone on the doorstep about Cyril and they agree that it's best now that Cyril's secrets are out in the open. It makes it harder for others in power to keep dirty secrets. The conversations about his long reign of power in Rochdale – he had a huge political influence in the town for fifty years – continue to this day in pubs, over the garden fence and on social media.

More and more stories have subsequently emerged and many national and local journalists have continued to investigate Cyril's time in Rochdale. One of these was Ed Howker, who has been writing stories on Rochdale for years and was the first to expose Cyril's close links to asbestos bosses in the *New Statesman*. He developed a strong interest in Cyril and went on to produce the Channel 4 *Dispatches* documentary, 'The Paedophile MP: How Cyril Smith got away with it'. I spoke to him at length about Cyril and was fascinated as to why he kept jumping on the train from London to come to Rochdale. 'Cyril Smith was the stuff of nightmares,' he told me. 'No one was strong enough to stand up to him. He was able to subvert the law and democratic politics. He is a fascinating figure.'

After the Channel 4 documentary aired in the autumn of 2013 I started to see a growing acceptance of what had happened in the town. Even the most stony-faced deniers could see the evidence in front of them. A welcome realisation was dawning.

I'm still stopped and asked about Cyril in the most unlikely places. On one occasion I was even pulled up in the swimming baths by someone swimming in the next lane to me and asked how Cyril had got away with it for so long. 'I don't know,' I spluttered, stopping to get my breath. As I paused for breath I looked up and down to see swimmers all around enjoying the new £11 million facilities at Rochdale Leisure Centre. It's a fantastic place. Only months before it had opened a Liberal Democrat councillor had argued that it should be named the Sir Cyril Smith Sports Complex. Thankfully the suggestion had been rejected.

Common sense was finally winning the day.

Chapter 9

Pursuit

Soon after stories of Cyril Smith's abuse of children made national headlines in late 2012, after my speech to Parliament, I began to get phone calls from former police officers. 'Don't think we didn't try to get him in the dock,' one said to me straight away. 'We knew he was guilty and we did all we could to make him face charges.'

Some gave me their names and told me about their time in the force, but others were more circumspect. 'I'll lose my pension if I tell you what I know,' said one. All were united in one thing, though. They wanted to set the record straight. 'We investigated Cyril in the late 1960s and as far as I'm concerned he's guilty,' one former officer told me. 'Don't make out the police turned a blind eye to this stuff. We were just as disgusted as you. But people at the top blocked our efforts. They said it wasn't in the public interest to pursue this.'

Soon I was getting calls from all over the country. And the stories that former officers told me became more harrowing by the day.

Even as far back as the late 1950s, the police had their suspicions about Cyril. One officer, Mike Smith, who was in CID for twenty-five years, said that Cyril's newsagent on St Mary's Gate, which he sold in 1959, had been under surveillance for a few days because there had been concerns that boys were entering by the back. He also confirmed that Cyril's mother was eventually banned from coming into the police station, as part of her role as cleaner for the council. The police station was housed in the town hall at the time and she was known to go through the bins looking for any information that would help Cyril.

Paul Foulston's story was the first to really raise the ante, though. A young detective constable with Thames Valley Police in the 1970s, he worked in the police for fifteen years before retiring after a serious road traffic accident left him with a broken back.

Now sixty-six, he has good memories of his time in the police and speaks highly of his detective sergeant, who has since passed away. But, after all these years, there's one thing that still bothers him. Cyril Smith's abuse was covered up.

In 1976 Foulston and his detective sergeant were working on a murder case together and drove out to south-west London one morning to interview a suspect at Ashford Remand Centre. When they arrived and got out of the car, a Rover 3500 police car came racing round the corner, tyres squealing, and blocked their way. Two men jumped out and approached them. They were Special Branch officers from the Metropolitan Police.

'They'd obviously been alerted by someone at the remand centre that we were coming and they told us straight away we were forbidden from speaking to the suspect,' Foulston recalls.

This didn't go down well with Foulston's detective sergeant. 'He was furious. He told them to piss off and get out of the way. This was a murder investigation and he wasn't going to be sent home by these guys.'

A furious row ensued and the standoff lasted several minutes. 'They were arrogant in the extreme and treated us like a couple of yokels from the provincial forces.' His detective sergeant dug his heels in and eventually the two Special Branch officers backed down. 'They said we could eliminate the suspect from our inquiries but we weren't to ask him about Cyril Smith under any circumstances,' explained Foulston.

This puzzled the pair of them. They hadn't bargained on an overweight Liberal MP being thrown into the equation. What had Cyril Smith to do with the murder they were investigating? Nothing, said the two men from the Met. 'Just don't ask the suspect about Cyril.'

As far as Foulston and his detective sergeant were concerned, Cyril Smith was irrelevant. They shrugged in agreement and headed off inside Ashford Remand Centre.

Ashford had started off as a school but in 1961 it was turned into a remand centre and included the Sex Pistols' Sid Vicious among its prisoners. Known now as Feltham Young Offenders Institution, after its merger with Feltham Borstal, it's one of Britain's most notorious youth jails.

For Foulston, this should have been a routine visit. He did this stuff all the time. But out of hundreds of interviews this one would stick in his memory forever. He and the detective sergeant went through the process of interviewing their suspect, a teenage offender. 'He had nothing to do with the murder,' Foulston remembers. 'He was in prison at the time it was committed. He'd been flagged up by someone from the incident room as a potential lead, but there was nothing in it.' They were about to wrap up, Foulston recalls, when his colleague caught his eye. There was one more question they wanted to put to the suspect.

'What do you know about Cyril Smith?'

Up until now the teenage boy had been calm and helpful throughout the interview but he quickly became agitated. His eyes burned and the left side of his face started to twitch. He looked at both the officers angrily, his eyes bulging. Then he unleashed a tide of vitriol.

'It took us by surprise,' admits Foulston. 'He was Cyril's ex-boyfriend and was furious at how Cyril had discarded him. He was completely off the wall.'

Over the next few minutes, the teenage suspect told the two police officers how Cyril would groom boys. He was one of them, and had come to see Cyril as his boyfriend. Cyril, he said, liked them young with tight sphincter muscles. When their sphincter became looser as they got older, he would ditch them.

'I can't forget the graphic detail,' Foulston tells me. 'I was disgusted.'

On the way home the two of them talked about Smith in the car. 'I remember my thoughts at the time,' he says. 'It was the bloody system protecting their own.'

As police officers, he said, they did not like the thought of anyone being above the law. But they still had a murder to solve and they had to park Cyril to one side. 'When you're young and there's case after case coming at you, you move on. But as I've got older I often think about that case. I was proud of my detective sergeant that day. He told Special Branch they were protecting a Member of Parliament above a murder inquiry and they could piss off.'

It was what happened years later that left a bitter taste. In 1988 Foulston opened his newspaper and looked at the honours list. The MP that Special Branch had tried to protect over a decade ago was set to become Sir Cyril Smith.

'If the establishment knew what he was up to and could award him a knighthood, then there is something seriously rotten, isn't there?'

Foulston certainly wasn't the only one who knew of Smith's guilt. It later transpired that there were files of evidence incriminating him that had been ignored by the Director of Public Prosecutions. In 1979 the Director of Public Prosecutions told *Rochdale Alternative Press* that they could not 'confirm or deny' receiving these files. They were common knowledge among politicians and police. I'd heard all about these files but no one had seen them. Officers had told me there'd been numerous investigations into Smith, but they had always been knocked back.

On 21 November 2012 I decided it was time that serious questions were asked about these files. At Prime Minister's Questions, I asked David Cameron if he would commit to publishing all files on Smith and ensure that a police investigation took place into any cover-up.

The Prime Minister looked nervous as he rose to respond. These were 'serious allegations about a former Member of this House', he said, justifying Foulston's suspicion that the establishment instinctively looked to protect their own. 'If anyone has information or facts they should take them to the police,' he continued, getting into his stride. 'That is the way we should investigate these things in this country.'

I was disappointed, but not surprised. The same answer was trotted out when I asked again about Smith at Home Office questions, this time by the Liberal Democrat minister Jeremy Browne. Ministers were closing ranks. I was beginning to think any police files on Smith were locked in a vault somewhere destined never to see the light of day. There certainly seemed no political appetite for them to be made public. I guess they figured it wouldn't do for a politician to be outed as a paedophile.

Then I received a phone call from Greater Manchester Police. 'It's regarding the questions you're asking about Cyril Smith,' a senior detective within the Public Protection Division announced when I picked up the receiver. 'We could do with having a chat.'

'Certainly,' I said. 'I'd be happy to meet. But I don't think I'm going to get anywhere with finding these police files.'

The line went silent for a few seconds.

'That's what I want to talk to you about,' he replied. 'I have them here in front of me.'

A week later two police officers, one from Greater Manchester Police and one from Lancashire Police, came to meet me to discuss Cyril Smith. They didn't bring the files with them but we spent a good hour talking about them.

The files, I learned, were clear about one thing. Cyril was guilty of using his position to abuse boys. The language of the report, I was told, was 'extremely forthright'. This eighty-page report had been sent to the Director of Public Prosecutions on 11 March 1970. A week later it was returned with a note recommending no further action be taken. Three months later Cyril stood as the Liberal candidate in the general election.

That was it then? Cyril had immunity? He could carry on abusing as he pleased because the Director of Public Prosecutions didn't think it was in the public interest to put a local politician in the dock?

The officers shrugged. I could tell that Cyril wasn't a big priority for them. Resources were stretched, they explained, and, since Savile, there had been a surge in the reporting of historic sex crimes. There were plenty of live paedophiles that they wanted to bring to justice instead of chasing dead ones.

That I could understand. To some extent policing, like politics, is the art of the possible. But what about the victims? Cyril had left a trail of misery and shame in Rochdale and elsewhere as he'd abused any boy he fancied. Wasn't it fair that the crimes against them by Cyril should be recognised at last?

The officers nodded. There was to be a 'Gold Meeting' on Monday to discuss Cyril Smith and it was likely they would put out a statement acknowledging that they believed he should have been prosecuted. They would pay a visit to Cyril's surviving family members first to forewarn them. Once the statement was released, victims would get apologies.

I sat back and pondered. It would represent quite a breakthrough for the police to admit this. We agreed to speak the following week.

It was then that the politics of the police and the Crown Prosecution Service took over.

It had been agreed that Greater Manchester Police and Lancashire Police would put out a statement to the effect that they believed Cyril Smith should have been prosecuted for abusing boys. But the CPS got wind of this and realised this wouldn't portray them in a good light. The attention would immediately focus on them. Their public relations machine went into overdrive and a damage limitation plan was quickly conceived.

They moved swiftly to trump the planned announcement by GMP and Lancashire Police with one of their own. Before the police were able to express their grievance with the justice system and state their view that Cyril should have been prosecuted before he became a Member of Parliament, the CPS rushed out a statement. The gist of it was, 'we do things differently these days'.

If we'd known what we know today, announced Nazir Afzal, Chief Crown Prosecutor for CPS North West, then Cyril would have been prosecuted.

It made plenty of headlines and it proved to the public beyond doubt that Cyril was guilty. But it got the CPS off the hook. They were on the front foot. Their statement contained a lengthy legal explanation as to why 'the evidential threshold for charging was higher than today'. There is some truth in this, but it didn't tally with the stories I'd heard from Foulston and others of people at the top intercepting evidence, making sure files were removed and police being told to drop their inquiries into Smith. Everything I was hearing pointed towards a cover-up and now the CPS were claiming it was all down to different legal values at the time.

'It is important to note,' the statement concluded, 'this way of thinking bears little resemblance to how such cases are assessed today.' The fact that I'd seen clear evidence earlier that year, in the Rochdale grooming scandal, that victims were still being treated in the same way as the victims of Cyril Smith made a mockery of this claim. Forty-seven girls had been victims of appalling sexual abuse that had gone on for years. It could and should have been stopped far sooner. The victims, some as young as thirteen, had cried foul to the police and the CPS ignored them, too.

Another story ended up much lower down in the CPS-driven headlines that week: the admission by Lancashire Police that on three separate occasions files were passed to first the DPP then the CPS containing details of abuse committed by Cyril, but on each occasion no prosecution was pursued. Three times? It was beginning to look as though Cyril was untouchable.

But while the CPS had suddenly established a firm grip on the narrative, and commentators began to debate whether sexual abuse was understood well enough in the 1970s, there were still plenty of police officers determined to get their side of the story across.

One of these was Jack Tasker. He phoned my office towards the end of 2012 and told me he had been assigned to investigate Cyril Smith in the late 1960s. His weathered, raspy voice got my attention immediately and a few weeks later we met for coffee in east Manchester. There was something about him that told me he was the real deal. Jack had spent twenty-five years in the police and his experiences were mapped out for all to see on a craggy, expressive face. He looked every inch an ex-detective and I listened attentively as he began to tell me his story.

A former CID officer with Lancashire Constabulary, Jack was stationed in Prestwich, a town within the borough of Bury, a few miles north of Manchester city centre. 'We did all the murders, the big jobs. We went out and about all over Lancashire,' he told me. It quickly transpired that Jack had a strong sense of justice. So strong that he'd even helped prosecute fellow police officers in the past. He did not believe in turning a blind eye to corruption.

The fact that Tasker was not based in Rochdale was the reason he was summoned to see his boss, Chief Inspector Derek Wheater, in the summer months of 1969. 'It was a Monday morning and me and my colleague, Detective Tom Courtney, came into work and were told to go up to the third floor straight away to see Derek Wheater,' he explains. 'I remember we looked at each other in the lift blankly. We thought we'd done something wrong.'

Wheater told them to sit down and then got straight down to business. 'Do you know the politician, Cyril Smith?' he asked. They thought for a second and nodded. 'He's been abusing boys for years. We've had three goes at him but every time we've been blocked. I want to bring him in and I need two officers who are not known in Rochdale to do it.' He paused and looked both of them in the eyes. 'I want you and Tom to do it.'

All previous statements had been confiscated, Wheater added, and he wanted them to interview boys again who'd made complaints about Cyril and get fresh statements.

Jack and Tom nodded. Pursuing murderers, thieves, politicians. It was all the same to them.

Over the next few months they interviewed eight boys who'd originally complained about being abused by Cyril. 'We found them convincing. I believed them. Obviously Wheater believed them as well,' said Tasker. It looked a straightforward case as far as he was concerned, but he hadn't reckoned on the network of spies and obstructive forces Cyril had at a local and national level to protect him.

Once they'd gathered all the statements the time came to bring Cyril in. 'We called him and told him we'd like to see him at Rochdale police station,' he recalls. 'He knew what it was about.'

A few days later Cyril turned up with his solicitor and sat across from Jack and Tom in a police interview room. A large reel-to-reel tape recorder was placed on the table between them. 'We went through the case with him and he looked very agitated,' Tasker remembers. Although they weren't based in Rochdale, he was aware that Cyril was a politician whose career was in the ascendancy. 'I'd seen him in the newspaper. Even then I think he was on TV, too. He was a big man with a big mouth, but he wasn't so confident that day,' he recalls. 'I got the impression that if it went to trial he would crack.'

Under the hanging lamp Tasker could see beads of sweat

start to form on Cyril's jowly face. He looked a worried man. 'We had him,' said Tasker, 'that much I remember clearly. He said "this will kill my mother". I think he thought the game was up.'

When Cyril stood up to leave there was fear in his eyes. He knew the police had been pursuing him for a long time now and the net was closing in.

It was Thursday evening and the light was beginning to fade. But by Monday he'd given them the slip again.

Tasker and Courtney shared a police car and after the weekend he remembers waiting to be picked up by Tom to take him into work. Pale sunlight shone through grey clouds and the clinking of empty bottles in crates made him look up to see a milk float whirring past.

'It was just a normal morning,' he says. 'We got in about 8.30 and the station duty man came out to tell me that there were two men waiting in my office.'

This came as a surprise to Tasker. He wasn't expecting anyone and it was highly unusual for someone to wait in his office. Things became stranger when he entered to find two officers sat behind his desk. They were chief superintendents from the Lancashire Constabulary headquarters in Hutton. Tasker sensed there was something wrong straight away.

'Who are you?' they asked.

'More to the point,' Tasker responded, 'Who are you? You're in my office.'

They identified themselves and asked where DC Courtney was.

'He'll be here any minute,' said Tasker. 'What is this about?'

They looked at each other and leaned forward. 'You've been doing an inquiry into Cyril Smith, haven't you?'

'Yes,' nodded Tasker.

'Where are all the statements?'

'In the drawer there, locked.'

'Open it.'

'I think I'd better get in touch with my boss first…'

'You've no need to speak to him. This has come direct from the chief constable.'

At that point, Tom arrived. He shot a glance at Tasker as if to ask what was happening, but was told by their two guests to take a seat.

'DC Courtney. Glad you could make it. We're taking over the Cyril Smith inquiry. We want everything you've done on it. Every scrap of paper, every statement, every recording, every lead. Give us everything.'

Tasker knew he had no choice and opened the drawer.

'They took everything,' he tells me forty-three years later. 'They went through every file. After they'd bagged it up, they asked, "Is that everything? If it isn't everything, and we find out that you've held something back, then there will be trouble." I asked them what was going to happen now and they said they were handling the case and as far as I was concerned the inquiry was over. Then they left and we just sat there looking at each other, wondering what had happened.'

Once Tasker was sure they had left the building he picked up the phone to his boss, Chief Inspector Wheater. 'He told us we'd better come over.'

When they got to his office and told him what had

happened, Wheater slumped in his chair and stared impassively ahead. He looked deflated. 'If it's from the chief constable,' he sighed, 'then that's the end of it. There's nothing we can do. You'd better accept it.'

A fortnight later Tasker and Courtney were split up and sent to different parts of Lancashire.

The files, says Tasker, went to Hutton and were buried. They never heard anything again. The next thing he knew, he was watching Cyril Smith on television with his arms aloft in triumph after winning a shock by-election. He was the new MP for Rochdale.

Tasker finishes his coffee, puts his cup carefully back on the saucer and stares out of the window. 'That's the first time I've told that story in years,' he says softly.

For a few moments we're both silent. 'Where do you think the orders came from?' I finally ask.

He taps the cup in front of him and looks up. 'I had the idea that what we were investigating was the tip of the iceberg,' he said. 'I think there were others and it must have come from the very top. It's only those kind of people who could do that.'

What struck me then, as it does now, is the powerful sense of injustice felt by officers who'd been foiled by higher forces that were protecting Cyril. The disgust you hear in their voices as they talk about turning the television off years later whenever Cyril popped up is genuine. The anger they feel hasn't softened over the years. They are genuinely sickened at what happened.

Whoever was helping Cyril then, it was yet another narrow escape. He'd walked out of the police station on

Thursday knowing his goose was nearly cooked. By Monday he was laughing again and free to carry on as before.

With stories such as Tasker's mounting up, I'd spend weekends and evenings phoning back dozens of officers and witnesses to Cyril's abuse. What on earth had been going on for so long in Rochdale? More to the point, how many people up the chain knew what Cyril was up to? The stories I heard were astonishing. It was obvious that Cyril had a secret life, but the scale of his perversity seemed to know no limits.

John Hessel's story was another that stuck with me. Now running a pub in Scotland, he managed a bingo hall in Northampton in the 1980s and remembers one evening seeing a woman crying over the table during a game. 'She was on her own and just sobbing uncontrollably,' he remembers. 'It was disturbing the other players so I asked her to come into the back for a coffee.' As John handed her a box of tissues in his office and tried to calm her down, she told him she worked in the local police station as an administrator. She'd had a bad day, she explained, wiping the tears from her eyes and apologising. She shouldn't let these things get to her, she said, but it wasn't every day a politician was brought into the station and put in the cells. That politician was Cyril Smith.

His car had been pulled over on the motorway and officers had found a box of child porn in his boot. The police were naturally disgusted and wanted to press charges. But then a phone call was made from London and he was released without charge.

Senior officers had threatened the officers involved with

dismissal if he was not released immediately. The mood was tense and sullen as officers stood back while Cyril breezily walked past them to freedom. All the staff who knew about it were threatened with the Official Secrets Act if they discussed the matter any further. It had shocked and upset everyone and her tears were a mixture of disgust and anger that a politician could get away with something like that. Once again Cyril walked out of the police station knowing he was a protected man.

In 2012, in a search through the Director of Public Prosecutions' files by the CPS, a file containing a police referral of allegations relating to indecent obscene publications came to light. For good measure, in the same files a referral relating to the Public Bodies Corrupt Practices Act was also found.

I subsequently met with the Director of Public Prosecutions, Keir Starmer, to discuss this and, on the eve of his departure from the role, he asked me to direct all my queries to his team, which I did. I promptly got an email back saying they had been passed on to the Metropolitan Police, where they remain unanswered.

Cyril's secret life was remarkable and I began to wonder how he'd managed to sustain it without it ever becoming public knowledge. The map of his misdeeds showed that he abused from Rochdale to London. If things had gone quiet in Rochdale after his narrow escape at Cambridge House then it was simply because he'd moved on to pastures new.

After Cambridge House, he also began to take more risks, as Ron Foynes testified. A member of the Royal Military Police Company based at Rochester Row in central London in the late 1970s, Ron got in touch to share what he said was an open secret at the time.

'Cyril Smith was into young boys, we all knew that,' he said. 'We heard plenty of stories about him.'

These stories would be shared at the Corporals Mess bar where they'd eat and socialise with the Royal Parks Constabulary, whose police station was in St James's Park just behind the Guards Memorial opposite Horse Guards Parade.

'I distinctly remember conversations in the bar where Parks officers explained how they carried out observations and arrests on the male public toilets in the park close to the junction of Marlborough Road and the Mall,' he said. 'These toilets were a regular meeting place for homosexuals and young male prostitutes after dark.'

On a number of occasions police officers had detained Cyril Smith after he was caught 'in acts of gross indecency with young lads' at these toilets, Foynes explained. On each occasion, they'd been told by those higher up the chain of command to discontinue their inquiries due to the status of the individual concerned.

How many times had Cyril been arrested or pulled in by police only to be released as soon as the phone call from high office was made? I wondered if he actually got a thrill out of being caught knowing they couldn't pin anything on him because he was a protected man.

A clear picture was now emerging. Tales of Cyril's rapacious sexual appetite weren't confined to a corner of Lancashire. All over the country people knew about his interest in boys. Derek Smith was an instructor at Sussex Police and remembers in the 1980s one of his colleagues actually using Cyril's case as part of a training session for other officers on child abuse.

'She talked about Cyril not being convicted as an example of how you had to get as much evidence as possible if you wanted to charge someone that had an important social status. She told the room that there were 144 complaints of child abuse against Cyril but he still couldn't be convicted,' he said.

Senior officers were furious when word spread that Cyril's case was a part of the training. 'She was moved on to Harrogate with a threat of discipline hanging over her. All instructors, even those in charge of the driving school and IT training, were threatened with dismissal if Cyril's name was ever mentioned again,' he said.

Smith compares these continued attempts to prevent anyone from talking about Cyril to Ryan Giggs's ill-fated attempt to gag the press from discussing his affair in 2011 with a super-injunction. 'Everyone knew about it,' he said. 'You couldn't stop it spreading.'

By the late 1980s copies of the file that had been sent to the DPP in 1970 containing allegations of Cyril's abuse had been distributed between officers all around the country. Such was their disgust that many were part of a letter-writing campaign to high street banks urging them to remove him as the public face of their Access credit card campaign. 'It may well have worked,' said Smith, 'as he was later dropped from that campaign.'

Smith's conclusion underpins this scandalous political cover-up. 'Honest police officers simply had nowhere to go with the information they had.'

I was beginning to understand how they felt. Getting to

the bottom of this sorry saga looked an impossible task. The CPS, the Metropolitan Police and government ministers had all made it clear that no information would be forthcoming from them. Questions would remain unanswered. Mistakes of the past were going to be left there.

But why had so much effort been put into keeping Cyril's misdeeds hidden from public view? What had he done to be worthy of this level of protection? 'I just don't understand it,' one of the country's leading child abuse lawyers told me, shaking his head in exasperation. 'What was so important about Cyril?'

That remained the million-dollar question – and I've yet to hear one single satisfactory answer. Later, as I flicked through old editions of the *Rochdale Alternative Press*, which had famously challenged Cyril in the 1970s, one cover image caught my attention. It was Cyril, as a huge blimp, floating above Rochdale Town Hall. Comical, absurd even, this image perfectly encapsulates the stranglehold he held on the town. Even now, his presence seems to hang over Rochdale and we still have some way to go to be completely free of his malign influence.

For some, that influence had been passed from one generation to another. I remember getting a moving call from a mother one afternoon who told me how Cyril had abused her father in the 1960s. He'd passed away recently, she said, and hadn't made it to see Cyril outed as a serial abuser. Even in his final years he used to speak about Cyril. The intervening years had done nothing to dim his memory and he still could remember what Cyril did to him at Cambridge House.

While I struggled to comprehend how Cyril's influence had allowed him to bend the law for so long, I knew one thing for certain. His enormous popularity and working-class appeal should never be underestimated.

One caller, a former dog-handler with the Metropolitan Police, said Special Branch officers had long shared the police's irritation at Cyril being able to avoid prosecution, but there was a simple explanation. The DPP was worried that Cyril might be able to do something remarkable if he went to trial. He might have been able to win public sympathy for paedophilia.

This sounds incredible now but the former police officer went on. 'They knew how popular he was in Rochdale and thought it might backfire. They thought ladies in Rochdale would be offering their children up in a show of support.'

My head was spinning at the thought. It sounded complete lunacy. But if you followed this thinking down the rabbit hole into 1970s Wonderland you quickly had to acknowledge there were more than a few advocates for paedophilia.

The Paedophile Liberation Front and the Paedophile Information Exchange were two of the more high-profile liberation campaigns that sprung up at the time, seeking to reclassify paedophilia as 'intergenerational relationships'. One of the leading members of the Paedophile Information Exchange was the British diplomat, Sir Peter Hayman, who was later jailed. These weren't simply loony fringe sects. They were affiliated to the National Council of Civil Liberties (NCCL), now known as Liberty, and would pop up frequently in the media. Part of their strategy, as their chairperson, Keith Hose, freely admitted, was to 'seek out as much publicity for the organisation as possible' and 'the only way to get more paedophiles joining PIE' was 'to make paedophilia a real public issue'. To this extent they succeeded. They had hundreds of members, possibly as many as a thousand, and were influential. In 1978 they sent every Member of Parliament a copy of their booklet, *Paedophilia: Some Questions and Answers*. News of their existence spread. The national media reported on their views and the NCCL seemed sympathetic to their cause. Most alarmingly, a letter published in the NCCL house magazine, *Rights*, in 1982, argued that more needed to be done to champion paedophile rights. 'Consensual sex between adults and children is simply people of different age groups being nice to each other,' the author claimed. Worryingly, it seemed that a fair few on the left, including some who have subsequently become key figures in the Labour Party, were fooled into giving this hideous group shelter. All of which helped Cyril's cause and kept him hidden from scrutiny. It seems unthinkable now, but groups like these tried to water down parliamentary bills to protect children from child abusers and academics loudly championed their cause. Cambridge professor Donald West was among those leading the charge of the child sex abuse lobby. It was 'unwise', he argued, 'to over-dramatise institutional abuse'.

With this sickening liberal wind behind them, it was hardly surprising that ugly networks quickly grew to protect and provide for paedophiles of a high social status. Secret parties, underground grooming activities and vile associations all developed out of these thriving networks and the

Elm Guest House in south-west London soon became the centre of a VIP paedophile ring.

Raided by the Vice Squad in 1982, allegations of child abuse were never followed up at this ostensibly quiet lodging in Barnes. Only after recent political pressure in Parliament has a police investigation finally started to look into allegations of boys being trafficked from a nearby care home run by Richmond Council to be abused at the Elm Guest House by a paedophile ring. There has been much speculation as to who was part of this sordid club, but the Metropolitan Police has confirmed that Cyril Smith visited the premises.

This was later confirmed to me when I was passed the details of someone who was forced to work at Elm Guest House in the early 1980s as a masseur. 'He knows all about Cyril,' my source told me. 'See if he'll speak to you.'

The man, who was sixteen at the time and understandably doesn't want to be named, answered straight away. 'How did you get my number?' he demanded. There was fear in his voice. He warned me of the dangers of digging too deep into what went on at Elm Guest House. 'The police told me not to say anything about it. You know what happened to Carole, don't you?'

Carole Kasir ran Elm Guest House from 1979 to 1982. Paedophiles from all over the country would attend parties there and boys were sexually abused. It was raided by police in 1982 and shut down. Years later, Kasir threatened to expose all the people who'd attended her parties. Soon afterwards she was found dead of an insulin overdose.

The fear in the former masseur's voice is genuine and not for the first time I wonder whether victims of abuse can ever feel safe no matter how much distance they put between themselves and their abusers. I learned that Cyril had visited Elm Guest House several times for sessions with this sixteen-year-old lad. He liked to receive oral sex and, on one occasion, got stuck in the sauna and had to be hoisted out. The people who attended and were booked in for sessions with young masseurs all had nicknames. Cyril was given the sobriquet 'tubby'.

Cyril's loyal fan base back home had no idea of the sickening circles he was moving in. Another victim has gone public to say that Cyril had a friendship with notorious paedophile and founding member of the Paedophile Information Exchange, Peter Righton. As the co-author of the book, *Perspectives on Paedophilia*, which championed the right of adults to have sex with children, Righton was later to become the subject of a BBC programme entitled *The Secret Life of a Paedophile*.

Sometimes I reflect on what Jack Tasker told me, about why he thought the investigation was closed, and think he's probably right. Cyril was a part of a bigger story and I'm sure he wasn't the only high-profile figure, or even politician, involved in preying on and abusing young boys all over the country. Even now, over three years after his death, it seems as if the police are still in pursuit of Cyril Smith. And, as was the case then, Cyril remains one step ahead and is still protected. The sense of injustice felt by honest officers who wanted him exposed remains. But with Special Branch documents still under lock and key and kept secret for national security reasons, no one is in a hurry to own up to mistakes of the past.

It soon reached the point that whenever an email flashed up in my inbox with Cyril Smith in the subject line something tightened in my stomach. I felt a visceral reaction. It felt as though he was pursuing me, too. I was affected by the anguish of some of the victims. Sometimes I just felt despair. There were no easy solutions in sight. He was dead and was never going to face justice. Even getting an acknowledgement from the police and CPS that he should have been prosecuted was only a pyrrhic victory for the victims. It was all too late.

Many people who got in touch were happy finally to unburden themselves to someone who gave them a fair hearing. I wondered how many other public figures over the years had received calls and letters about Cyril and not acted on them. I imagined there were a few – and not all of them would have been Liberal politicians. There had been a consensus of fear in the town for years among all parties. No one dared challenge Cyril and there were plenty of people in positions of power who knew what he was up to.

When I became the parliamentary candidate for Rochdale I had known nothing of Cyril's double life. But it wasn't long after I'd started my campaign to become the town's MP that I began to hear the rumours. When I started to ask questions a fellow Labour MP approached me and told me to leave Cyril alone. 'Don't attack him, steer clear of him,' he said. 'It's not worth it.' It wasn't just the words that irritated me, it was the look that followed them. It more or less said, 'Play the game, this is how it works and if you want to join our club then obey our rules.'

Too many senior politicians shared this view. It was as though Cyril had them all under a spell. For me, these rules were archaic and I think the public knew that local democracy wasn't functioning properly. They could sense that a cosy club was in place that was too inward-looking. Cyril had turned local politics into freemasonry.

In the lead-up to the general election there was one attack on me that the Liberals employed again and again. I was 'an outsider', they said. They put this on leaflets, they ensured it was quoted in the local newspaper and they told everyone they met when out campaigning. 'He's an outsider, he's not from Rochdale. He's not one of us.'

It's true, I wasn't from Rochdale. But I was hardly someone from the Home Counties that had been parachuted in. I had been born fourteen miles away and lived all my life in Lancashire.

But I knew what they meant. I didn't do politics like they did and I didn't share their values. And as far as I was concerned this was good news for the town. Rochdale needed a break from the past.

You don't give up three years of your life and make huge sacrifices that affect your family to try and become a Member of Parliament if you don't believe passionately in politics. And you can't passionately believe in politics if you turn a blind eye to cover-ups and continued malpractice. The two positions simply can't sit together.

I knew that and that's why, as soon as the first victim of Cyril Smith approached me, there was no turning back. Every email, every phone call, every meeting uncovered more about his double life. And the more I found out the more I realised the harm he'd done and continued to do, even though he was no longer here.

I came to realise that this wasn't just about abuse, it was about power. Cyril exercised far too much power in Rochdale and he'd left a dreadful legacy.

When major politicians stand down from office they often set up foundations to make sure any cause they have advocated continues to be advanced. The Thatcher Foundation and the Tony Blair Faith Foundation are two examples. In Rochdale the Cyril Smith School of Politics operates without walls, classrooms and books. There are plenty of members and the funds have poured in for a long time. But it's a different model of foundation entirely. It relies on disciples of a ghastly style of politics continuing to initiate new recruits into Cyril's way of doing things. The school had existed for too long and it was time to close it down.

I'd spent many months wading through abuse, despair and wretched politics in pursuit of Cyril's identity and the more I persisted the more revelations turned up. I had just about gone as far as I thought possible, and I wasn't sure if I had the stomach to deal with much more, when a key piece of the jigsaw I'd almost given up on finally turned up.

I got access to the police files on Cyril.

It was in a restaurant in London when I first got sight of them. They were placed in front of me by a journalist and I put the menu down and started to devour every word.

There was plenty there that I already knew, having pieced it together from other sources, but there was one section that quickly grabbed my attention.

Henry Howarth had succeeded Cyril as mayor of

Rochdale in 1967 and was the leader of the Rochdale Liberal Party. In a police interview with Detective Sergeant Jeffrey Leach, he offered some robust advice to the police regarding the prospect of charging Cyril with child abuse.

'May I offer a personal opinion,' he begins. 'I sincerely hope that this matter is not prosecuted before the court. In my opinion, as a Justice of the Peace, it is not court worthy. The prosecution can do no good at all and the backlash will have unfortunate repercussions for the police force and the town of Rochdale. It is no secret that Cyril and I are buddies and not only politically.'

In other words, the leader of the local Liberal Party was threatening the police.

Notes from Detective Sergeant Leach underneath this account acknowledge as much. 'The veiled threats and innuendoes contained therein,' he remarks, 'reflect Howarth's general attitude to this inquiry.'

I'd already known that Cyril was leaning hard on the police, but I didn't know that the local Liberal Party was doing the same. What 'unfortunate repercussions' for the police could Howarth possibly have had in mind as, like Cyril, he tried to bully the police into dropping their investigation? Was this the kind of relationship that local politicians had with the police at the time? Who was the law working for? A small group of politicians or the people?

Reading on it quickly became apparent that even Leach had doubts about Rochdale police. Referring to the evidence given by the council's children's officer Lyndon Price, Leach casts doubt on whether Rochdale's Chief Constable Patrick Ross ever acted upon it.

'It is quite feasible,' he notes, 'that Mr Ross would keep it to himself because of the status of the man involved.'

The suspicion he shares is clear for all to see. Cyril had police officers worried.

The files also offered some clues as to the weak defence Cyril was prepared to give if the matter went to court. Under questioning, he tried to claim *loco parentis* where the boys were concerned. They were on his property and in all matters medical and relating to general discipline Cyril claimed the boys had signed off legal responsibility for him to care for them. In other words, Cyril could do whatever he wanted at Cambridge House. Leach knew only too well that no court in the land would buy this.

'In my opinion it's without merit. It will not withstand even superficial examination,' was how he put it in comments underneath.

Concluding, Leach seemed confident of a prosecution. Under questioning by police officers, Cyril 'had difficulty in articulating and even the stock answers he offered could only be obtained after repeated promptings by his solicitor'.

Like Tasker, Leach had firmly believed that Cyril would crumble in court.

'Were he ever to be placed in a witness box he would be at the mercy of any competent counsel,' he remarked.

Unfortunately, the Director of Public Prosecutions did not share the same confidence. In a letter to Lancashire Police in 1970, Sir Norman Skelhorn said he did not consider there to be a reasonable prospect of a conviction. Referring to the statements by Cyril's victims, he said, 'The characters of some of these young men would be likely to render their evidence suspect.'

It may as well have said that as long as a high-profile local politician decides to abuse boys of lowly social status then there is zero chance of him ever being prosecuted. It more or less outlined a code of conduct for abusers. Stick to vulnerable people from broken homes and the law will give you a wide berth.

The injustice contained in these words is as strong now as it was then. It was a loophole so huge that even some-one as gargantuan as Cyril could skip through. If anything can best attest to the law being an ass then this was it.

I can understand why the DPP might have been nervous about bringing such a high-profile case to court, as Cyril certainly had his supporters. But I refuse to believe that insufficient legal tools were available to make a prosecution.

It was a colossal error that would compound the injustice felt by victims and allow Cyril to repeat the same pattern of behaviour time after time. Knowl View, Elm Guest House and other abominable cases of abuse could and should have been avoided.

Chapter 10

The Dog That Didn't Bark

Among the many obituaries that celebrated the life of Cyril Smith after his death, Michael Meadowcroft's in *The Guardian* was the first to give a hint that Cyril wasn't as popular within his party as he was with the general public.

Unlike the generous praise lavished upon Cyril by many of his colleagues, the former Liberal MP for Leeds West eschewed clichéd tributes to offer a plain and at times brutal appraisal. A 'difficult colleague', 'addicted to self-publicity' that colleagues were ashamed of campaigning for because he was 'uncomfortably to their right' were some of his candid observations. He even alluded to the allegations of Cyril abusing boys that reached *Private Eye* from the *Rochdale Alternative Press* in 1979. But he didn't dwell on them. They 'appeared to have no effect on his electability' was his only observation.

When Meadowcroft appeared before *Dispatches* on Channel 4 a few years later, he elaborated more on this final observation, giving a telling insight into why his colleagues had turned a blind eye to serious allegations of child abuse.

'There were whispers before that there were problems,' he said of the *Private Eye* article about Cyril in 1979, acknowledging he'd heard rumours that Cyril 'liked boys'.

'I don't think we did much about it, maybe we should have at the time but we didn't,' he added.

If the rumours were true they expected something to happen in Rochdale at the 1979 general election. When it didn't and Cyril romped home to another comfortable victory the party relaxed and ignored it.

The 'persistent freemasonry of the House of Commons' that Churchill had complained about nearly seventy years previously was still very much in evidence. Only this wasn't a case of covering for a drunk Prime Minister, as Churchill had observed in 1911, when he'd seen colleagues try to hide the fact that Prime Minister Asquith was so drunk he could barely speak. This was covering for a paedophile.

'Essentially as long as a colleague turns up and votes the right way we don't really do much about their own problems,' Meadowcroft concluded.

For the journalist who conducted the interview with Meadowcroft, this chilling confession spoke volumes about the rotten culture within politics. 'His admission that no one was willing to take the claims seriously, as long as Smith voted in the right way, tells us as much about the practice of politics as it does about senior Liberal Democrats today,' said Liz McKean.

Meadowcroft was the only colleague of Cyril's prepared to go on the record and answer McKean's questions about why reports of Cyril's abuse were not acted upon in Westminster. 'They were all too happy to heap praise on Smith after he died,' she notes, 'but refused to address any of our questions.'

An ex-*Newsnight* reporter who'd previously worked on the

exposé of Jimmy Savile as a paedophile, McKean said the *Dispatches* programme left a lasting impression on her.

'In all my years of reporting I have never met so many middle-aged and elderly men so close to tears. Decades have passed since Cyril Smith abused them and they have never got over it. In all cases they've been left with the wretched legacy of childhood abuse – the sense of shame and inadequacy.'

The comparisons between Savile and Smith, she says, are plain to see.

'Both men, who knew each other, were working-class northerners, outside the establishment and yet eventually a significant part of it. They used native cunning to manipulate their way into positions of influence over vulnerable young people – and their professional success and powerful personalities helped ensure they were never held to account.'

After interviewing Meadowcroft for the programme, McKean and her team were struck by the sense among other politicians that Cyril's abuse had been known all along.

'A telling moment came when my colleague was filming shots of Westminster for the programme,' she says. 'A former Conservative Cabinet minister from the 1980s asked him what the film was for. When he was told he shook his head and said twice: "We all knew, you know."'

Meadowcroft's honesty lays bare the uncomfortable truth surrounding Cyril within the Liberal Party. Many in his own party did not like him, but they were prepared to tolerate his dark side, or sexual peccadilloes, as they viewed it. Rumours of his abuse had certainly filtered through to many in the party, including the leadership. But the allegations were crowded out by one extremely attractive attribute of Cyril's – that he had the electoral Midas touch.

Cyril's stunning by-election win in 1972 kick-started a Liberal revival and an impressive string of by-election victories followed. Rochdale hadn't seen a Liberal MP since Ramsay Bryce Muir won in 1923 and even then he didn't last long, being voted out at the next general election the following year. Cyril had achieved a remarkable breakthrough ensuring that the party could finally begin to build on the foundations that Jo Grimond had laid over a decade earlier. He soon became one of the most famous faces in politics and, while publicly many in the party were reluctant to recognise his remarkable contribution to their success, they were only too aware of the difference he made.

Gazing out over the Thames from the historic Pugin Room in Parliament, Lord Ronnie Fearn of Southport acknowledges as much. As the MP for Southport on two occasions, from 1987 to 1992 and 1997 to 2001, he was one of many Liberals to benefit from Cyril's Midas touch. 'He certainly helped me become an MP,' he says. 'When he came to Southport in 1987 people would be coming out of their houses just to see him. Everyone wanted to see Cyril, he was more popular than the leader of the party at the time.'

Looking back at that election he fondly remembers Cyril coming to his house for afternoon tea. 'He broke my couch just by sitting on it,' he laughs. 'The legs broke. We both thought it was hilarious.' When the pair went to canvass voters, people would swarm around him on the street. 'They all wanted to shake his hand and say, "I've met Cyril Smith." He helped me win and get a 2,000 majority that year.'

Cyril's size was a big asset, he admits. People would spot him from the other end of the street and they'd make a beeline for him straight away. His size literally forced people to notice him. 'When you go through the voting lobby the doors only half open to allow one person through at a time,' he said. 'When Cyril went through they had to open the double doors to allow him to get through.' To this day he remains the fattest man to ever sit in the House of Commons.

His obesity may have caused complications in the voting lobby and was too much for Fearn's couch to bear, but it added substance to what was essentially a weak campaigning operation in his party.

'He'd campaign everywhere,' beams Fearn. 'I don't think he ever said no to anything.'

'But what about the allegations of abuse? Surely you must have heard the rumours,' I pressed.

'There are always rumours against someone that popular,' he responded dryly. 'Our Cyril? No. I refuse to believe it.'

I'd begun to find there were all sorts of reasons why Cyril's abuse of boys was ignored. Some, like Fearn, saw him as a miracle worker and refused to countenance his darker side. Others, no doubt, were still reeling from the knowledge that their leader in the 1970s, Jeremy Thorpe, was caught up in an explosive sexual scandal in his own right. Thorpe ended up in court in 1979 accused of conspiring to murder a stable boy, Norman Scott, with whom he was having an affair. He was ultimately acquitted but forced out of public life. It left a deeply unedifying pall over the Liberals and no doubt his colleagues were keen to get some distance between this scandal rather than face up to the equally scandalous activities of Cyril Smith.

The episode is compellingly documented in Freeman and Penrose's book *Rinkagate*, which reveals how MI5 were already monitoring the activities of politicians at the time. We learn, for example, that Thorpe had been vetted in 1960 because he was being considered as best man for the royal wedding between Princess Margaret and Antony Armstrong-Jones. He never became best man as the report concluded that he had 'homosexual tendencies'.

A further sign of how political networks operate in Parliament was shown in a Liberal MP's approach to a Labour Home Office minister calling for a police inquiry into Thorpe and Norman Scott to be stopped. The book discloses how Peter Bessell approached George Thomas asking for the Norman Scott file to be destroyed. Bessell went on to meet the Home Secretary, Frank Soskice, who was sympathetic to his claims that a 'ghastly man' was out to destroy Thorpe. Soskice later confirmed that the inquiry would go nowhere. The allegations were buried for now, but they would return to haunt Thorpe.

Thorpe's dalliance with Norman Scott clearly gave Cyril a fright. He was chief whip at the time the story finally became public and raged against the injustice of what he called 'insinuations and slanders' forcing his party leader out of public office. When journalists called Cyril for a comment on the remarks made by the former male model, Scott, over his relationship with Thorpe, he said his blood went cold. Knowing full well that it could just as easily be him facing calls from the media over his relationships with young men,

Cyril decided to go on the attack. It was scandalous conduct by the media, he complained, to be hounding a man over something so ludicrous and irrelevant. He went on to say in his autobiography that he firmly believed a politician's private life was his own affair. Skeletons, he argued, should stay in people's cupboards unless it could be proved they had an adverse effect on their political judgement. He was getting his defence in early. Even though Cyril's private life involved him wrecking lives and trawling round schools and youth clubs in search of vulnerable boys that he could have his way with, he remained of the view that it was no one else's business.

The Liberals handled the Thorpe affair badly and an indication of how they might have dealt with the allegations about Cyril abusing boys can be seen in the secret internal investigation into Thorpe carried out by David Steel and fellow Liberal MP Emlyn Hooson in 1971.

Considered by many to be a sophisticated cover-up, when the allegations became public a few years later the politicians involved in the investigation blamed everyone else except themselves. No one in the Liberal Party, it appeared, wanted to know what was going on. Worse still, the leader of the party at the time when rumours of Cyril's paedophilia were raised went on to ensure Cyril got a knighthood. Despite efforts by the Cabinet Office to prevent it being known that David Steel nominated Cyril for a knighthood, the Information Commissioner's Office recently overturned the decision to redact Cyril's knighthood nomination papers and disclosed that Steel helped get Cyril knighted in 1988. Furthermore, the Information Commissioner concluded that it was in the public interest for this to be known because the person who nominated Cyril would have been aware of rumours about him at the time.

To begin to even try and understand why Steel dismissed such serious rumours you have to consider the zeitgeist of the 1970s. There was a febrile mood in the party and a sense that British institutions were under threat. The establishment was being battered by scandals and now the Liberals were in the firing line. Freeman and Penrose's book brilliantly captures the mood at the time through an explanation from Peter Bessell MP, a former Liberal. Anyone with public prominence, he explained, automatically acquired a measure of immunity denied to everyone else. This strange code certainly benefited Cyril, although it couldn't stop a growing sense of anxiety engulfing him.

I believe Norman Scott haunted Cyril. Cyril saw how Thorpe was publicly humiliated and destroyed by the scandal and he knew there was a grave risk of someone else, like Scott, emerging and doing the same to him.

Over thirty years later, when the Guardian Media Group were downsizing, Cyril wrote to the *Rochdale Observer* complaining about the decision to move his local newspaper to Manchester. In a bizarre Freudian slip, he wrote that 'Norman Scott would be spinning in his grave'. He had meant to say John Scott who established the Scott Trust Limited, which owns the Guardian Media Group.

In the end, Cyril was right to worry. People would come out of the woodwork a few years later, but their stories would never reach the mass media or cause anything like the damage Thorpe had suffered. Cyril would carry on relatively unscathed and he had plenty of people more than willing to protect him.

But while the Fearns of the world were too blinded by Cyril's electoral talents to notice any wrongdoing, I figured there were still plenty of others like Meadowcroft who were not overawed by Cyril's celebrity status.

One of these was Lord Tony Greaves, who served on Lancashire County Council for twenty-five years and was mentioned in Meadowcroft's obituary as one of the Liberals uncomfortable at campaigning for Cyril.

Like Meadowcroft, he, too, was asked to write an obituary for a national newspaper after Cyril died. He refused because of 'political reasons'. By this, I'm led to believe that he didn't want to criticise Cyril publicly for fear that it might be damaging for his party. As I listen to him squirming over the phone, the hypocrisy is obvious. Greaves despised Cyril. He's quick to disassociate Cyril from the Community Politics motion he advanced, saying Cyril had nothing to do with a national movement within the Liberals to put power in the hands of ordinary people. And he's quick to make the point that he hopes there will never be another politician like Cyril Smith again. But he was happy to allow his party to bask in the glory of Cyril's populism in the immediate aftermath of his death, with successive party stalwarts queuing up to praise Cyril as some sort of national treasure.

Despite my invitation for him to set the record straight and give an insight into the real Cyril Smith from the view of those within his own party, he politely declines for the same reason as he turned down the opportunity to write his obituary. 'I don't want to do it for political reasons.' He would be too critical of Cyril, he said, and that wouldn't do.

I'd reached the conclusion that the Liberals had truly come to a sorry pass when senior figures in the party were reluctant to denounce child abusers for political reasons.

There had been enough of these weasel words by now. As George Orwell said in his seminal work *1984*, the aim of the party was to extinguish once and for all the possibility of independent thought. It was mission accomplished for many in the Liberals. Cyril Smith was the elephant in the room and his party were tiptoeing around him, afraid of confirming what they'd long suspected – he wasn't fit to represent them in Parliament.

In the weeks following the revelations about Cyril Smith, Liberals would actively avoid me in Westminster. Some would get out of the lift when I got in. Others would just stare ahead, bristling with indignation.

As leader of Rochdale's Liberals in 1969, Henry Howarth had known all about the serious allegations hanging over Cyril and had threatened the police with 'unfortunate repercussions' if he were prosecuted. Soon after, Cyril was made the Liberal Party parliamentary candidate for the 1970 general election. No wonder Cyril conceded it was a time of acrimony for the party and he was by no means the unanimous choice. How many members knew he'd been the subject of a police investigation into child abuse? A year later the Liberal leader, Jeremy Thorpe, personally asked Cyril if he'd stand in what was then an anticipated by-election in Rochdale the following year.

As Cyril's success continued throughout the 1970s

his penchant for boys became an open secret. Journalists discussed it in Westminster bars; even Dominic Carman, the son of the barrister that defended Thorpe in one of the biggest sexual scandals of the decade, who would himself stand to try to become a Liberal Democrat MP, knew about it.

But still no one raised the alarm.

Stephen Moore was a Labour councillor in the 1970s who would go on to lead Rochdale Council. In the mid-1960s he visited a friend at Cambridge House and remembers being told he'd have to leave at around 9 p.m. when Cyril arrived. 'I was there when Cyril did arrive once and he went straight upstairs to the lads' rooms. It did look odd,' he said. 'All the lads would disappear around then.'

Moore shudders at what he now knows must have happened, but says they were all completely oblivious to the crimes he was committing. Even Moore's father, who was the town clerk at the time, had personally given a donation to Cyril to establish Cambridge House.

It wasn't until many years later that he was told of what Cyril had been up to by journalists working for the *Rochdale Alternative Press*. By then, Cyril's juggernaut was unstoppable and his popularity was such that people just couldn't bring themselves to believe it.

'He was enormously active and very visible,' he said. 'We found it very hard to campaign against Cyril. There was a real frustration. We wondered what you could do to expose this guy.'

The added complication, he admits, was that most people did not understand the real nature of his abuse and the

Labour Party was loath to attack Cyril for being gay. From both sides of the political spectrum, there was a reluctance to confront the allegations for different reasons.

From the Conservative standpoint, Cyril's boasts – and he could be brazen – about his chastisement of unruly boys appealed to a sense of restoring discipline. Punishments for deviation from moral rectitude were generally seen as a good thing.

Cyril had successfully managed to dress up his obsession with spanking, bizarre medical examinations and groping of boys' testicles as some sort of necessary action required to restore discipline.

From the Liberal/Labour standpoint, rumours of Cyril's liaisons with boys just confirmed that, like other politicians in the town, he was gay. The climate at the time was a lot more ambiguous on paedophile activities than today and a number of paedophile lobby groups had convinced radical gay rights activists that they shared similar goals of sexual liberty. This fed into what was mistakenly deemed to be a progressive agenda.

Political confusion from both sides of the spectrum on the true nature of Cyril's abuse ultimately created a vacuum where his activities escaped any effective scrutiny and there was no real effort to hold him to account.

Then there was the fact that Rochdale had a turbulent political scene where frequently no party enjoyed overall control of the council. 'A lot of horse trading would go on,' says Moore. 'People from all different parties talked to each other a lot.' The dog didn't bark because the culprit was well known to all.

Add to this the fact that if people ever publicly referred to the rumours swirling around Cyril, he would have his tanks on your lawn in no time at all. 'I had three solicitor's letters off Cyril for things I had said publicly or on a leaflet,' explained Moore. 'He never followed them up but he was always throwing his weight around like that, making it clear that he was ready to fight. It silenced a lot of people.'

On top of which, Moore said there had been a feeling among Labour councillors at the time that nature would soon take care of Cyril. He was so grossly overweight that few thought he would be able to carry on in public life much longer. There was a temptation 'to keep your head down and wait for him to go', he admits.

But he carried on – and on. He kept winning election after election and his bandwagon showed no sign of stopping. Cyril had the constitution of an ox. He wasn't going anywhere.

Cyril's image, certainly among the town's establishment, was such that it afforded him a further protection. The 'Mr Rochdale' epithet he'd successfully cultivated led to him being viewed almost like family. Few politicians are able to achieve 'Father to the Nation' status. Gandhi, Lincoln and Mandela are obvious examples. Cyril pioneered a more parochial model. He was an 'Uncle to the Town', a constant, smiling avuncular presence that people came to accept as one of their own. And just as research shows that sexual abuse within the family is often covered up out of shame, rather than protecting the abused, then so was Cyril's abuse covered up. It would be too damaging to the town. Mr Rochdale couldn't be a paedophile, could he? It would not be in the town's best interests.

I spoke to politicians from all three main parties who were around during the height of Cyril's powers and they all more or less said the same. No one really knew the full detail. Cyril was too powerful. Nothing could be done. He should not have got away with it and it mustn't happen again. There was a lot of hand-wringing, but not much evidence of action ever being taken.

I was continually struck, though, by the number of people in his party who clearly took a dislike to Cyril. Away from his Rochdale fiefdom where hype and hogwash ruled, Liberals further afield showed no hesitancy in challenging Cyril's ridiculous views.

The *Liberator* magazine was closely associated with the Liberals and generally seen as representative of the views of Young Liberals. In 1978 it ran an opinion piece entitled 'Unjust Cyril' that was critical of Cyril's close relationship with James Anderton, the controversial chief constable of Greater Manchester Police. Anderton was an extremely divisive figure who would go on to accuse people with AIDS of 'swirling around in a human cesspit of their own making'. He also showed open hostility to Labour politicians, something that no doubt endeared him to Cyril. In Anderton's view, the Labour Party was the vanguard of a left-wing conspiracy to weaken the police. In almost biblical language he frequently raged about how left-wing subversion was hastening the downfall of Western civilisation.

Cyril referred to him as one of the best policemen 'in the world' and said any attacks on him were 'disgraceful'. The *Liberator* was not impressed.

'The law is clearly not as fair as we would like it to be,'

their comment piece argued. 'To sweep criticism under the carpet in assaults on those who seek to advance our justice is to attack democracy not defend it. Cyril Smith's blanket condemnations are as bogus as his declarations of support are short-sighted. We can only hope he never makes the bench.'

No doubt many more rank-and-file Liberal members would have found Cyril's views on Anderton's policing, capital punishment and abortion very much at odds with liberal principles. But what did the leadership make of him? Jeremy Thorpe had called him a 'bit of an ass' and David Steel and Cyril famously didn't see eye to eye. Cyril dismissed him as a 'drawing room politician', and then declared he wouldn't campaign in any constituency that had voted for Steel to become leader of the party. Steel found him hard to control and always seemed faintly exasperated by him. Yet, strangely, he still felt it necessary to push for Cyril to be knighted.

In the modern era, Paddy Ashdown seemed indifferent to him and Menzies Campbell said that Cyril hardly ever came to Parliament. His record of attendance was appalling. For a man who'd enjoyed such a high media profile and was one of the few people in the Liberal Party who could generally be viewed as a household name, he seemed to be somewhat underappreciated. And Cyril knew this. 'I don't believe I have ever been acceptable to the Liberal Party establishment. I was handy to trot out to attack the Labour vote because I was working class,' he said in 1985.

But there were some in the top ranks of the party, I discovered, who did appreciate him and valued his contribution enormously. That's why it was all the more difficult for them to speak now.

When I first approached the then deputy leader of the party, Simon Hughes, to speak about Cyril, his face dropped. Cyril's fall from grace had affected many in the party. But he agreed to do it, and when we met in Portcullis House a few weeks later he seemed genuinely sad at the admission by police that Cyril should have been charged for abusing boys.

Unlike some in his party, he made no effort to excuse Cyril's behaviour. 'There is no reason to doubt the evidence. It was very wrong and unacceptable,' he says ruefully.

He says concerns had never been raised with him and insists that David Steel must have asked Cyril questions about the rumours when they first surfaced. There can be no excuses for Cyril avoiding justice, but the reason he got away with it, he suggests, has less to do with internal investigations within the party and more to do with the actions of the police. After all, the police had investigated Cyril before he was selected as a parliamentary candidate.

'I'm hopeful we're in a period where the police are not as respectful of authority anymore in a way in which they might have been previously,' he says mysteriously. 'Even now I don't think we have a completely perfect police system.'

When I press him further on whether details of Cyril's darker side were ever presented to him, he makes a strange admission. 'Cyril stayed at the National Liberal Club in London when he was in Parliament,' he says. 'I remember David Penhaligon [a Liberal MP who was killed in a car crash in 1986] telling me once that Cyril had told him, if you stay at the National Liberal Club, never invite anyone into your room because people would get hold of the wrong end of the stick.'

I wasn't quite sure what to make of this, and Hughes wouldn't offer any clues. But I'd already heard enough stories about goings-on there. It wasn't just the activities of its conman owner George de Chabris that were raising eyebrows at the time.

A Liberal since 1971, Hughes says he remembers Cyril's by-election win in 1972 well. He subsequently made a number of visits to Rochdale to support Cyril and recognises that his victory was a springboard for Liberal success across the country. In taking a working-class Labour seat in an urban area, it broke new ground.

Not surprisingly, he credits Cyril's strong attachment to Rochdale as the reason behind his success. 'Local representation is important in our party,' he said. 'Cyril was a working-class representative of his community. He looked like he came from Lancashire, sounded like he came from Lancashire and acted like he was from Lancashire. Once Gracie Fields had gone he took over the place.'

There is clearly a feeling of admiration in his voice and Hughes makes no attempt to hide his respect for Cyril. Even though his condemnation for Cyril's abuse was sincere he's still willing to share the warmth he felt towards Rochdale's longest-serving MP. Like Scott Fitzgerald's dictum that the test of a first-rate intelligence is the ability to retain two opposed ideas in mind at the same time, he shows no discomfort in moving from criticising Smith to positively eulogising him.

'I saw him as an uncle or godfather in the party,' he admits. 'When Cyril came to party conference he was the main event. I didn't come from a political family and I was thrown in at the frontline very soon after I got here. Cyril was always very supportive. "Don't be a bloody fool" was a phrase he would use often.'

Adding that Cyril was 'never part of the establishment', he says Cyril remains a great example of a type of MP that's still sorely needed.

'There are some places that clearly need someone to fight for them,' he says. 'Other places don't really need an MP. I represent a place with more council properties than anywhere else in England and I'm clear that my social duty is to my constituency.

'For Cyril, Rochdale was his place. He was passionate and emotional about it. We need more people in politics like that with bottom lines. How many MPs are there who are prepared to put their constituencies first and challenge their own party?'

His question goes unanswered, but I know what he's driving at. The idea of an MP that's highly visible in their constituency, very vocal about local people's concerns and a champion for the town is much more attractive to most people than a remote parliamentarian that you might hear late at night on Radio 4's *Today in Parliament*. For too many politicians these days the constituency can be almost an afterthought. Some MPs don't even live in their constituency and only visit once a month for surgeries. The ideal of a democratic umbilical cord linking politicians to their community has sadly become almost a quaint notion.

Hughes's fervour for community politics is genuine and I decide not to remind him of Cyril's willingness to sell the health concerns of working-class people in Rochdale for 1,300 shares in the town's asbestos factory. Or his failure to put the needs of vulnerable boys first ahead of his twisted sexual appetite. There is no point.

Deep down Hughes knows this. He has the look of someone who's still coming to terms with the fact that his mentor was a monster. But I don't discount the fact that Cyril no doubt helped and inspired him. And I also believe that while he did a lot of damage Cyril also, at times, did some good. If there's one painful lesson that all politicians must realise it's that the electorate are not fools.

As our conversation comes to an end and we both finish our coffee, Hughes makes one more mention of the police. 'For victims to come forward the police needs to be more independent,' he says.

A few days later his comments assumed more significance after it was announced that he would be joining the government as a minister of state for justice. Hughes now had the opportunity to put right some of the wrongs of the system that had failed Cyril's victims.

Cyril's victims were never able to get justice and some have since left this world, broken and distraught. Others live on, troubled by the past. Over fifty years on from Cyril's first known victim I'm not convinced the system has improved that much. Vulnerable victims don't have the confidence to come forward and those who've been abused often have little faith in the criminal justice system. As Hughes fully knows, there is an awful lot of work to do to make it fit for purpose. The fact that only 53 per cent of paedophiles who were convicted for sexual activity with a child under thirteen were jailed in 2012 is a chilling reminder of the incompetence at the heart of the justice system.

Cyril abused people both as a Labour councillor and then as a Liberal MP and no political party was ever able to stop him. To ensure history doesn't repeat itself it's vital we take away the responsibility to root out anyone abusing their power in that way from a party political establishment fraught with freemasonry. We have to make sure the police are able to make prosecutions free from political influence.

This change has to come. We owe it all victims. I can only hope the uncomfortable spectre of Cyril Smith gives Hughes the motivation to drive it through.

Chapter 11

Sorrow

There had always been a ruthless side to Cyril. He'd fought hard for everything he'd got in life and was prepared to trample over anyone who got in his way. But layers of charm, northern bonhomie and all-round tomfoolery had long masked this. His ruthless core was hard to detect. As he aged, though, this side to him became more apparent. Bit by bit, the charm and big personality began to fade. Journalists made the trip to Emma Street far less frequently now and he hardly ever saw the TV cameras anymore. He hadn't sat on a chat show host's sofa in decades. Sometimes he'd try to rekindle the old magic when the local newspaper called, but his well-trained act wasn't what it used to be. There was something missing. He could still put on a bit of a show but he struggled to make the same impression. He was out of practice and his tuxedo hung at the back of his wardrobe gathering mould. All that was left was a bitter old man.

Politics is all about harsh truths. He knew that all too well. But this was one he didn't want to face up to. The show was grinding to a halt.

He'd look in the mirror sometimes and recoil at the face looking back at him. Jolliness and vitality used to be written all over Cyril's face. A smile permanently danced on his lips. Hunger shone in his eyes. But that face had gone. The flint-faced, gaunt reflection now before him had bitterness written through it. Where once his eyes were ablaze with passion they now seemed hard and lifeless. His craggy face was like granite, the eyes mean-spirited.

Cyril had never retired from politics. He couldn't do it. He'd built a career on keeping dark secrets hidden away and his life depended on it. He'd controlled his town for years and people in high places feared him. It had to remain that way. His secrets would have to stay hidden and he'd make sure people knew to carry on keeping their mouths shut.

But his controlling modus operandi was beginning to come unstuck. The sophisticated network he'd call upon to ensure that favours were done and problems dispatched no longer had the same power and influence. His disciples and fixers weren't as many and the cult of Cyril had lost its lustre. He could no longer expect unquestioning obedience. The age of deference was coming to an end.

And so Cyril became reckless. He'd always taken risks but that was when he was on top of his game and his mojo was humming. There was a strange method to his madness then. Now an irrational bitterness guided his actions. He was lashing out at everyone.

He'd attempt to intimidate people that he perceived to be political enemies who weren't anything of the sort. He'd try and force council colleagues to push through policies that were unwise and unpopular. And he'd fire out hostile letters to anyone he believed represented a threat to his shrinking power base.

He reached such a stage of paranoia that he was even writing abusive letters to priests.

Father Paul Daly is a priest at St Joseph's Church in Heywood and was the recipient of a strange letter from Cyril in 2006. He'd been working there for two years at the time and, as he didn't even live in Cyril's constituency of Rochdale, he was somewhat surprised to find a hand-written letter from the godfather of Rochdale politics in his postbag.

He was even more taken aback when he read through its contents. 'It was an angry letter,' he explains, 'and he said he'd heard that I was using the pulpit to tell people to vote Labour. He called me a disgrace.'

As he tells me the story now there is still disbelief in his voice. 'I would never tell people how to vote,' he says, half laughing at the suggestion. 'He must have got the wrong end of the stick. I'd given a sermon on something to do with poverty that he took exception to.'

Stunned at receiving a rebuke from 'a giant figure' of the Rochdale political scene, Father Daly immediately phoned him to try and find out what lay behind the letter.

'I remember calling him Sir Cyril and he seemed to calm down straight away,' he says. 'He admitted that he must have been misinformed and went on to tell me that he was a personal friend of every priest in Rochdale.'

He laughs about the incident now, but says even then he got the impression that Cyril was a figure 'that people were generally in awe of and trod warily'.

That much had long been known to me, but stories of how he was still trying to exert as much political influence as possible, albeit in a rash and clumsy manner at a time when he was pushing eighty, struck me as very odd.

I began to ask around, speaking to local politicians who had been active long enough to know what was happening.

'It was because his power was going,' explains Councillor Ashley Dearnley in the canteen at the town hall one morning. 'He knew the whole thing was about to collapse.'

As the leader of the Conservative group in Rochdale and a councillor since 1982, Dearnley had long been accustomed to Cyril's mood swings and strange behaviour. 'There were some people that genuinely feared him,' he says, sipping his tea. But in Cyril's final years he knew one thing was certain. His iron grip on the local party was slipping.

'People left the Liberal Democrats when Cyril died,' he said. 'They wouldn't have dared when he was alive because it would have upset him. If you went against him he would try and destroy you and use every dirty trick in the book. He ran the Liberal Party in Rochdale from his house in Emma Street. It wasn't a healthy situation.'

It didn't sound like one. The impression I got was of a party moulded by fear. When I'd arrived in Rochdale it looked like a solid, efficient machine. But in reality it was a house of cards that could fall apart at any minute.

It didn't take long after Cyril died for it to do just that. The fear factor had gone and the party imploded. Within months nine Rochdale Liberal Democrat councillors had resigned, ensuring they brought down the first Liberal–Conservative council since David Cameron and Nick Clegg formed the government. It was incredible.

For Dearnley there had long been a *fin de siècle* feel to

Cyril's faltering operation, but it had managed to stay on the road way past its sell-by date. Looking back, like others he notes that Cyril combined ruthlessness, charm and skilful networking to maintain his powerful grip on the town for so long. It was a smart blend and it wasn't just temper and fits of rage that sustained him; there could be a surprisingly kind and considerate side as well.

'He wrote letters to everyone,' he explains. 'Some of these were very kind. He wrote a letter of support to Paul Flowers [former Co-op bank chairman] when he had difficulties and I remember when my grandma died the first letter I got was from Cyril. He said he knew how much I'd done for her and I could have no regrets because I had looked after her. It was very touching.'

When Dearnley became leader of the Conservative group he was advised by the previous leader Pam Hawton to always try and keep Cyril onside. 'If there was an issue and you needed support I would go and talk to him at his house,' he says. As long as he was informed of the problem first, more than likely you'd get his support. Cyril always needed to feel at the centre of Rochdale politics. If you put him there, he'd back you to the hilt.

In Rochdale everyone has memories of Cyril, but one is universally shared. The sight of him lumbering around Rochdale market in his carpet slippers. 'I remember seeing him there,' smiles Dearnley. 'Cyril seemed to know everyone's name. He certainly knew how to rub shoulders and shake people's hands. People saw him as Mr Rochdale. He couldn't do anything wrong.'

But this wasn't the only political skill that Dearnley

observed. 'He needed to milk the Conservative vote to win here and he did it well,' he admits begrudgingly. He remembers watching him on *Question Time* once and calling him afterwards to congratulate him. He'd pressed all the Conservative buttons. 'He didn't put a foot wrong.'

But there was another side to him that no one, including Dearnley, could avoid. 'He had a real rotten side. When we went into coalition with Labour he was vicious. The attacks were constant. He made one of our councillors go in front of the Standards Committee over nothing and it made her ill.' If he saw any opportunity to go on the attack he'd seize it.

This was the side I'd come to see. The Cyril Smith that presented himself to me when I arrived in Rochdale was a crotchety old man clinging on to the past. He had a furious appetite for political combat and seemed to relish the prospect of taking on newcomers.

I used to continually wonder why he was still so involved, at a time when he should have been getting his affairs in order and enjoying the twilight years of his life. But I hadn't realised there was one small matter that consumed him. That of securing his legacy and trying to find a successor.

Cyril's slippers were big ones to fill all right. Liz Lynne had already crumpled under the weight of expectation when she'd succeeded him in 1992. 'I'll never forget her sitting in the front room of my house after losing the seat five years later, crying her eyes out,' Cyril told the *Daily Express* in what was said to be his last ever interview. 'She's not what I'd call a flamboyant personality or even a political personality,' he added for good measure. It was clear that she didn't measure up to his style of politics.

Sue Rothwell worked for Liz Lynne and was at Cyril's house on the night he refers to, when Lynne lost at the 1997 general election. 'Harry Wild was there,' she recalls. 'Cyril told us to bring fish and chips. He gave Liz a pep talk and told her to go out and face the music. She'd have to put on an act and be strong.' He sent her to the count knowing she'd lost.

Cyril had held the seat for twenty years before he stood down. As far as he was concerned it was still his seat. But five years later it had gone. No wonder he was disappointed.

When Cyril had first emerged as a major political force to be reckoned with in the 1950s he'd taken Rochdale by storm. He was soon everywhere and everyone knew his views. Now Milquetoast ninnies who weren't fit to lace his boots surrounded him. The more I continued to speak to Rochdale politicians, or locals connected to politics who knew Cyril, the more apparent it became that he'd become frustrated at the lack of any kind of able successor that could carry his torch.

The local Conservative councillor Ann Stott remembers this well. Her husband Rodney was Cyril's long-suffering agent and she would hear plenty of stories about Cyril's fruitless efforts to build a lasting legacy.

'He had a group of mainly young people that he called the Magnificent Seven,' she says. They were all ambitious Liberals and he thought that one of them would become his successor. But they all faded away. Some lost interest, some simply weren't up to scratch and none of them could match Cyril.

Much to Cyril's annoyance, his faith in these aspiring leaders was misplaced. There was no Steve McQueen,

Charles Bronson or Yul Brynner in his Magnificent Seven. He simply couldn't find anyone with the character or personality big enough to carry his torch.

It wasn't the first time that Cyril had shown bad political judgement. He'd vociferously backed John Pardoe over David Steel in the contest to become Liberal leader after Jeremy Thorpe in 1976. Steel easily cruised to victory and the oft-mocked Pardoe went on to play the fairy tale Liberal Prime Minister in BBC Radio 4's Christmas pantomime before losing his seat at the next general election.

Cyril had a bad habit of backing the losing horse and frustration began to cloud his judgement, so much so that he even turned on close friends – including his agent, Stott.

Rodney had been with Cyril a long time. An ambulance crew member and councillor who'd been first elected in 1973, in Cyril's ward no less, the pair hit it off straight away. As his agent, Rodney drove Cyril everywhere. 'He was always taking Cyril somewhere. They went to London to do a cooking programme, they went to do *Question Time*, it was non-stop,' remembers his widow Ann.

When Cyril retired the pair of them would tour the world aboard the *QE2* cruise liner. Even in these luxury surroundings, with spas, a ballroom and theatre on board, Cyril would still wander around in his carpet slippers. He and Rodney would play croquet on the games deck and marvel at the art works and murals in the Grand Ballroom. It was a long way from the combative cauldron of Rochdale politics.

When Rodney became mayor in 1995, Cyril helped him raise a record £87,000 for charity, more than any other mayor before or since. His well-thumbed contacts book was pulled out and calls were made to make sure Rodney's fundraising efforts would surpass all expectations.

'Cyril used his connections very well,' Ann admits. The Duke of Westminster came to speak at a fundraising dinner. So did the Archbishop of Canterbury and the controversial ex-chief constable of Greater Manchester Police, James Anderton. Cyril even managed to convince the former Home Secretary and Conservative MP, Sir Leon Brittan, to go out of his way and come to Rochdale to help. His networking paid off. Cyril was constantly in his tuxedo and the great and the good turned out in force. The money started to roll in.

But it wasn't all tuxedos and cruise liners and their relationship wasn't always an easy one, as Cyril had got into the habit of making ever-increasing demands on Rodney.

In 1983 Rodney was hospitalised after a serious accident at work. A fire had blown back in his face leaving him with terrible burns. As he lay recovering in a bed at Birch Hill Hospital, Cyril began to get impatient. A general election was looming and he couldn't have his agent out of action. This was no time to be laid up in bed.

His impatience finally got the better of him and he walked into the Victorian hospital and demanded to be shown to his bed. He paced the corridors of the former workhouse until he found his heavily bandaged agent lying prone in the burns unit. 'Come on, lad,' he boomed. 'You can't stay in here forever, there's work to be done.' Rodney sat up and protested but Cyril wasn't listening. He called a nurse over and got him discharged that day. 'He's my agent, there's an election coming up and I need him,' he told her. 'He'll be right as rain, don't you worry.'

As Stott's widow relates this tale you can sense the bitterness in her voice. 'It was very painful for Rodney,' she says, 'but Cyril wouldn't listen.'

But much worse was to come and the lack of concern that Cyril had shown that day should have acted as a warning for what he was capable of.

'I'd seen the nasty side of Cyril before,' admits Ann. 'If someone disagreed with him he could be very vitriolic.' But his ruthless side went much further than arguing with opponents. Cyril had to make decisions that were in his interest. He was constantly plotting and looking to stay one step ahead of his rivals and this meant that his judgement couldn't be clouded by sentiment. Tough decisions sometimes had to be made and to hell with the consequences.

In 2004 Rodney Stott had a stroke and became seriously ill. He was still a councillor at the time and as he began to recover he started to return to council meetings and carry out his duties for his ward. Rodney had been involved in local politics a long time and his commitment to public service was hardwired into him. Going to the town hall and helping shape local decisions was important to him and helped aid his recovery.

But Cyril Smith had other ideas.

Still obsessing about his legacy he remained on the look-out for prospects within the Liberal Democrats that might be able to continue his work. One of these prospects was a local hairdresser. Behind the scenes Cyril started to agitate for Rodney to be deselected and replaced by his preferred candidate.

With local elections looming and Rodney's ward a rock-solid Lib Dem seat, Cyril moved in for the kill and ensured that his preferred candidate, who would go on to resign as part of the collective hara kiri among Lib Dems after Cyril died, was selected as the candidate instead.

Thirty years of friendship counted for nothing. Rodney was out in the cold and Cyril's barmy game plan had ended his career in the party.

'He was not happy,' recalls Ann. 'He felt betrayed and that's why he went and joined the Conservatives. He'd joined the Liberals in 1969 and given them a lifetime of service. But to be treated so shabbily at the end by Cyril...' Her voice trails off for a second. 'He deserved better than that.'

Their friendship never healed and in April 2010 Rodney died, aged seventy. At the time, Cyril was very ill in hospital. Five months later he too passed away.

Stories like this characterise Cyril's later years. As power and prestige drained away from him, he became bitter and obsessive. The loyalty and friendship others had given to him didn't matter. Power and his potty legacy was all he cared about.

He'd sit in front of an electric bar fire in Emma Street, plotting and scheming, his face creased with worry. He'd be on the phone constantly, directing operations and ordering around his dwindling troops. But it was to no avail. The game was up. Cyril could never find a successor cast in his own image. That kind of politician was bordering on extinction.

For over fifty years he'd given all his energies to Rochdale politics. And what had he built? Rodin had spent years creating his masterpiece, *The Gates of Hell*; James Joyce took seventeen years to write *Finnegans Wake* and it took many years for the Dutch masters to perfect chiaroscuro painting.

Cyril had spent half a century building a poisonous legacy that had started to crumble to dust before his very own eyes.

All that remained was sorrow.

That much was evident when I made the journey across town to visit Maureen Cooper at her home in Norden. Neatly dressed, diminutive and with a stern, no-nonsense matron's air about her, she had agreed to talk about Cyril when I'd met her at the Cenotaph on Remembrance Day a few weeks earlier.

Maureen succeeded Cyril as chair of Rochdale Childer, which he'd founded in 1969 to help vulnerable children. I wanted to hear her view of Cyril and also to find out the origins of her charity. After all, Cyril founded it at a time when police were investigating him over child abuse allegations.

I was astonished to be told that Cyril had been approached by a priest from the Catholic Children's Rescue Society and asked to set up the charity to help them. The fact that he was completely unsuitable for the role didn't seem to enter anyone's head. Cyril had, naturally, agreed but insisted that it be non-political and non-sectarian. He named it after the old Lancashire word 'childer', meaning children.

As Cooper tells me this in her living room, she frequently gets up and down to show me flyers, pictures and awards that demonstrate the good work the charity has achieved over the years. It ensures that poor children in the borough are able to wake up on Christmas Day and get presents like everyone else. Families can apply to their fund for bedding, stair gates and other household items. They also help ensure children are able to go on holiday. In some cases they've even helped children learn to play the piano. 'We're a grant charity for children who need help,' she explains. Last Christmas they distributed well over £1,000 worth of presents.

At its peak, Cyril was a major driving force. 'I saw him as a trusted friend,' she says. 'If we wanted to do something, like get a minibus for disabled scouts, then before we had chance to discuss it Cyril would have found a solution. He knew how to make things happen and was very good at raising funds.'

Blessed with entrepreneurial flair and great contacts, Cyril's irrepressible zeal instantly won people over – and you can see why. 'He wouldn't listen to arguments why we couldn't do something. There was always a way. He'd say "why not?" and find a way to make things happen.'

Listening to her memories of Cyril, he sounds like the kind of MP every charity would want fighting their corner. But the awkward pause as her praise comes to an end reminds us both that ultimately this wasn't the case.

She hands me her latest leaflet and watches as I glance through the content. 'For the first time ever we never mentioned Cyril,' she says, in a voice full of regret. 'We had Cyril taken out of the leaflet and I feel terrible for it.'

I say nothing. Regardless of how capable a fundraiser he was, the idea of Cyril fronting a children's charity seems as abhorrent to me as Jimmy Savile presenting children's TV programmes.

'I feel sorry for his family,' she continues. 'I feel sorry for Norman [his brother].'

She doesn't mention the victims.

'But the charity will go on without Cyril.'

Do you think that's what he'd want?

'When Cyril started this I felt I owed it to him to keep it going.' Cyril had helped her continue training as a teacher, she explains, by persuading the local education authority to allow her to do further study. 'He did command loyalty,' she says. 'I felt I owed him.'

Many people I'd spoken to across Rochdale had expressed similar sentiments. Cyril had a way of making people feel obligated. People who knew him felt they'd almost entered into an unspoken contract with him. They were beholden to him and were always on the end of a phone for when he'd call favours in.

In 2002 Cooper had been awarded an MBE for services to children across Lancashire. Cyril was one of her nominees. She's proud of her work and powerfully conveys the reward it brings.

'When I go to a house to deliver Christmas gifts and I'm told that they wouldn't have anything if we hadn't come then that means everything,' she says.

She begins to tell another story of a child she'd met that always wore wellington boots. They were too small and the rim around the top had started to cut into the young girl's legs, causing them to bleed. When she brought her new shoes the young girl's face lit up. She'd never had a pair of new shoes before. 'The look in her face when she told me that … these things you don't forget,' she recalls.

I nod, sadly. My surgery is full of difficult stories like this every week and I'm acutely aware of the poverty in Rochdale. It's a town with enormous challenges.

As I drink the coffee her husband has made, I think of

the absurdity of the situation we're discussing. How did Cyril get involved in children's charities? What right had he to mix his sordid desires with this kind of valuable work? Like Savile, it provided cover for his shameful proclivities. But at what cost?

'You know, I asked Cyril about the rumours,' she says quietly, breaking the silence. 'He said the boys wouldn't have a bath and he had to smack their bottoms to get them to do it. That was the full tale. I didn't think it was as bad as it turned out to be. There was no suggestion of sexual abuse.'

I nod sympathetically. I'm not here to interrogate. I'm here to listen.

'He asked me to be a governor at Knowl View School,' she continues, 'but I said no.'

The mention of Knowl View sends a shiver down my spine and her eyes narrow, as though she can read my thoughts.

'I would have liked to have condemned him for what he did, to his face,' she says.

I sip my coffee. It must be hard coming to terms with what happened, I say.

'I don't know what to believe sometimes,' she says, her voice a mixture of anger, regret and confusion. 'I feel abused myself. I still like him because of what he did for me. I could go to him with any problem. I feel I've lost a friend.'

There are many more like Cooper across Rochdale going through the same conflicting emotions: publicly disassociating themselves from Cyril but privately struggling with regret, anger and a residual sense of loyalty. There is a strong sense of sorrow and shock. I often see people's eyes widen as they try to explain how the realisation dawned upon them.

'I would have trusted him with my own children' is a phrase, usually uttered in disbelief, which I've heard a lot.

But as uncomfortable as it is listening to key figures in our civic life expressing their sadness and incredulity at Cyril's double life, their sorrow is nothing compared to that of the victims. It is just not the same thing.

I know many people in our town feel betrayed by Cyril. But the victims feel as though Cyril stole a part of their youth from them that could never be replaced – and they've been living with the shame of it ever since.

Our town as a whole is still coming to terms with Cyril's abuse but, in time, I think we'll be a lot stronger for confronting it. As a politician you look at your town's potential and you strive to find ways for communities to achieve more and for everyone to get on in life. You look at the hurdles that lie before people and think of how these can be cleared to make opportunities easier for them to seize. But some hurdles are virtually insurmountable. Many people in Rochdale are already battling against tough odds. But living in an environment where sex abusers prey on vulnerable people makes the odds of leading the kind of lives that most aspire to all the more difficult.

Cyril has also done a lot of damage to politics and trust in the political process. There was a time, and I know there was never a golden age, when people wanted to believe in politicians more so than now. Some politicians captured the public's imagination and Cyril was one of them. People wanted to believe in politicians back then. Now they actively want to distrust politicians and have little faith in them.

As we come to the end of our conversation, I thank

Cooper for her time and wish her all the best with Rochdale Childer. In all of these meetings I'd learned something more about Cyril's legacy. I was beginning to think I had a strong understanding of the damage he'd caused by now. But as I put my empty coffee cup back on its saucer and get up to leave, she made me realise I'd overlooked one terrible consequence.

'You know the worst thing,' she said, as she handed me my coat. 'It's terrible to have to teach children to trust no one. That's what we have to do now.'

As the door closed behind me all sorts of emotions crowded my mind. Cyril had betrayed so many people who'd believed in him. He'd done an incredible amount of harm and managed to keep most of it hidden. Across town, children from Knowl View School that had committed suicide lay in their graves. Ex-workers from the Turner Brothers asbestos factory that had died painful mesothelioma deaths were there, too. It was an appalling legacy. How did he live with himself? What sustained him?

The answer was simple enough. Cyril lived by his own bewildering code. It was a kind of corny show business formula. Despite now being consumed by bitterness, as well as his gradually deteriorating health, in his last years he threw what remaining energies he had into trying to keep his foolish act going. He still managed to keep up appearances and never missed an opportunity to revel in the razzmatazz, even when he turned eighty.

This was a milestone deserving of a special occasion. Jimmy Cricket dusted off his best 1980s gags to entertain guests at a special party at the town hall. Cyril's favourite cheese pie was served and Jim Bowen appeared on a screen overhead paying tribute to the great man. Celebrity life coaches Nik and Eva Speakman, who make a living out of resolving pop stars' problems with time-travel treatment, turned up with a special gift. A DeLorean car. This was back to the future all right. The huge 'Nice One Cyril' banner shook under the tumultuous applause. A message from the Liberal Democrat leader, Nick Clegg, was read out. 'You were a beacon for our party in the '70s and '80s and continue to be an inspiration to the people of Rochdale,' he gushed.

A more ludicrous scene would be hard to imagine, but this was standard farce for Cyril. He'd been doing this for years. It was the only way to keep the demons at bay.

For the last ten years of his life the threat of being exposed as a child abuser had continued to hang over him. It never went away. But Cyril kept himself busy and ensured that his life continued to take a very different course to the silent torment of a generation of Rochdale boys. The show must go on.

And so his daft antics continued. On one such occasion, Cyril made his way to a recording studio across town and squeezed into a vocal booth to perform one of the most bizarre duets ever heard. Standing alongside the 4ft 9in. actor, Don Estelle, star of *It Ain't Half Hot Mum*, Cyril crouched down and the two of them leaned into the microphone. Then they began to sing the Laurel and Hardy film song, 'The Trail of the Lonesome Pine', for Don's new CD.

In the blue ridge mountains of Virginia on the trail of the
lonesome pine
In the pale moonshine our hearts entwine
Where she carved her name and I carved mine
Oh June, like the mountains I'm blue
Like the pine I'm lonesome for you
In the blue ridge mountains of Virginia
On the trail of the lonesome pine.

They only needed one take. The pair high-fived and Don
smiled. 'That was great, Cyril. Just perfect.' Cyril winked.
And they both burst out laughing.

Afterword

Not so long ago I met with a Member of Parliament who was complaining that being a politician wasn't all it was cracked up to be. He'd been elected to Parliament in 2005 and subsequently gone through the expenses scandal and seen public faith in politics continue to wither away.

Before he was elected to Westminster he'd been leader of his council. 'I was respected then. People looked up to me. Now people shout abuse at me from across the road. It's awful,' he told me.

As cautionary tales go, this one paints a bleak picture of politics. But it's one I've come to believe we must accept. We don't need deference in politics anymore and if the price we have to pay is abuse shouted from a bus top window when we get off the return train from Westminster then so be it. There is no great prestige attached to being an MP anymore. Politicians have to earn the public's respect and that's how it should be.

Deference to authority has allowed a multitude of sins to go unnoticed. In Cyril Smith's case it effectively gave him carte blanche to go around abusing vulnerable boys. The observation by former Liberal MP Peter Bessell that anyone with prominence in public life automatically acquired a measure of immunity exposes the criminal double standards at the heart of public life. Bessell, of course, was reflecting on another scandal in his party regarding its leader Jeremy Thorpe, but his comments touch upon a wider truth.

Politicians cannot moralise and pass judgement on the rest of the nation while ignoring indefensible behaviour among their colleagues.

Instead of protecting and reinforcing the establishment, as some obviously believed was the reason why the likes of Cyril Smith had to be given immunity, this blind spot has done the reverse. It discredits our political institutions and gives the impression that Parliament is a cosy club where everyone covers each other's back – and crimes like child abuse are swept under the carpet. I'm still astonished at the amount of run-ins Cyril had with the police. He's been questioned about offences relating to public lotteries, child abuse, electoral fraud, bribery and pornography – and yet was never properly held to account.

Some will no doubt argue that things have changed. The cover-up of Cyril's abuse was a long time ago. The values of the 1970s are a lot different to the standards expected in public life today. People wouldn't stand for that now. Awareness of child abuse has improved tenfold. No one would tolerate this kind of behaviour among colleagues, surely?

I would like to believe this view, but all the signs I've seen suggest it's not the case.

A number of police officers told me that Cyril was just the tip of the iceberg and, unfortunately, I expect more stories of Cyril's abuse to emerge. I expect in time we'll hear that there were more abusers in Parliament, more terrible cover-ups and it won't be just one political party that's guilty of harbouring abusers.

Abuse of power cuts across all party lines – and there is no greater abuse than using political power to prey on the most vulnerable.

I'm in no doubt, though, that Cyril benefited from being in a minority party where scrutiny of his behaviour was concerned. From a media perspective the Liberals have all too often been seen as an afterthought – and as a result haven't been held properly to account. Even books about Liberals are usually written by Liberals. As David Torrance observes in his biography of David Steel, the Liberals have by and large charted their own history. Some of this is long overdue a rewrite. Myths need to be torn down.

There remains a great irony in that while the job of politicians is often to bring the country to face up to hard truths – now more than ever – and deal in practical reality, politicians are often unable to face up to hard truths in their own party.

One person who did have to confront a particularly hard truth was T. Dan Smith. In 1977 when Cyril was embroiled in the machinations that led to the Lib–Lab Pact and MI5 were taking a close look at Cyril's police files, T. Dan Smith was stepping out of Her Majesty's Prison in Leyland to begin a new life as an ex-offender.

Just as Cyril was known as 'Mr Rochdale', T. Dan Smith had been known as 'Mr Newcastle' in the 1960s. Both were working-class, charismatic politicians with big voices that the media loved. But then the brilliant political career of

'Mr Newcastle' was cut short and he was sentenced to six years' imprisonment for accepting bribes.

He took up art while in prison and had plenty of time to reflect on his mistakes. On his release he learned to taste humility and lived on the fourteenth floor of a tower block. He went to work for the Howard League for Penal Reform and campaigned for the rights of released prisoners. Flawed, more humble and wiser, T. Dan Smith's modest later years stand in marked contrast to Cyril's undignified struggle to cling on to power.

It was as though Cyril was trapped in time. The heady days of the 1960s and '70s, when cameras followed his every movement and his stock was at its highest, acted as a powerful drug and he refused to let go, intoxicated by memories of the power he held and desperate for one last hurrah.

Strange birthday parties, DeLorean cars, arguments with priests, the betrayal of old friends and a bitter struggle to try and convert asbestos-contaminated land into homes and a children's day-care centre acted as the bewildering backdrop to his final years.

I often wondered what a spell in prison would have done to Cyril. I think he would have emerged stronger for it.

Just as Maureen Cooper had wanted to condemn Cyril to his face while he was still alive I, too, would have liked to have done the same. But by the time I was convinced the rumours were absolutely true he'd long gone. Although the truth is now known and the victims' stories have finally been heard there is no sense of any justice being achieved.

The victims I've spoken to say they're relieved that Cyril's past is now out in the open and they no longer feel as

burdened by the dirty secret they've carried for years. But
the sense of shame remains and I know this will never be
expunged. People who've been abused carry this wherever
they go. You can see it weighing down on them as they
speak, hear it in their voice. It follows them like a shadow.

Many have subsequently said that there will never be
another politician like Cyril Smith and I don't doubt that.
But, as one of his victims reminded me recently, there's no
way of preventing others carrying out similar deeds.

'People are always drawn to personalities. They're the ones
with the most power – and politics needs personalities,' he
said. 'There's no easy way round it.'

He's right. As political apathy threatens to undermine
the legitimacy of our democracy the best antidote is often
found in personalities with a strong connection to their
constituencies who portray themselves as local champions.

The painful irony we both acknowledge is that the sense
of theatre, individuality and big personality that people like
Cyril brought to politics is more needed than ever.

But I think we're coming to the end of an age where
personality had such an intoxicating effect on people that
it left them almost hypnotised. Personalities will always
be needed to enliven politics and make a strong connection with voters, but no one is quite as in thrall to political
personalities these days. Mesmerised faces taking in every
word that politicians say are a thing of the past. No one is
dancing unquestionably to a political tune. No snakes are
being charmed from their basket. And, thankfully, no caps
are being doffed.

As blind deference no longer determines a significant

part of people's worldview, earned respect has become the challenge facing everyone in public life.

And that's what gives me grounds for optimism. It may not be the police or political parties that prevent another Cyril Smith from building a rotten power base. It will be people in every community motivated by a healthy and unstinting scepticism. They know, as Albert Einstein once said, that 'blind belief in authority is the greatest enemy of truth'.

Amen to that.

Epilogue

Unfinished Business

I hated every day in Buckley Hall Young Offenders' Institution. But I did look forward to playing table tennis. It was the only respite we got, and I knew I was better than everyone else. Don't get me wrong, there were some good lads in there and I had to work hard to win. But once I got into the zone, swinging my blade like a man possessed at that little white blur zipping back and forth across a matte wooden top, working the corners, attacking anything short, well … the result wasn't in doubt.

I was completing a six-month detention sentence when we were told there'd be an annual tournament for the inmates. It was December 1974, I was about to turn seventeen and I had nothing else to look forward to that Christmas. The fact that we were now playing for something gave me an extra edge. Games that had previously been tight became hopelessly one-sided. What had looked like a tough tournament was becoming a procession. When I got to the semi-final, I couldn't wait to get started. I was at the table five minutes before my opponent arrived, bouncing up and down, listening to my trainers squeaking on the gym floor. I wanted to get it over with.

It didn't last long. I won comfortably without breaking sweat. I was already thinking of the final and mentally weighing up my likely opponent as I shook hands and turned to head back to my cell. But there was a screw blocking my way.

'Dave, I want a word with you.'

'What is it?'

'It's about the final. We've scrapped the other semi-final because you'll be playing someone else now. Not one of the lads here. Someone very important. And you're not to win, got it?'

He fixed me with a hard stare. His jaw was furiously chewing gum.

I didn't say a word. I was confused.

'Don't go playing like that tomorrow. OK? If you don't lose there'll be trouble.'

I nodded.

'Can I go now?' I asked.

He waved me back to the cell, cuffing my head roughly with the back of his hand as I passed.

I was disappointed, but I didn't think anything more about it. You get used to the screws' daft games when you're inside. They're always trying to mess with your mind, make things harder than they are. You learn to ignore them. Treat them with the contempt they deserve.

The next day we were all assembled in the hall and told to sit and wait. I had no idea what was going on but I had a bad feeling about it.

There was suddenly a commotion, and in burst this huge guy. He was in a suit and the top brass were all over him. They were fawning around him like he was royalty. I hadn't a clue who he was. One of the lads said he was a politician but it didn't mean anything to me. I just couldn't believe how big he was. He was like the Michelin man. I'd never seen anyone that fat before.

I was still trying to work out what was going on when he started to amble towards me.

'Come on, Dave,' a screw barked at me, pulling the chair from beneath me. 'You're about to play Mr Smith. Get on your feet.'

I picked myself off the floor where he'd unceremoniously dumped me and grabbed my bat.

By now this Mr Smith character was at the other end of the table. But he didn't stop there. 'Hello lad,' he bellowed, and extended his hand. I went to shake it but he pulled me towards him and embraced me. 'Good to see you,' he smiled, as I disappeared into his vast midriff. 'May the best man win.'

I just wanted to get this over, and without thinking I raced into a 7–0 lead. I wasn't even trying and he still couldn't win a point. This Mr Smith guy was hopeless. I looked up and the screws were glaring at me. I could feel their hostility eating into me. I'd better slow down. So I mishit a few shots, made it as easy as possible for him. But he still couldn't take advantage. Before I knew it I was leading 10–4. I was sweating now. If I won another point and beat him I'd be in serious trouble. I didn't even dare look at the screws' faces. I had to lose big time. So I hit shots long, into the net, wide. Anywhere but in. Everyone could see I was throwing the game. When Mr Smith finally won, he held up his arms and cheered. The screws clapped politely, but all the other inmates were unmoved. Silence filled the hall.

'Well done, lad. You pushed me all the way there,' he said, striding towards me and lifting me off my feet. He buried my head in the giant folds of fat that smothered me and fondled my buttocks. He held me close to him for what felt like hours but was probably a few seconds before dropping me back to earth. I was gasping for air.

'*Congratulations, sir,*' I said through gritted teeth. *I wanted to smash his face in.*

'*Well done, Dave. Now get back to your cell,*' a screw snapped, ushering me towards the door.

I ran back to my cell and shut the door firmly. It was my birthday that day. I was seventeen years old and I lay on my bed for hours, staring at the ceiling and wondering what had just happened. What on earth was a person like him doing in a place like this?

•   •   •

As I listened to this story from a man in his fifties, sitting in his living room on the Langley estate in Greater Manchester, the same thought crossed my mind. The whole thing sounded a farce. 'Did you ever find out why he was there?' I asked.

'No,' he said, lighting a roll-up and sucking the smoke deeply into his lungs.

Dave was the first person to tell me about Cyril visiting Buckley Hall Young Offenders' Institution. Several months had passed since we'd completed the first draft of this book, and I was beginning to feel we'd barely scratched the surface. This was a much bigger story than either of us had imagined. Other stories about Cyril's connections at Buckley Hall would soon start to filter through to our office. But it was the look of bewilderment on Dave's face as he explained Cyril's unexpected appearance at a teenagers' table tennis competition that made me want to find out more. I'd heard too many stories like this by now. There was something equally surreal and sinister about Cyril's appearances. The images passed through my mind in a chilling montage. Cyril popping up at a school for children with learning difficulties and wandering around the dormitories; Cyril fondling boys while handing out football trophies; Cyril wandering around Buckley Hall Young Offenders' Institution. I was reminded of a famous Raymond Chandler quote: 'He looked about as inconspicuous as a tarantula on a slice of angel food cake.' Why couldn't anyone see what was happening?

I soon found out what was going on where Buckley Hall was concerned. If Dave was more bemused than anything at Cyril's presence there, the next person I spoke to had a far more painful experience to share.

When I first heard from Steve, I immediately knew he'd had a very different experience at Buckley Hall. His faltering voice told me that what he was about to relate would be extremely distressing. He arrived there at the beginning of the 1980s as an eighteen-year-old – and it didn't take long before he came across Cyril. But they hadn't met over a ping-pong table. Cyril had walked into his cell one afternoon and quietly closed the door. Before Steve had time to question who this giant of a man was, Cyril was in his face, scolding him for bad behaviour.

'You've been a bad lad, haven't you?' he hissed. 'I hear you've been giving other lads cigarettes. We know it's you, so hand them over.'

When Steve protested that he hadn't got any cigarettes, Cyril made him take his clothes off.

'I need to search you thoroughly,' he told him. 'I can't be doing with liars.'

When he was naked, Cyril ordered him to bend over. Then he abused him.

The experience was more than Steve could bear. He trashed his cell and screamed for hours. He beat his fists against the door until they bled. But no one would believe him and he was eventually taken to Strangeways Prison in Manchester and put in solitary confinement.

I was now convinced that Buckley Hall Young Offenders' Institution had massively failed in its responsibility. One police officer told me he suspected Cyril had keys to the place. I was told he made frequent visits. No one challenged Cyril and I have no doubt he was able to wander around the place and prey on boys for years. But he didn't do this all by himself. His frightening operation at Knowl View School revealed he wasn't alone. He had accomplices and it was one of these, his long-time partner in crime Harry Wild, who eventually gave the game away.

When Walter MacGowan walked into my office last summer, he cut an imposing figure. Nearly seven foot tall, the former director of operations at Buckley Hall must have been a sight to behold in his prime. He'd been governor at Strangeways Prison before he worked in Rochdale, and had a fearsome reputation. 'I was over eight foot tall when I was in riot gear,' he chuckled, as I handed him a cup of tea.

By the time MacGowan arrived at Buckley Hall in the mid-1990s, it was no longer a detention centre. It had become a private prison for adult males, and the new director soon acquainted himself with the lay visitors appointed to the independent monitoring board. Their role was to monitor day-to-day prison life and ensure that proper standards of care and decency were maintained. They had unrestricted access to the prison and could talk to any prisoner they wanted. One of these visitors was Harry Wild. His appointment would have been signed off by the Home Secretary of the day.

'He'd been appointed on the understanding that he was an ex-colonel in the Life Guards and a director at ICI,' explained MacGowan. Admitting he was suspicious of Wild the first time he met him, he told me that this impression was soon justified after a prisoner accused Wild of groping him.

When MacGowan confronted Wild with the accusation, he didn't deny it. Although Wild pleaded for clemency, MacGowan was unmoved and threw him out of the prison. MacGowan subsequently met with the chief constable of Greater Manchester Police, Sir David Wilmot, and warned him about Wild. His intervention ensured the police looked into Wild and investigated him for child abuse at Knowl View School. At the time, Wild had been recommended to be the next High Sheriff of Greater Manchester and it certainly killed off his chances of taking this ceremonial position. But it also revealed something else.

'I found out he was a total imposter,' recalls MacGowan. 'He was never in the Life Guards or a director at ICI. Someone up the chain had been fooled. I'd like to know who recommended him to the Home Secretary.'

I thought I was coming to the end of Cyril's story. But MacGowan's visit confronted me with a barrage of further questions. I knew by now that these sexual predators were incredibly manipulative and were able to inveigle themselves into all sorts of places where they had no right to be. But how far had they burrowed into the establishment? And were they really pulling the wool over the authorities' eyes that easily? By now it had become public knowledge that the chair of the Paedophile Information Exchange was working as an electrical contractor in the Home Office in the 1980s and stored information there. I was beginning to wonder if stories like these were just the tip of the iceberg.

'You know, Harry Wild used to arrive at the prison in a chauffeur-driven car,' said MacGowan, as he finished his tea and got up to leave. 'I found out it wasn't a chauffeur. It was his neighbour. It was quite an act. He fooled a lot of people. But just imagine if he was a terrorist.'

In my eyes, paedophiles are no different to terrorists. They have the same destructive monomania and often possess remarkable depths of guile and cunning. Thankfully, 2014's Queen's Speech recognised this with a new crackdown on child abusers that ended the distinction between their activities and those of terrorists. But there is more to be done, particularly where powerful paedophiles are concerned. They are extremely dangerous because they are so manipulative. And in Cyril's case, there seemed no end to the lessons I was forced to learn about his devious cunning.

Soon afterwards, the BBC journalist Tom Bateman discovered a letter written by Cyril Smith to the director general of the BBC in 1976, urging the BBC not to investigate 'the private lives of certain MPs'. He also wrote to the then Home Secretary Merlyn Rees, asking him to ensure the BBC was not using public money for 'muck raking'. The brass neck of this man knew no bounds.

Fresh examples of breathtaking chutzpah by Smith now began to present themselves on a weekly basis.

Next, I discovered he'd even used his local newspaper to groom boys. In 1978, Cyril had placed a story, which appeared on the front page of the *Rochdale Observer*, stating that he was offering a free place to a public school for a young boy from a single-parent family.

The boy who won this scholarship is now the same age as me and got in touch to share his heartbreaking story.

After his mother had made contact with the newspaper, Cyril visited the family and said he wanted to offer a place at Reed's School in Cobham, Surrey to her eleven-year-old son. Further still, he promised to take him to see London for the first time and give him a tour of his new school.

Imagine the boy's excitement, then, when shortly afterwards Cyril returned to pick him up and take him on the train down to London. 'I was very nervous,' he remembers, over thirty-five years later. 'I remember sitting on the train watching Cyril demolish this huge breakfast of eggs and bacon. I was overwhelmed by it all.'

Once they'd arrived in the capital, they quickly made their way to the Houses of Parliament, where he was introduced to the leader of the Liberals, David Steel. This was a dizzying programme for a boy who hadn't yet reached puberty. He saw the famous green benches, gazed on the statues representing mercy and justice in the House of Lords and admired the frescos in the Royal Gallery. The vastness of the place captivated the young boy. If Cyril had set out to impress, he'd certainly delivered. As they wandered around the Palace of Westminster together, no one batted an eyelid at the sight of Cyril alone with an eleven-year-old boy.

Later, after he'd taken him for a quick tour of his new school in Surrey, Cyril took him to the Liberal Club over the Embankment on the River Thames, established by

Gladstone nearly 100 years earlier. They'd walked for miles and the boy was tiring now. It was getting late. 'Let me show you to your room,' Cyril smiled and led him up the famous cantilevered marble staircase.

As Cyril led him into a modest-sized room with one bed, the boy froze, realising that they'd be sharing. 'I thought that perhaps, err … we'd have our own separate…' but the boy didn't finish. Cyril put his finger to his lips and shushed him. He lifted him onto the bed and began to undress him. The boy knew this was wrong. Especially when Cyril insisted he take his underpants off. As Cyril attempted to fondle him, the boy fought him off. He was shaking with fear.

It was going to be a long night.

When he returned home, the boy told his mum he couldn't go to Reed's School. He didn't want the place that the town's MP had offered him. She couldn't understand and was initially resentful. She begged him to reconsider. 'This is a wonderful opportunity for you,' she argued. But she sensed something was wrong and eventually let it lie.

The experience soured the young boy, and his attitude towards school changed overnight. He became withdrawn and lost interest in his studies. He flunked his exams at sixteen and spent years in the wilderness. It took him a decade to get back on track.

As we talked about these awful events that he'd clearly tried very hard to forget about until that day, I sensed how difficult it was to look back. Exhuming a buried past can bring back some painful memories. 'My mother blamed herself,' he said quietly. 'I didn't tell her for ages and it's been hard for her. She blames herself for leaving me alone with Cyril.'

'But he was the town's MP,' I protest. 'How could she have known?'

No matter how many stories I heard about Cyril, I never ceased to be shocked. Every case was different and every one of them could have been prevented.

By now I'd decided it was simply impossible that others in his party did not know about Cyril's behaviour, and a reckoning of sorts was needed. After hearing this story, I decided to write to the Liberal Democrat leader, Nick Clegg, urging his party to hold a proper investigation into who covered up Cyril's abhorrent actions.

I thought we'd reached a stage where everyone now realised the past must be confronted. But Clegg's response disappointed me. Taking a Pontius Pilate approach, he disowned all responsibility, refused to open an inquiry and said no political party could do justice to the breadth and scope of these allegations.

It felt like another door slamming in our faces. And you could almost hear the sound of bolting and double bolting on the inside.

But no amount of locks and bolts could keep this story from being heard now, although it continued to fall on deaf ears where the political establishment were concerned. It didn't take long before I found myself driving through the leafy suburbs of south Manchester to hear yet another story about Cyril, this time one of the clearest examples yet of the fact that people in his party must have known about his double life.

Sitting in a hotel bar with a steaming pot of tea and a photo album to leaf through, I warmed to Julie straight away. A widow in her sixties, she was a former Liberal activist and her passion for campaigning remained undimmed as we talked freely about modern politics. It didn't take long, though, before the conversation turned to the 1970s and, in particular, the Manchester by-election in 1979. As she pointed to photos in the album before us of campaigners stuffing envelopes in her flat, she began to tell me the story of how she'd met Cyril.

'The Liberals had enjoyed a good run of election results. David Alton had been elected in the Liverpool by-election and even though we knew we weren't going to win Manchester we wanted to put up a good fight,' she recalled. As there was no Liberal group in Manchester, the party had piled up to Prestwich to use Julie's flat as a campaign headquarters. During the campaign, activists poured into her living room to address envelopes for a constituency-wide mail-out and to discuss doorstep strategy. David Alton was one of the first MPs to turn up and lend his support. And then, on another night, they were told that a Liberal grandee would be coming round to help. It was Cyril Smith.

'We were all excited that Cyril was coming round,' Julie says. 'He was a local celebrity and everyone knew him. We called the parents of our Young Liberals and told them Cyril would be popping round. Lots of people wanted to come.'

So when the evening of Cyril's visit came around, her flat was full of party members, including a good number of younger teenage activists. 'Cyril was late, I remember that well,' she recalls. 'We thought he wasn't going to turn up. Then there was this pounding at the door and the next minute he was lumbering up my stairs with the regional organiser, who was acting as his chauffeur. He made a grand entrance like he always did and made sure everyone knew he was here. He had to be the centre of attention.'

He'd been invited to rally the troops and boost morale. But he was to have the opposite effect and it didn't take long before things turned sour.

'He was very crude,' says Julie. 'He told smutty jokes and put my back up.' After he'd broken one of Julie's chairs, she moved him across the room. By now he was getting very lewd and loud, she recalls. 'People were getting uncomfortable. They started looking over at me.' He'd moved so he was sat next to a fourteen-year-old boy and she watched with horror as his hand moved slowly towards the youngster's groin area.

He yelped and jumped into the air.

Everyone stopped what they were doing and stared at Cyril. And one person in particular decided he'd seen enough. Julie's husband, who had recently retired as a police inspector for Greater Manchester Police, had watched events unfold from across the room. There was no doubt in his mind: Cyril had to leave.

While Julie took the young boy into the kitchen to calm him down, her husband put his hand firmly on Cyril's shoulder, leaned in close and whispered in his ear. 'He told him not to make any trouble and go quietly,' explains Julie. 'Cyril knew he had no choice. He got up and quickly made his way out without any fuss.'

The next day, her husband phoned the Liberal Party regional office and told them what had happened. 'He wanted to make an official complaint because Cyril's behaviour was totally inappropriate,' she says. He then phoned the Liberal Party headquarters in London and had the same conversation. 'I know my husband got through to David Steel's office,' she adds. 'He wanted this story to get through to the top of the party. He was very explicit about what had happened.'

He told the police too. But they decided not to follow the matter up.

The Liberals, on the other hand, realised the seriousness of the matter and Julie soon had a knock on her door. A few days later, a Liberal organiser came round to see them both. 'He was very uncomfortable,' she remembers. He offered to give them £200 in expenses, quite a sum in those days, to cover any inconvenience they'd suffered. 'That was more than I earned in a month as a teacher,' she adds.

At the time they both looked at each other aghast. They knew he was trying to buy their silence and turned him down flat. 'We wouldn't take a penny,' she says, the disgust still there in her voice.

It was a watershed moment. They were both keen Liberal activists but their interest in the party died there and then. Her husband had even stood in the local election for the Liberals. But not any more. They didn't want to belong to a party that brushed incidents like this under the carpet.

I looked at the photos before me, capturing the events of that night three and a half decades ago. Sepia images frozen in time. There was one of Cyril with a large smile plastered across his face. And another of the boy he'd groped. My gaze switched between the two as Julie began to reminisce about her late husband. Looking at the teenager's innocent face in the photo, you could understand her anger.

The image of that young boy resurfaced in my mind a few months later as I sat in Millbank House in London. There was plenty to mull over from the last few months as I waited outside Lord Steel's office, drumming my fingers on the table before me. There were lots of things I wanted to ask him about. I'd agreed to meet the man who'd led Cyril's party when allegations of his abuse first emerged – and he was running late.

Just as I was trying to work out what questions to prioritise in the limited time we had left, I heard footsteps and saw the smiling septuagenarian former Liberal leader coming towards me. 'Sorry I'm late,' he said amiably, and we both hurriedly made our way into his office and got down to business.

It was well known that there was bad blood between Cyril and David Steel, but Steel was quick to recognise how important a figure Cyril had been for the Liberals. 'You have to remember the background to Cyril coming in the party,' he told me straight off. 'We had a bad election in 1970; we were down to six MPs. A little puff of wind and we would have been almost obliterated. That by-election [when Cyril won Rochdale in 1972] was the start of the revival.' But while Cyril was an electoral asset, his popularity came with a price, and Steel's voice hardens as he describes the problems Cyril caused him. 'He was very difficult to deal with,' he sighs. 'I had several run-ins with him, as you know. When I became leader he said he wouldn't speak in any constituency that voted for me.'

I ask if Cyril was a bully and he nods. 'There was a bit of that, yes. He was used to getting his own way. Partly because of his size, he had a demeanour that would put some people in awe of him.'

This seemed a suitable juncture to bring up Cyril's double life, and Steel didn't hesitate in recalling the time he confronted Cyril about child abuse allegations he'd read about in *Private Eye*.

We were having dinner in the Members' dining room and I said, 'Cyril, what's all this in *Private Eye* about?'

Cyril said, 'Yes, it's true I was interviewed by the police, but you see I had this role in relation to the children's home as a councillor.' There was no more to it than that.

There was a momentary silence between us as I digested this explanation and the lack of curiosity he showed in accepting it. Then I asked him about Julie's account of her husband reporting Cyril groping a boy at a Liberal by-election campaign meeting. 'I never heard anything about this,' he counters. 'I don't think they would have spoken to anyone in my office. I never heard anything more about that kind of thing after the *Private Eye* article. Not even whispers.'

What about the eleven-year-old boy Cyril had taken to Parliament the year before and introduced to Steel before he went on to molest him at the Liberal Club? 'I may well have met him but I wouldn't have known he was going to spend the night with him,' he answers. Some of his poise has gone now and he suddenly seems older than I thought. Riverbed creases wrinkle and line a face that's been in politics for over fifty years. In interviews I've heard previously, Steel has often sounded prickly and defensive. But not today. This is not the defiant, bullish Steel I heard interviewed by Martha Kearney on Radio 4 about Cyril Smith last year. There's a sense of resignation to his voice. 'I feel sick about it. It was all new to me when this broke. Quite horrifying.'

Again we share an awkward silence. 'Did no one ever tell you what Cyril was up to? In the police it seemed an open secret.'

'No, they didn't,' he holds his hands up in a gesture of surrender. There's still no defiance in his voice. 'My brother was a police officer and he never said anything. I had protection officers when I was leader and no one said, "There's something funny about this Smith guy." Whether people were protecting me, I don't know.' There's a mixture of bafflement and sadness in his voice.

And that's the mood that follows me as I shake hands and leave shortly afterwards. Nobody ever sees truth except in fragments, a great social reformer once said. That's what I was left clutching. Pieces of a puzzle that was much bigger than I'd ever anticipated. I'd spoken to social workers, survivors of physical and sexual abuse, police officers, politicians, local businessmen and -women and countless community figures. I'd listened to former friends and enemies of Cyril. I'd heard visceral truths and grappled with a story that operated in the shadows. It was never meant to be told. Yet still I felt part of me was stuck in no man's land. It was as though I could see a clear explanation of why Cyril had been protected and why he'd always managed to get away with crimes against boys. But it was surrounded by fog and no one was going to take me there. Certainly not David Steel.

In the weeks and months that passed, this gnawed away at me. I had a sense of unfinished business. I was busy with plenty of other things. But it remained in the back of my mind and I always looked eagerly through emails and the list of calls that had come in for me, wondering if anyone had contacted me with fresh information that could lead to a breakthrough.

It didn't take long before I was driving through snow on

the M62 over into Yorkshire to meet another former police officer with an incredible story.

By now, my world seemed to revolve around two types of people. Former police officers who knew all along that Cyril was a paedophile and were seemingly powerless to do anything about it. And politicians who claimed to know nothing about the fact a paedophile was operating among them but could have done plenty about it.

I'd begun to brace myself when I sat down with ex-officers to talk about Cyril. There was always a bit of suspicion at first. 'I don't like politicians or journalists,' Karl told me matter-of-factly as he handed me a coffee and dropped a sugar lump into his. But as we got talking, his guard gradually lowered and he told me everyone in the police had heard about Cyril's antics with boys. As he began to tell me of the conversations among fellow officers about Cyril, one incident in particular grabbed my attention.

In the early 1980s, Karl went on an intensive ten-week CID training course at Bishopgarth House in Wakefield to learn about criminal law. They were long days, he explains, with lots crammed in and guest speakers to talk about specific areas of the police. One of these was from the British Transport Police. Over 100 officers were sat in a horseshoe-shaped auditorium as the officer turned to the overhead screen and began to play some security footage to illustrate how transport police could detect crime at key transport hubs around the country.

'It was late and we were tired,' Karl recalls. 'Some of us were yawning. Others were making choo-choo noises, mocking the speaker.' Then suddenly on the screen overhead, footage from Euston concourse caught their attention. 'He was showing us some footage of a guy approaching young boys at the station. It was clear he was up to no good. It was a dirty old man trying it on with boys.'

No one was yawning or making choo-choo noises now. A murmur of recognition travelled around the room. 'That's Cyril Smith,' someone piped up. 'Everyone realised it was him,' said Karl.

'So you were being shown a training video of Cyril Smith grooming boys?'

'Pretty much, yeah,' he shrugged. 'I guess they were trying to show us that Big Brother is watching you and could provide some useful evidence.'

'But didn't you wonder why no one was doing anything about Cyril?'

'I thought at the time someone should be doing something about this, but you don't step on other people's toes. I presumed transport police were dealing with it.'

This wasn't the first time I'd struggled to believe what I was hearing when listening to accounts from police officers on what they knew about Cyril Smith. I'd felt the same astonishment when Derek Smith told me about 144 complaints of child abuse being made against Cyril, and I felt equally amazed when I met another ex-officer back in Lancashire a few weeks later to discuss another Greater Manchester Police operation in the late 1990s.

This time the rain was hammering down in the Pennines and we huddled round a heater in a small deli, waiting for hot drinks to be served. John had worked on Operation Cleopatra, which was launched in 1997 to investigate child abuse in children's homes and schools across Greater Manchester.

One of the schools they looked at was Knowl View, where Cyril had abused boys, and in 1999 John submitted a file recommending Cyril be prosecuted for child abuse.

But once again this fell on deaf ears. 'They decided not to pursue Cyril Smith and I never saw my report again,' he explained.

I sat back and slowly took in what I'd just heard. Another officer, Mike Smith, had previously told me he'd investigated Cyril Smith in the 1950s after they'd heard reports of boys going into the back of his newsagent's. Now I knew he'd been investigated as recently as 1999. For well over forty years the police had pursued Cyril. How could he possibly be investigated for so long and never be charged?

It seemed lots of people knew what Cyril was up to and all the signs indicated that this went right to the top. It soon emerged on BBC's *Newsnight* that Cyril had been arrested in the early 1980s after police had caught him on camera abusing fourteen-year-old boys at a flat in Lambeth. Incredibly, he was able to walk free again. A duty sergeant who wanted to keep him in custody was reprimanded; officers were forced to hand over all their evidence and were warned to keep quiet about their investigation or face prosecution under the Official Secrets Act.

The dam was now beginning to burst, and more and more stories like this were being told. Police officers even called a radio phone-in to talk about how investigations into child abuse featuring Cyril Smith were stopped by bosses just as they were about to make arrests. As more official documents began to enter the public domain, we suddenly discovered that the former Prime Minister Margaret Thatcher had been personally informed that police had investigated Cyril's abuse of boys before she awarded him a knighthood in 1988. In documents that the Cabinet Office tried to suppress, newspapers revealed that Thatcher had been explicitly warned that awarding Smith a knighthood could damage the integrity of the honours system. Incredibly, she ignored these warnings and went ahead and knighted him.

I'd heard too many stories by now. Looked in the eyes of far too many experienced detectives to know that this was a problem that must extend further than Cyril Smith. I knew there must be other politicians involved. Why else would Cyril be protected?

Other stories were now appearing in the newspapers linking MPs with the murders of children during depraved violent orgies. A pretty bleak picture was forming. I spoke to other officers about this and pressed everyone who came to me about it for information. But one thing held them back. There was an incredible fear of speaking out.

As the stakes were getting higher, I sensed a greater nervousness about sharing information on criminal investigations. I'd be passed on to colleagues who'd panic when I approached them and suggest I talk to someone else. Everyone I came across seemed to be touched by the same anxiety.

And then I realised why.

The phone rang one afternoon and a woman said she wanted to talk about the child abuse stories she'd seen in the newspapers. She was a lawyer who used to work in Barnes and had represented a young client who had worked at Elm Guest House. My ears immediately pricked up and I moved to take the call somewhere more private.

'I'd been asked to go to Barnes police station one afternoon', she explained, 'to represent a young lad who was being questioned by the police.' When she got there she found the young lad looking very uncomfortable. 'The police began to give him a hard time. The questioning was getting a bit aggressive.' When she stepped in and said as much, the police officer took her to one side.

He pulled out a police statement and flung it at her in disgust, she recalled. 'He was angry and told me to read it because that's why he had to push the lad.'

Up until that moment, she didn't know much about what had happened at Elm Guest House. But as she began to read the statement before her, a chilling realisation of how serious this was began to dawn on her.

'The statement was from a young man and detailed how his father had raped him and then told him that he would be raped by other men there,' she said. 'Among those who had raped him included politicians.'

After I'd finished the call, I stared out the window for a long time. Where this dark journey was taking us, I had no idea. But I suspect some people didn't want it to carry on much further. We were getting dangerously close to things that powerful people did not want ever to be made public.

But, similarly, I was beginning to get the impression that people in power didn't even want others talking about things that were now a matter of public record.

Former Special Branch detective Tony Robinson was one of the first to speak out about MI5's interest in police files on Cyril Smith. His decision to go public on how a sex abuse dossier had been seized by MI5 had posed tough questions on the role of the security service in dealing with sexual abuse allegations made against politicians.

But when I spoke to him more than a year after he'd decided to speak out, there was anger in his voice as he described a call he'd received out of the blue from Lancashire Police towards the end of 2014.

Now recovering from a serious illness, the frustration and tiredness in his voice were palpable. 'A young officer called me and wanted to talk about Cyril Smith,' he said. 'I've been retired thirty-one years and never heard anything from the police. And now I suddenly get this call. It was obvious they were trying to warn me off. I found it very unnerving.'

I could fully understand now why officers were extremely nervous about going public on what they knew about Cyril Smith and other politicians who had been investigated over sexual abuse. A febrile mood was forming in police circles and I could only imagine the kind of calls that were being made, the pressure they were being put under.

'Everyone's trying to keep a lid on it,' Robinson complained. 'We really need to clean out the Augean stables.'

As long as they remained filthy, as long as files were fed secretly into the shredders and people were warned to keep quiet about what they knew, I was sure there would be consequences. In January 2015, hundreds of survivors of sexual abuse gathered in Parliament as part of a child abuse rally to fight for justice. It was a raucous, passionate affair and a sense of angry determination to unmask abusers shook the walls of the biggest committee room in Westminster. It was rammed and people stood in the aisles and sat on the floor, listening attentively and cheering on the speakers.

As I finished speaking and sat down, I looked out at this impressive crowd of committed campaigners. A movement was slowly building and I could sense the public mood changing. People had had enough of establishment cover-ups. They were tired of files going missing, charges being dropped and inquiries going nowhere. Everyone could see there was very little appetite by the authorities to get to grips with the problem. It seemed that some people could get away with anything. That had to change.

Feeding off the energy before me, my mind went back to the renowned protest in Belgium in 1996 when 300,000 people had marched on the streets of Brussels against the authorities' handling of a major paedophile scandal. People came from all over the country that day and carried white flowers as a symbol of innocence and purity.

We all knew by now that a scandal was brewing, and the size of it seemed to be growing by the day. Cyril wasn't the only one, of that much I was sure. There were other parliamentarians who'd led double lives and abused children while presenting a picture of respectability to the public. It would take time for the truth to fully emerge, but it was futile trying to keep a lid on it and pretend there was nothing to see. Sticking with a culture of denial was dangerous. The public wouldn't be easily fobbed off this time. Sooner or later, public anger would spill over if cover-ups continued. And maybe it wouldn't be long before the same rhythmic thud of boots on the streets that Cyril had grown up hearing as part of Depression-era social protest was heard once more.

Select Bibliography

In writing this book we have drawn upon numerous interviews and a wealth of material. We have been fortunate
to gain access to many unpublished documents including
legal reports. Here is a list of key published materials:

Published works

Ashdown, Paddy, *A Fortunate Life: The Autobiography of
Paddy Ashdown* (London: Aurum, 2010)

Benn, Tony, *The Benn Diaries 1940–1990* (London: Arrow
Books, 1996)

Campbell, Menzies, *Menzies Campbell: My Autobiography*
(London: Hodder & Stoughton, 2008)

Freeman, Simon with Barrie Penrose, *Rinkagate: The Rise
and Fall of Jeremy Thorpe*, (London: Bloomsbury, 1997)

Gardiner, Juliet, *The Thirties: An Intimate History of Britain*
(London: Harper Press, 2010)

Li, C. K., West, D. J. and Woodhouse, T. P., *Children's Sexual
Encounters with Adults: A Scientific Study* (Buffalo, NY:
Prometheus Books, 1993)

Michie, Alastair and Hoggart, Simon, *The Pact: The Inside*

Story of the Lib–Lab Government 1977–8 (London: Quartet Books, 1978)

Moules, Joan, *Gracie Fields: A Biography* (Chichester: Summersdale, 1997)

Orwell, George, *Coming Up for Air* (London: Victor Gollancz, 1939)

Thumin, Janet, *Inventing Television Culture: Men, Women and the Box* (Oxford: Oxford University Press, 2004)

Torrance, David, *David Steel: Rising Hope to Elder Statesman* (London: Biteback, 2012)

Smith, Cyril, *Big Cyril* (London: W. H. Allen, 1978)

Trippier, Sir David, *Lend Me Your Ear* (Durham: Memoir Club, 1999)

Tweedale, Geoffrey, *Magic Mineral to Killer Dust: Turner & Newall and the Asbestos Hazard* (Oxford: Oxford University Press, 2001)

Periodical

Rochdale Alternative Press

Home Affairs Select Committee, Localised Child Grooming inquiry (House of Commons)

Broadcasts

Dispatches: The Paedophile MP: How Cyril Smith Got Away with It (Channel 4), 12 September 2013

Sunday Supplement: Nice One Cyril (ITV Granada), 2003

BBC North West Tonight, Obituary by Jim Hancock (BBC One), 2010

Man Alive: Santa Claus for a Year (BBC Two) 1966/7

Index